ADMINISTRATIVE MANAGEMENT AND PLANNING

ADMINISTRATIVE MANAGEMENT AND PLANNING

Compiled & Edited
By
Dr. R.K. Pruthi

DISCOVERY PUBLISHING HOUSE
NEW DELHI-110002

First Published-2005

ISBN 81-8356-009-1

Published by

DISCOVERY PUBLISHING HOUSE
4831/24, Ansari Road, Prahlad Street,
Darya Ganj, New Delhi-110002 (India)
Phone: 23279245 • Fax: 91-11-23253475
E-mail:dphtemp@indiatimes.com

Printed at
Arora Offset Press
Laxmi Nagar, Delhi–92

Preface

Sound planning leads to efficient management. Planning is a co-operative, collective co-ordination and co-ordination is the first principle of management. Planning has rightly been defined as the process of determining the objectives of administrative effort and of devising the means calculated to achieve them. Why planning? What is planning? Its kinds, process, origin and functions. The purpose of management, its techniques and dimensions.

In this book an attempt has been to collect interesting, innovative and import material for our general readers as well as for the use of students and teachers.

We record our acknowledgements to the authorities on the subject who have directly and indirectly influenced us in completing this work.

Librarians and their staff members have rendered every possible co-operation. We thank them all.

With me, my publisher and his staff members have worked hard. Our readers satisfaction with the book will be our best reward.

R.K. Pruthi

Contents

1

Introduction

In this chapter we shall trace the historical evolution of Public Administration as a field of inquiry and also explain different traditions in the development of Public Administration. We have identified three traditions, viz. Absolutist, Liberal Democratic and Marxian, in the evolution of Public Administration.

The classification is done for educative purposes rather than for the purpose of explaining their empirical implications. The analytical frame, we hope, will enable you to have a broad perspective on the developments in Public Administration considered in terms of the impulses, ideological or otherwise behind them.

We introduce you to diverse traditions in the practice and theory of Public Administration. Such a diversity ahs arisen mainly because of differences in not only the history, culture and levels of development at various societies but also the impulses shaping them at different times. Before discussing them in detail, let us briefly consider the importance of the study of the evolution of Public Administration.

Evolution refers to a gradual unfolding of development of things in the course of time, when the past, present and future are considered in tenns of a continuum, the steady of the past or of history becomes all the more significant. The past not only foreshadows the present but also serves as its matrix.

History, in the words of E.H. Carr, is an unending dialogue between the past and the present. In this sense, the study of history has a contemporary relevance. Indeed, it is necessary for the understanding of the contemporary status of the subject and the critical issues therein, the genesis of which may be found in the past.

There is much truth in the saying that 'a phenomenon can be understood only in a historical context'. Again, the study of different phases and traditions in the evolution of Public Administration may also help in applying the 'lessons' or the indicators of the past to the consideration of the development of the subject in the present. Broadly, the study of evolution fulfils both theoretical and pragmatic purposes. From the theoretical point of view, it helps to locate the subject in a broader frame of reference and from the practical point of view it facilitates the use of the knowledge of the past to further the development of the subject in the present.

ABSOLUTIST TRADITIONS

In this section we shall discuss the absolutist tradition which antedates the other two-Liberal Democratic and Marxian. Absolutist tradition refers to administrative traditions of absolute monarchical regimes, where all powers are concentrated in the monarchy. The earliest work concerning it is Kautilya's *Arthasastra, the most important work on Public Administration in ancient India*. We confine our discussion to the Indian, tradition mainly for two reasons. Firstly, sufficient information is not available or the absolutist administrative traditions of other Asian societies. Secondly, the students of administration should be acquainted with their own traditions in the field of Public Administration.

According to tradition, Kautilya, also known as Chanakya and Vishnugupta, was the Prime Minister of Chandragupta Maurya (322-298 B.C.) who founded the Maruya Dynasty of Magadha (Bihar), Kautilya's treatise known as Arthasastra may be regarded as an ancient Indian text-book of practical politics. It, according to some, ranks in importance with Manusmriti and Kamasastra and forms a triad with them in dealing with the three imperatives of the social philosophy of that time—Dharma, Kama, Artha. It deals mainly with the Science Polity, which, according to Kautilya, is a combination of Science of Wealth and Science of Government.

Vittasastra (Economics) and Dandanithi (Statecraft). To Kautilya, finances provide the sinews of government and financial considerations are paramount in the government's a activities. Thus, his treatise adopts the political economy approach to the understanding of the problems of governance. H.V.R. Iyengar described Arthasastra "as an exceptionally able dissection both on the aims of the State as well as on practical means by which these aims can be achieved". Arthasastra is both an analytical and a perspective document revealing amazing perception and mastery of detail.

Kautilya's Arthastra mainly discusses three aspects of the science of Public Administration, viz. the principles of Public Administration, the machinery of Government and the management of personnel. The principles of administration are not explicitly dealt with in Arthasastra. They are implied by the functions of the monarch, ministers, etc. as detailed in it. The machinery of Government as described in the Arthasastra is mainly related to the monarch, his relations with ministers, etc. The problems of higher level personnel receive greater attention than the lower level functionaries in Arthasastra.

Kautilya spelt out the importance of the science of Public Administration. According to Kautilya, an administrator can adopt the art of Public Administration only if he is conversant with the science of Public Administration. So it is necessary for the King, the Crown Prince, the High Priest and the ministers to be conversant with the science of Administration. He emphasised the principles of authority, obedience and discipline as being central to the administration of the state. He considered principles like division of work, hierarchy and coordination important to the mechanism of internal organisation. Further, Kautilya is, perhaps, the earliest known thinker to recognise the importance of statistics in administration.

Kautilya made a systematic study of the society and did not blindly accept the current views based on faith and tradition. Ancient Hindus held that the Vedas constitute the sole source of law. But Kautilya laid down four distinct sources of law, namely, sacred scriptures, the rules laid down in Arthasastra, customs and edicts of kings. Each of these he considers more authoritative than the one preceding it. He explicitly states that when the sacred law is in conflict with the corporal law the latter should prevail. Arthasastra is secular in its tenor and puts politics in command over religion. According to Kautilya, religious considerations should not outweigh political considerations. The king according to him, should strive and maintain the stability of the State and increase his power and material resources by policy or subterfuge. To this end he even proposed an elaborate system of recruiting spies and training them. Some of these propositions of Kautilya are termed Mechiavellian. Here it is interesting to note the observations of H.V.R. Iyengar, who said that "Kautilya was honest and stated frankly what today is hidden under dubious veil of secrecy".

Kautilya's 'Ideal State' was something like a modern Welfare State under an all powerful ruler. He clearly required the State to provide for the maintenance of children, women, the old, the infirm and the disabled. The State was to run agricultural farms, help the artisans, and exploit the forest wealth and mineral resources for the benefit of the people at large. Indeed, the basics of 'Welfarism' can be traced in Kautilya's Arthasastra.

Kautilya advocated a strong centralised authority vested in the monarchy. As pointed out by N.P. Inamdar "the principles governing the democratic Public Administration are in many respects different from the principles underlying a monarchical Public Administration described in Arthasastra, as the sources and the configurations of authority in the two systems are different'. The administrative system as discussed in Arthasastra centres on the king. His orders are unquestionable. His interests are supreme. He is the source of authority for all institutions. The fading away of the monarchical form led to other traditions to explain and understand the administrative systems in democratic societies. However, it should be noted that the traditions of Public Administration as established by Arthasastra are significant for its emphasis on the Science of Public Administration and systematic analysis of the art of governance.

LIBERAL DEMOCRATIC TRADITIONS

Traditionally, the origins of Public Administration as a separate area of inquiry are traced to Woodrow Wilson's essay. The Study of Administration, published in 1887. His essay marks the beginning of systematic investigation into the field of Public Administration.

Since then the study of the subject passed through various phases, each phase characterised by a particular paradogmatic approach. Broadly, seven phases are identified for understanding the evolution of the subject in the broad paradigm of liberal democracy. Let us briefly discuss each one of them.

Politics—Administration Dichotomy Approach

Woodrow Wilson, the father of modern Public Administration, considered politics and administration as separate processes and attempted to conceptually distinguish between the two areas of study. A similar attempt was made by Frank Goodnow, another exponent of the dichotomy approach who observed that "politics has to do with policies or expressions of state while administration has to do with the execution of these policies". This distinction is made between policy making and policy execution. Policy making is regarded as the realm of politics and execution as the realm of Public Administration.

Further, politics and Public Administration are differentiated on the basis of their institutional locations. The location of politics is identified with the legislature and the higher echelons of government where major policy-decisions would be made and the larger questions of allocation of values decided upon. The location of administration on the other hand is identified with the executive arm of government—the bureaucracy. The processes of administration, it was argued, have a certain regularity and concretness above them, which can be successfully investigated. Thus it is possible to develop a science of Administration.

Structural Approach

This approach is marked by the tendency to reinforce the idea of politics—administration dichotomy and to evolve a value free? Science of Management.

The 'Public' aspects of Public Administration was virtually dropped at this stage and the focus was almost wholly on economy and efficiency. The questions of 'value' were not considered important to the new science of Administration Politics as practised by the politicians was considered irrelevant.

Scientific Management for the efficient handling of the 'business' of administration became the focus of interest.

Principles of management were worked out as readymade aids to practitioners. The administrative practitioners and the business schools joined hands to emphasize the mechanistic aspect of management unaffected by the predictions of politicians and the failings of human beings.

The approach emphasised the structure of the organisation. Structure is a device through which human beings working in an orgination are assigned tasks and related to one another. It is believed the the effective functioning of the organisation depends upon the structure that a group of human beings build and operate. The structural approach was criticised for the ambiguity of its principles absence of scientific validity and its mechanistic approach to human problems.

Human Relations Approach

The Hawthorne experiments pioneered a movement which came to be known as the Human Relations Approach to management. Its impact on Public Administrate was much more widely in the postwar petrol than before. The approach to organisational analysis drew attention to the formation and effect of work groups in the organisation the force of informal organisation is the formal setup the phenomena of leadership and conflicts and cooperation among groups in the organisational setting. In short, the human relations approach brought out the limitations of the machine concept of organisation in 'Scientific Management' thought. By drawing attention to the social and psychological factors of work situation, it underlined the importance of the "human side of the enterprise".

The social psychological has extended the concern of human relationists by bringing in additional knowledge about the sensitivity to human components. It is aimed at bringing about: (1)

greater organisational productivity or effectiveness, and (2) greater human happiness and increased self-realisation. Prominent writers advocating this approach include Abraham Maslow. Douglas McGregor, Rensis Likert and Chris Argyis. The human relations approach has been criticised for its manipulative orientation. It is alleged that the aim of the movement is to manipulate the man in organisation to achieve higher productivity. It is also criticised for ignoring the institutional and social system variable in understanding the organisation.

Behavioural Approach

Herbert Simon's Administrative Behaviour' is a critique of the older Public Administration. More importantly, it sets forth the rigorous requirements of scientific analysis in Public Administration, Simon's conclusion about some of the classical Principles' was that they were unscientifically derived and were "no more than proverbs." He rejected the politics administration dichotomy, and at the same time brought in the perspective of logical positivism for the study of policy making and the relation of means and ends. Reflecting the perspectives and methodology of behaviouralism in psychology and social psychology. Administrative Behaviour pleaded for the enforcement of scientific rigour in Public Administration. The substantive focus was on "decision-making", and as Simon insisted. "If any theory is involved it is that decision making is the heart of administration and that the vocabulary of administrative theory must be derived from the logic and psychology of human choice".

Simon's approach provided an alternative definition of Public Administration, and widened the scope of the subject by relating it to Psychology. Sociology, Economics and Political Science. In the development of the 'discipline he identified two mutually supportive streams of thought. One was engaged in the development of a pure science of administration which called for a good grounding in social psychology, and the other in the development of a broad range of values and in working out prescriptions for public policy. The second approach was, in Simon's view, analytically far-ranging. It would imply the assimilation of the whole of Political Science and Economics and

Sociology as well as Public Administration. Thus Public Administration, he feared, might lose its identity in the second approach. But he favoured the co-existence of both the streams of thought to the growth and development of the discipline. As he said, "there does not appear to be any reason why these two developments in the field of Public Administration should not go side by side, for they in no way conflict or contradict. But the workers in this field must keep clearly in mind in which area, at any given time, they propose to work".

Development Approach

The ecological approach to the study of administration originated in the wake of the emergence of the Third World and increasing realisation of irrelevance of most of the western organisation theories to the study of administration. To quote Robert Dahl, "The study of Public Administration inevitably must become a much more broadly based discipline resting not on a narrowly defined knowledge of techniques and processes, but rather extending to the varying historical sociological economic and other conditioning factors... This suggestion has been taken up as a challenge and efforts have been made in the study of Public Administration in the developing countries in a bid to "establishing propositions about administrative behaviour which transcend national boundaries". Such efforts have given rise to Comparative Public Administration and Development Administration.

Public Policy Approach

The Social Sciences' general concern for social engineering has resulted in the laying of emphasis of public policy. The study of Public Administration has also been influenced by the public policy perspective. The abandonment of politics administration dichotomy made the public policy approach agreeable to administrative analysis.

Evidence from the practical world of administration has brought out the criteria of a close nexus between politics and administration. As governments seek to formulate and implement more and more welfare programmes, the promotion of policy studies in public Administration gathers momentum. At this stage, the study of Public

Administration has been gaining in social relevance no doubt; but its boundaries as a descriptive study are not as clearly distinguishable now as they used to be in the olden days of politics—administration dichotomy. The discipline, to many Public Administration analysts, has gained in vigour and vigour; but it has suffered a crisis of identity with diversification and strength.

Political Economy Approach

Another development in the study of Public Administration is brought about by the adoption of the political economy approach to the analysis of administrative problems. This is associated with the moving of Political Science closer to Economics in the interest of greater theoretical cohernece and better policy guidance. Economists like Anthony Downs and Gordon Tullock have gone over the boundary by experimenting with the application of economic methods and models to political problems. Thus Public Administration as a branch of Political Science and on its own has moved towards a liaison with Economics.

The liberal democratic tradition in the evolution of Public Administration as described above shows that, starting with an assertion of independent identity, it has moved towards the assimilation of ideas, methods and techniques of different Social Science disciplines. Thus the scope of the discipline seems to be broadening while the question of its identity remains unanswered.

A CHART INDICATING THE DIFFERENCES BETWEEN VARIOUS APPROACHES

Politics-Administration Dichotomy Approach	*Structural Approach*	*Human Relations Approach*	*Behavioural Approach*
1. Politics and administration are distinct	1. A value-free Science of Management	1. Emphasis on the human side of the enterprise	1. Deals with the "inside" human being with a focus on his values and rationality.
2. Politics is concerned with policy making, administration with execution of policy	2. The focus is on economy and efficiency	2. Brings out the limitations of the machine concept of organisation	2. Decision-making is considered to be the heart of the administration

3. The location of politics is legislature and the Cabinet the location of administration—the executive arm of the government	3. "Public" aspect of Public Administration was dropped	3. Emphasis on the social and psychological factors of work situations	3. Widens the scope of the subject by relating it to Psychology, Sociology etc.
4. A value free science of management	4. Emphasis on the structure	4. Deals with the relationship among the people working in organisation	

Development Approach	*Public Policy Approach*	*Political Economy Approach*
1. Emphasis on the study of the developmental aspect of the administration	1. Emphasis on Public Policy structure	1. Emphasis on the application of economic methods and models of political problem.
2. Emphasis on historical socio-economic, political factors which condition development	2. With the formulation and implementation of welfare programmes policy study assumes greater significance	2. Empahsis on the Public Administration's closer interrelationship and interaction with politico-economic policies.

MARXIAN TRADITIONS

The October Revolution of 1917 generated debate among the Marxists on the role of bureaucracy in Russia. But the Marxist interest in the bureaucracy, organisation and management became pronounced only in the decade following the Second World War and developed in a number of directions.

We have to go back to Marx to understand the classical Marxist view of bureaucracy. Although Marx has not paid much attention to the concept of bureaucracy, his views on bureaucracy and its relation to the power structure of the society found in his major works provide an important clue to the understanding of the later developments in the Marxist thought on bureaucracy. His ideas on bureaucracy figure mainly in his work. The 18th Brumaire of Louis Bonaparte. His ideas about bureaucracy can be understood when considered within the general framework of his theory of class conflict, the crisis of capitalism, and the emergence of communism. In the wider context of class struggle Marx regards bureaucracy as an instrument of the dominant ruling class, promoting its particular interests. Its existence and development thus have a transient and parastic character. From this point of view bureaucracy and further bureaucratisation become unavoidable in a society divided into classes. Marx envisaged that with the abolition of the classes, the Sate and its bureaucracy would 'wither away'. The "withering away" of the bureaucracy would mean its gradual absorption into the society as a whole. Thus instead of having an oppressive structure, Marx visualised that in a Communist society, the functions of the bureaucracy would be taken over by the members of the society themselves. The administrative tasks shedding their exploitative character would come to mean administration of things and not of people. This philosophic stance of Marx has had a great influence on his followers as well as on his critics.

The October Revolution of 1917 in Russia and the establishment of socialist government in many countries of the world in subsequent years led to experimentation with Marxian ideas. There has been in the socialist world a proliferation of bureaucracy and a growing tendency to apply western management techniques. Lenin viewed the strengthening of the centralised bureaucracy in post-revolutionary Russia as an indication of the immaturity of socialism and the inadequate development of forces of production, Lenin like Marx considered it a traditional phenomenon. In contrast, the critics of the system have put forward theories regarding the bureaucracy as a "New Class". i.e. a newly emerged class in Soviet Union and other socialist countries ruling in the name of proletariat.

In is indisputable that Marxion studies of bureaucracy, its organisation and management have added a new dimension of the study of Public Administration and helped to develop it. The attempts of Stewart Clegg and David Dunkerly, Nicos Mouzelis, Braverman, and many others to build a radical organisation theory have led to some significant advances in the study of Public Organisation. Indeed, the Marxian traditions have placed the study of Public Administration in the wider perspective of social transformation.

The evolution of Public Administration was examined in the framework of absolutist, liberal democratic and Marxian traditions. The State in the ancient times was dominated by an absolutist monarchial system for a long time. Kautilya's Arthasastra describes the science of administration in relation to the authoritarian monarchy. Some of the principles of administration described in 'Arthasastra' have relevance to the present time probably because of the continuation of authoritarian traditions in the modern state. The Industrial Revolution of the late 18th and 19th century resulted in the emergence eof a liberal democratic state in many parts of the world. The modern Public Administration is a by product of the liberal democratic state. Different phases in the evolution of Public Administration in a liberal democratic state reflect those of the social transformation in these societies. The events of the October Revolution of 1917 in Soviet Union resulted in the study of Public Administration from a Marxian perspective. The proponents and critics of Marxism and socialist practices have enriched the field of injury in Public Administration. The diversity of human experience in respect of governance and the ideological moorings of the people provide a battleground for the ideas and practices in Public Administration.

2

Management Information System

Management Information System is an integrated approach to the design and use of a computer-based information system that provides summary information and highlights exceptions for correctives decision-making. Readily available and up-to-date information is a vital requirement for facilitating correct policy-making and monitoring and control over various programmes. MIS also enables the management to take concurrent corrective action in ongoing projects.

COMPARATIVE POSITION

Measures Taken in Other Countries

Heralding improved MIS has been an inherent feature of administrative reforms effected in different countries of the world. In *Canada* an office of Information Management System and Technology headed by a Chief Information Officer was created for policy devolution, implementation and administrative re-engineering of the existing information systems. In 1994, the *Malaysian Government* introduced a Civil Service Link (CSL) as an on-line information database system to enable the general public to access information on government services at the touch of a button. This was preceded by massive computerisation and strengthened technology base in the management of public services. The ambit of administrative reforms in the *United Kingdom* included establishment of information systems in the principal areas of government departments like personnel records, finance, physical resources and procurement. An integrated approach to MIS was followed so as to share the available information between different government departments. Efficiency units were set up to determine departmental needs and recommend most suitable MIS for different governmental agencies. A body called the Government Centre for Information Systems was created for promoting effectiveness and efficiency in government through the use of information systems.

PRESENT STATE OF MIS IN INDIA

Ills Plaguing the Present System

Despite recent changes, government offices have not so far adopted Information Technology in a big way. Collection and compilation of information in government is being done on a very large scale by way of filing various returns, which engages, most of the time of field functionaries. However, this vast information is not fully utilised because of its bulk and its delayed availability. In government departments information technology is mainly used for document processing. While such systems have improved the efficiency of operation of processes of a repetitive nature, they have not been used either for decision-making of for planning, because of which the scope for enhancing the effectiveness of organisations as a whole has been extremely limited. Most of the departments have taken up computerisation of their operations in isolation and at times their systems are not compatible with the overall computer network of the government being operated by NIC. There is no effective mechanism for exchange of information between various ministries/departments. At times, the left hand does not know what the right hand is doing. The bulk of information gathered by the government machinery is not, therefore, utilised efficiently and effectively. Quite often, information, in spite of being available, has to be collected from the concerned offices due to cumbersome system of retrieval or the same information is sought more than once by the same office. The information so collected is hardly used for monitoring of projects or for taking corrective action or even to update data inputs for policy makers.

Desirable Attributes

Today the government machinery needs an MIS which will reduce duplication of efforts, streamline operations, Make standard, accurate and timely information readily available at all levels, integrate government operations across the country, and take care of routine and repetitive processes which presently account for nearly 80 per cent of all government activities. The government, in its role as facilitator, should also make relevant data available to the private sector to facilitate its business interests, within the country and abroad.

RECOMMENDATIONS

Developing a Computer Network

Each ministry/department should identify the type of information required at various levels for its designated functions and identify the sources for its collection. Thereafter an integrated software should be developed which should compile information fed by various sources and process it to facilitate its retrieval in the desired format by various functionaries. This will eliminate duplication in data collection, its compilation and transmission. The NICNET of the National Informatics Centre, which covers all the district headquarters in the country, should be utilised by all the ministries and departments of the central government. A common software should be devised by NIC for all government departments so that the systems being followed in different departments remain compatible. Even if individual departments have to develop specialised programmes for their specific functions, care should be taken to make their language compatible. The computers of various offices/departments should be networked so as to facilitate interchange of information between different offices/departments/ministries of the government. NICNET, Internet connectivity should be provided to heads of all field organisations. Proper safeguards should be incorporated within the system so that only authorised officers can access the information, to prevent misuse of leakage of information available.

Devising New Forms for Submission of Information

New formats should be devised for collecting information from field units by the head of office/ministry. These monthly formats should be exhaustive and contain complete information so that the need for calling details repeatedly from field offices is obviated.

Departmental and Functional Management Control Systems

A new system should be developed for department and functional management control. The system should interact extensively with information generated at the operations level to summarise and present it in the desired format. The reports generated by this system should cater to both routine as well as *ad hoc* queries essential for decision making.

Planning and Control System

For purposes of strategic planning control at higher levels, a suitable information system consisting of related information from external sources supplemented with data extracted from the operational level of the department should be devised. This system should have an inbuilt capacity to cater to a large number of unstructured and unanticipated requests and should be able to support 'What-If' analysis to enable users to develop their own models.

Specialised Software

Government departments should be given specialised software to perform functions which can lead to better analysis and results in time-saving.

Amendment the Existing Procedures

Necessary modifications should be made in the current system and procedures of the government to make them adaptable to computerisation and MIS.

Data Intelligence System

The data collected by government is quite exhaustive and can be of great use for private entrepreneurs in planning their operations. The government should develop a system whereby data having commercial value can be made accessible to private sectors for commercial use.

3

Autonomy and Delegation

The present trend the world over is towards granting greater autonomy and delegating more powers at all levels of the government. Perhaps the highest level of autonomy and delegation has been effected in New Zealand during the course of the reforms initiated in the last decade. Most of the government activities have been either privatised or are being run as State Owned Enterprises like private sector businesses conforming to commercial objectives alone. For the core activities that have been retained in Government, Ministers, enter into a contract with the Departmental Chief Executives wherein the output to be produced by the department and the price to be paid are specified. The Chief Executive, who himself is on a contract, has full powers to hire and fire his staff and to fix their salaries. All civil servants are employed on a contract, under which they are responsible to produce a certain number of outputs of specified quality at a certain price. In order to achieve such outputs, each manager has complete discretion over inputs and can prescribe work methods, devise systems, fix salaries, grant amenities and decide upon the number of his staff while remaining within his overall budget. The pay of the manager is also dependent on his performance. There are annual reviews and depending on their results his pay can be adjusted both upwards and downwards. Budgeting has become totally output-oriented, with the control of the Treasury limited only to a fixing of the total size of the departmental budgets.

AUTONOMY AND DELECTION—AN APPRAISAL

Feasibility of Introducing the New Zealand Model in India

While this kind of system may be the ultimate aim for any government of the future, it is doubtful if the present circumstances are conducive to its instantaneous implementation in India. Today we have a centralised system of Government that is premised on distrust. Whether it is the Ministry of Finance or the Ministry of Law or the Department of Personnel, they do not trust other individual Ministries to do the right thing. It is, therefore, necessary to refer everything important to these nodal Ministries. Whatever little autonomy the departmental heads seem to enjoy notionally is withdrawn by the Ministry of Finance under the guise of economy. Most important decisions of any consequence are taken either by the Cabinet or a Cabinet Committee or the Minister or the Committee of Secretaries.

Necessity for Delegation

Delegation of authority is critical to the cutting down of levels and the time taken for arriving at a decision. Only delegation can lead to reduction in the size of government which is central to the entire process of administrative reforms. Centralised control leads to wastage, as one set of rules cannot be equally applicable to thousands of diverse situations which obtain in a country of India's size and complexity. There is thus no doubt that delegation is the key to faster decision-making.

RECOMMENDATIONS

Decentralisation of Financial Powers

Presently, the most excessive centralisation of powers is seen in the matter of finance. All ministries have a Financial Advisor (F.A.) who is responsible both to the administrative ministry and the finance ministry. The F.A. assists the administrative Secretary in respect of the powers delegated to the ministry and the Secretary can, in theory, overrule his F.A. In practice, however, stringent restrictions have been placed in respect of exercise of delegated powers. Powers for creation of non-plan posts, reappropriation from plan to non-plan expenditure, expenditure on telephones, travelling allowance, entertainment, overtime etc. have been severely curtailed or withdrawn. This kind of total control is stifling and often acts as a barrier in achieving the allotted targets and goals. Accordingly, there is a need for the finance ministry to allow other ministries greater freedom and flexibility in financial matters. It would be more appropriate if the finance ministry approves the overall budget for different ministries and thereafter allows them sufficient flexibility to manage the financial resources in the most productive manner irrespective of the various heads under which it is spent. Simultaneously, all the powers withdrawn from the ministries during the last few years in the name of economy measures should be restored, with reiteration of the government's desire to effect maximum economy. The dual control over the F.As. should also be removed and they should work under the control of the administrative Secretaries as real financial "advisors" in respect of delegated financial powers.

Role of Ministry of Personnel, Public Grievances and Pensions

The Ministry of Personnel, Public Grievances and Pensions is the nodal ministry dealing with policy in respect of personnel matters. Due to common criteria prescribed by this ministry, there is a great deal of uniformity in the civil services, which is not always conducive to effective management of the functions attached to diverse departments. There is need for greater freedom in personnel matters within the existing system subject to the specified budget on pay and allowances. Individual departments should be allowed to determine the structure of their cadres within the existing pay scales without the intervention of the Ministries of Finance and Personnel. They should also be authorised to work out incentives applicable to their employees, within the parameters of general guidelines, like increments, lump-sum payments, productivity-linked bonus, etc. The departments should also enjoy greater freedom in respect of personnel who are specific to such departments and are not be found in other ministries. In such a scenario, the role of Ministry of Personnel would be confined to laying down general policy guidelines in respect of matters like recruitment, promotion, deputation etc.

Appointments Committee of the Cabinet

The approval of the Appointments Committee of the Cabinet should be sought only in respect of appointments of Joint Secretaries and above in the secretariat and appointments to posts carrying a pay scale equivalent to that of Additional Secretaries and above in the field offices.

Role of Committee of Secretaries

Presently there is a tendency to refer almost all important matters to the 'Committee of Secretaries'. This leads to avoidable delays and dilution of responsibilities. Individual cases should not be referred to the Committee of Secretaries. Only broader issues having wider ramifications should be taken up at their level. All administrative Secretaries should be delegated the complete and final authority for approval of projects, programmes, schemes, procedures etc. upto any limit within the overall budget. They will no doubt seek the advice of all those concerned before arriving at the final decision. This would ensure that the ministry responsible for a given task also has the necessary powers to achieve it.

Role of Secretaries

All administrative Secretaries should be given maximum functional freedom and financial flexibility as in the case of Chief Executives in New Zealand. Simultaneously, they should also be asked to commit themselves to targets and action plans for their entire tenure and held accountable for the same.

Delegation as a Prelude to Delayering

As a prelude to reduction of levels in the ministries, the posts of Director, Deputy Secretary and Under Secretary should be treated as one group and that of Joint Secretary, Additional Secretary and Secretary as another. An officer belonging to the lower group should submit the files directly to an officer of the higher group who should be delegated the necessary powers to take a decision on such matters. This will ensure that no file is dealt by more than two executives before a final decision is arrived at.

An Atmosphere of Trust

An atmosphere of trust has to be created throughout the administrative system, so that each rung of the Government feels motivated and responsible for the results in specific areas of responsibility. Power and responsibility should go together. Only in such a system can decisions be taken quickly and efficiently.

4

Leadership, Policy-formation and Decision-making

LEADERSHIP

The crisis of administration is the crisis of leadership. With the 'public' sector constantly on the increase, large and complex organisations are being built up under the aegis of the ever-expanding 'Welfare' State. All these organisations, big and small, need administrative leadership. More schools, more hospitals, more industries, more steel plants, more corporations, more institutes and laboratories call for one indispensable element, namely, administrative leadership.

Similarly, the successful implementation of thousands of programmes included in our Plan depends for their success on good leadership. Bernard is, thus, right in remarking "that the necessary production of leaders to the population has greatly increased." Growth in technology and specialisation too have made leadership complex. In the words of Seckler-Hudson: "The overwhelming significance of the problems of leadership has mounted with the revolutionary growth of such factors of size, complexity, specialisation, organisational entities, technical developments and social demands." Thus, the first and the foremost task of Management today is to provide leadership, that is, to direct, control, and co-ordinate the activities of a group of persons with a view to achieving the desired goals of the organisation.

Meaning and Nature

In spite of the overwhelming significance of leadership there is no unanimity about its contents. "Indeed, I have never observed any leader who was able to state adequately or intelligently why he was able to be a leader nor any statement of followers that acceptably expressed why they followed," says Barnard, and a person of his standing should know what he is saying. Leadership is often confused with personal preeminence. People tend to forget that leadership has a double meaning. A look at the dictionary meaning of the verb 'to lead' would show that the term is used in two different senses. In one sense it means "to excel, to be in advance, to be prominent;" in another sense it means "to guide others, to be head of an organisation; to hold command." A useful distinction can, thus, be drawn between personal leadership and management leadership. A person is born with the talent for personal leadership; he must learn management leadership.

It must be made clear at the outset that leadership should not be equated with command and fear. More than coercion, persuasion and inspiration motivate successful leadership. Leadership has, thus, been defined as "the activity of persuading people to co-operate in the achievement of a common objective." In a similar vein, Terry defines it as "the activity of influencing people to strive willingly for mutual objectives." In the words of Seckler-Hudson, "Leadership in large organisations may be defined as influencing and energizing of people to work together in a common effort to achieve the purposes of the enterprise." According to Barnard, "Leadership refers to the quality of the behaviour of individuals, whereby they guide people in their activities in organised effort." In his opinion, leadership "depends upon three things—(1) the individual, (2) the followers, and (3) the conditions." Very often we think of leadership as being chiefly personal in character. Undoubtedly, important though this aspect is, it alone is not enough. This much will depend on the quality and character of the followers. Mary Parker Follett has vividly described this relationship: "We have now to lay somewhat less stress than formerly on this matter of the leader influencing his group because we now think of the leader as being influenced by his group. One of our Chief Justices once said to me that he considered this reciprocal relation the main characteristic of leadership. I think it is one of the examples of what I have...called circular response. The currents go both ways. The channels should be kept open for the continuous flow to go on all the time. When it gets dammed up, effective leadership stops. That is, we should think not only of what the leaders does to the group, but also of what the group does to the leader. The third variable is the conditions in the background of which the leadership operates. Millett is right when he says that *"leadership is often made or broken by circumstance."* According to him, "The essential circumstances of leadership are twofold—political and institutional. By the political conditions of administrative leadership, we mean the need to be responsive to external political direction and control...By the institutional conditions of leadership, we mean the need to be responsive to the requirements of internal operation of keeping an administrative agency in actual running order."

Koontz and O'Donnell refer to three different approaches to leadership—*traitist, situationist* and *elementalist.* The traitist "adopted an inductive procedure, observing those recognised as leaders and enumerating the traits each possessed. Qualities held in common were assumed to be essential, and enumeration was offered as a standard for measuring leadership potential." Tead, Barnard and Schell are prominent advocates of this approach. The difficulty with this theory, however, is that there is no evidence of common traits of leadership. The traitists seldom agree on common qualities of leadership and thus, fail to furnish universally acceptable traits. The situationist approach is concerned more with evolving a method for identifying leaders: "Their starting-point is to assume that certain elements, such as, speech, intelligence, stability, and persistence, are essential in leaders. The next step is to place a candidate in a group and observe how he acts under trial situations that are constructed as realistically as possible." This approach has, however, been used only on an experimental basis for the selection of army and police officers in certain western countries, like Germany and the U.S.A. The proponents of the elementalist approach "are concerned with refining the concepts of leadership traits, correlating these with leadership success, and, thus, developing a value for each." Still others try to learn about the leader by studying his followers. Thus, a lot of research is going on in the field.

According to Barnard, a leader performs four main functions—(i) *the determination of objectives*; (ii) *the manipulation of means;* (iii) *the control of the instrumentality of action;* and (iv) *the stimulation of co-ordinated action.*

Qualities of Leadership

Almost every writer on Management has his own list. Thus, Barnard's list includes four qualities—(i) *Vitality and Endurance;* (ii) *Decisiveness;* (iii) *Persuasiveness;* and (iv) *Responsibility and Intellectual Capacity*—in that order of importance. His views on the limitations of intellectualism are interesting. He decries the present trend to put excessive emphasis upon intellectual attainments by selecting authorities. "We all know persons in and out of practical affairs of superior intellects and intellectual accomplishments who do not work well as leaders. In matters of leadership, for example, they prove to be irresponsible, non-decisive, non-persuasive. Moreover, we can observe that intellectual capacity rarely rises above physiological disabilities in active life, that the utmost perspicacity is useless for leadership if it does not decide issues, the persuasive processes must take full account of the irrational by which all are largely governed, that responsibility is a moral or emotional condition." Barnard's view in this respect has not gone unchallenged. Reading a paper on the political Executive at the Conference on that subject at the Woodrow Wilson School of Public and International Affairs, Princeton University (U.S.A.), Harlan Cleveland, till recently the Dean, Maxwell, Graduate School of Citizenship and Public Affairs, Syracuse University (U.S.A.), pointedly remarked, "I suspect that Mr. Barnard would agree that for the political executive, intellectual capacity should rank higher on his list than the last place. A political executive, unlike a business executive, cannot possibly delegate his thinking to a vice-president for ideas. It is a condition of survival in the jungle that he should do his own homework and be in intellectual command of he subject-matter of the programme for which he is responsible. When a congressional committee or an important 'veto group' wants to know the story and asks embarrassing questions, no understudy with a mimeographed statement will fill the bill." The same will apply to the Ministers in India. Cleveland's own list of attributes of leadership, in his own words, is: "Our political executive must be imbued with the public interest, he must be a leader of men, he must do his own thinking and be his own public relations man, and he should preferably have had some private experience." As the Hoover Commission's Task Force Report on Personnel and Civil Service (1955) noted, "His foresight must equal the hindsight of a host of critics.... The rules of the game of national politics allow no margin for error...To lead the life of a political executive of a high rank amidst the asperities of American politics is a test of toughness, of intelligence, and of devotion to the public interest." Millett enumerates these qualities as: "Good health, a sense of mission, interest in other people, intelligence, integrity, persuasiveness, judgment and loyalty." According to Terry, these qualities are—energy, emotional stability, knowledge of human relations, personal motivation, communicative skill, teaching ability, social skill and technical competence. According to Appleby, a good administrator has willingness to assume responsibilities; demonstrates continuing personal growth; is disposed towards action; is a good listener who asks pointed questions; works well with all sorts of people; seeks ablest obtainable subordinates; uses institutional resources—does not try to do it all and know it all himself; cares for power only as it contributes to effectiveness, chiefly as a reserve asset, has self-confidence, and so is ready to admit his limitations and errors; is hospitable to bad news as well as good; respects subordinates as much as superiors; constantly seeks to improve institutional performance; and in democratic governments he respect political processes and responsibilities.

In our opinion, a leader as the successful head of a big organisation, should possess the following attributes:

1. *Decisiveness.* Nothing is possible more damaging to the morale of an organisation than a vacillating, procrastinating, hesitating, indecisive chief;
2. *Clarity of Vision.* A leader must know what he wants and what he does not want;
3. *Far-sight.* A leader should be both far-sighted and far-seeing. He should be able to rise above and see beyond the existing situation;

4. *Unerring Judgment.* A leader's judgment has to be more correct than incorrect;
5. *Building up of Subordinates.* The extent to which an executive can change the baser human metal around him into shining gold is an index of his good leadership. He must win the confidence and trust of his staff and inspire them;
6. *Participative Management.* A leader should, of course, be a good organizer. In addition, he should also be able to create in the workers a feeling of participation in managing the organisation;
7. *Good Public Relations.* In modern age, this is a quality most needed. The executive should have the skill to sell his wares;
8. *Improvement in Consciousness.* The leader should be progressive and be enthused with the desire to improve performance of the organisation.

Development of Leadership

Now that Management has come to be regarded as a 'science' and a technique and accepted as a profession, the need for training managers has been universally recognised. It is true that traditionally, managers and executive leaders have been 'born' rather than 'made'. It is also true that 'coaching' by the boss and the school of experience have been the traditional modes of training, and, indeed, they will never cease to play their part. But the complex and technical nature of administrative processes has made a more systematic and better planned training programme imperative. In the words of Barnard, "I suppose no one doubts that without education the supply of leaders of organisations competent for conditions of the modern world would be wholly inadequate and many of us suspect that if we knew better how to train men, we should be much better able than we are to cope with the social dilemmas we confront." Barnard in his chapter on 'Education for Executives' makes a penetrating analysis of the needs of the executives and suggests methods to develop these requirements:

1. *Need for Broad Interests and Wide Imagination and Understanding.* This can be inculcated by a system of general

education supplemented by self-education on the part of the executives. Barnard suggests even giving them 'sabbatical leave' to brush up their knowledge and graze into fresher and wider pastures. In India, the government has already introduced general education at the university level and public servants are being encouraged to go on leave for education and training. Short-term courses, seminars, conferences, and workshops are being organised with the same end in view;

2. *Superior Intellectual Capacities*. A highly cultivated and trained mind is essential to understand the modern world of complex technologies and intricate techniques. This aspect is perhaps most amenable to formal education and training;

3. *Understanding Human Relations*. "The need of such understanding is of first importance to the executive; for human relations are the essence of managerial, employees, public and political relations; and in most cases, these rather than science, technology, law or finance are the central areas of the executive functions." According to Barnard, there are three aspects to this problem: (i) Appreciation of non-rational behaviour of human beings. Man, it must be remembered, does not always act rationally; quite often emotions determine his conduct. Intellectuals often tend to speak of the people as "stupid, dumb and animal-like"; but it is these persons with whom administrators have to deal. (ii) An understanding of the nature of general social system, and (iii) An understanding of formal organisations as organic and evolving systems. Organisations can seldom be built up on paper in accordance with some preconceived concepts for the simple reason that organisations consist of persons who cannot be left out of account in building up or running an organisation. All these three points are susceptible to formal instruction in educational institutions;

4. *Importance of Persuasion in Human Affairs*. The essence of administrative leadership, it has been rightly said, is not command but persuasion, particularly in a democratic society. This calls for training in the act of expression through writing, conversation or public speaking.

The question that now remains to be solved is how to educate and train executives. The magical effect of training and education should not be exaggerated. "The qualification of leadership that is subject to specific preparatory training for formal processes is the intellectual, including therein the inculcation of general and specific knowledge." Barnard draws a distinction between knowledge and skill in this connection, and regards the latter as more important. He defines skill as "the effective behaviour by which the appropriate adjustment to the infinite complexity of the concrete is established," and this, Barnard says, may depend more on experience or even intuition. It must be admitted that many attributes of leadership are not susceptible to formal training. They may either be discovered or grow out of experience.

How to Select Leaders?

This is a highly ticklish question. The very first question that arises here is: Are leaders manufactured or are they simply identified? In other words, is the task merely to discover persons with qualities of leadership and put them in position? Administration leaders today are secured by selection and not by formal preparation. But how to select such persons? Selection on the basis of written test is loaded heavily in favour of intellectual calibre. Selection on the basis of a prolonged psychological-cum-intelligence-cum-observation basis, as in the army, succeeds better in locating persons with skill of co-operation, co-ordination, leadership, organisation etc. The role of experience in building up leadership, however, should not be underestimated. In the words of Barnard, "Balance, perspective, and proportion in the senses relevant to leadership are to be acquired almost exclusively from responsible experience in leading." He suggests that administrator should be encouraged to gain experience in leadership outside the organisation they work in. Practice in leading is as important as in any other sphere. There is no substitute to a person's experience in carving out a place for himself against odds. In brief, proper method of selection, formal education and training and informal as well as formal experience will all be needed to create the requisite quality and quantity of leadership in modern society. The truth, however, remains that leadership is not given, it is assumed.

POLICY-FORMATION

Significance

The process of policy-formation is one of the central processes of government. According to Appleby, the essence of public administration is policy-making. The use of policies is vital in the task of planning a course of action. Policies supply the standard guides which help managers to plan, to act in line with legal requirements and to realize the desired objectives. Policies help the executive keep his activities within a 'prescribed framework of action'. As a matter of fact, policies give meaning to the objectives. The objectives of an organisation are usually couched in general terms. Policies give concrete form to these goals.

Meaning

The term is often used rather loosely: it is confused with rule, custom and decision. While it is true that a rule is a guide inasmuch as it prescribes the dos and don'ts, but rules, unlike policies are specific and rigid. A custom has been defined as 'a habitual course of action'. It is the way in which work is actually done. A custom just grows while a policy may be the result of deliberate action. However, customs and policies need not always coincide. A decision is usually taken within the framework of policy, that is, policy may involve a series of decisions. Similarly, a distinction should be made between policy and method or procedure. Policy is concerned with basic issue while method deals with the way of effectuating a policy. In the words of Terry, "A policy is verbal, written or implied basic guide to action that is adopted and followed by a manager." Dimock defines policies as "the consciously acknowledged rules of conduct that guide administrative decisions." Policy should be distinguished from the goal or the objective, on the one hand, and the operative steps, on the other. Thus, making every person in the country educated is an objective: compulsory primary education is a policy designed to realise the goal; and the opening of the schools and training of teachers, etc. are the steps necessary to carry out the policy.

Policy and Administration

It was Woodrow Wilson, who, in his essay, "The Study of Administration" published in 1887, attempted a rigid distinction between policy and administration. To him policy-making was a political function while administration was concerned only with the enforcement of policies. In his own words, "The field of administration is a field of business. It is removed from the hurry and strife of politics." Administration lies outside the proper sphere of politics. Administrative questions are not political questions. Wilson was followed by Goodnow, who provided detailed study of the distinction between the two, and influenced the course of administrative study for several decades. Even as late as 1926, White, in the first edition of his book, *Introduction to the Study of Public Administration*, made a clear distinction between policies and administration.

However, such a rigid dichotomy has since been disproved and disavowed. Opinion has veered round to the view that administration cannot be completely divorced from policy and *vice versa*. Luther Gulick was one of the pioneer advocates of this view. Above all, Appleby is the name most often associated with the thesis that politics and administration are inseparable twins. According to him, administration is politics since it must be responsive to the public interest. To quote his own words, "Administrators are continually laying down rules for the future, and administrators are continually determining what the law is, what it means in terms of action, what the rights of parties are with respect both to transactions in process and transactions in prospect.... Administrators also participate in another way in the making of policy for the future; they formulate recommendations for legislation, and this is a part of the function of policy-making." Public officials today are, thus, engaged both in policy-formulation and policy-execution, and government is a mixture of administration and politics all the way up and down the line. As Peter Odegard puts it, "Policy and administration are the Siamese twins of politics."

The pendulum, however, should not be carried too far to the other extreme so as to believe that there is no distinction between policy and administration. The fact is that the two functions are distinct even though the same person or persons may be performing them. A rough and ready and flexible distinction between the two is not only possible but desirable. It is in this sense that White defined public administration as "the enforcement of public policy". Louis Brownlow underlines this distinction when he says, "There is and always will be a difference between politics, on the one hand, and administration on the other, no matter how closely they may be related in democratic society."

Formation of Policy

Policy, it should be remembered, is not static and does not stand still. It is dynamic and is prone to constant changes. Policy is formulated in the context of changing goals, shifting environments and varying situations. Seckler-Hudson rightly regards every policy decision as a 'moment in a process'. In other words, policy-formulation is a continuous obligation, and the reformulation of policy in the light of experience is as important as its formulation in the first instance. Secondly, policies are 'not made in a vacuum,' that is to say, the policy-maker is not free to formulate policies arbitrarily; he is bound to take into consideration a number of factors. For example, the policy should be in consonance with the provisions of constitution as interpreted by the judiciary and the laws made by the legislature. The prevailing social mores, past traditions, customs, usages, conventions, and public opinions may also influence policy-making. At times, even international law and usage and world public opinion give a tilt to policy formation. Again, the policy of particular government agency has to get clearance from other agencies. Thirdly, there is bewildering variety of pressure groups constantly attempting to mould policies to suit their own interests. Integration of policies consequently becomes a necessary but difficult task. Lastly, a policy is nearly always the result of the co-operative efforts of many. In the words of Seckler-Hudson, *"Policies are arrived at, then, in all sorts of ways, conditioned by all sorts of matters."* The various organs that participate in the process of policy-formation are the legislature, the executive, the judiciary, chief executive, top administrators, all levels of hierarchy in administration, political parties, pressure groups, people, etc. It should be noted that in a given organisation there need not be only one point from where policies emanate; in practice the process is widespread all through the organisation. The whole process is, indeed, two-fold, namely, a working down from the rules at the top, and a working up from the persons affected. According to Gladden, four different levels in policy-making may by distinguished—(1) *political or general policy framed by the Parliament;* (2) *executive policy framed by the Cabinet;* (3) *administrative policy,* that is, the form in which the administrator carries out the will of the government; and (4) *technical policy,* that is the day-to-day policy adopted by officials in the working out of the administrative policy.

Policy-formulation in India

While the formulation of public policies under the system of Government in India, is concentrated in the executive, the various processes of policy-making are diffused over the entire system. The following are some of the important policy-making organs:

1. *Constitution.* All policies must be conformity with the constitutional framework. The Preamble declares the objectives while the Directive Principles lay down some of the basic policies;

2. *Legislature.* Its role is primarily that of vetoing, regulation and influence. It only helps in the determination of the final form of some of the policies. The occasions for exercising parliamentary control over policies are many and varies—law-making, President's address, general discussion on the Budget, voting of grants, interpellations, adjournment motions and resolutions. There are, however, limits to this control:

   (i) not every public policy requires legislative enactment; and

   (ii) the legislatures do not generally take initiative in sponsoring legislation;

3. *The Cabinet.* The formulation of public policy rests primarily here. It is the overall directing and controlling body, and all important problems of policy are, as a rule, considered by

the Cabinet. The policies for each Ministry are initiated and formulated by the Minister in charge. Within the Cabinet, the Prime Minister is the focus of policy-making;

4. *Planning Commission*. Though, legally a mere advisory organ, it has come to exercise significant influence over the formulation of public policies even in matters other than those of planning and development. Its advisory role extends over the entire administration;

5. *The National Development Council*, consisting, as it does of the Prime Minister and the Chief Ministers of States, is the highest policy-making body in the field of planning;

6. *Public Services*. The role of public services in matters of policy-formulation is threefold—(i) thinking out a policy for the execution of a particular objective laid down by the Executive and ensuring that it correctly interprets that objective; (ii) putting the policy into legislative forms; and (iii) translating the policy into action. They also advice and assist in policy-making;

7. *Judiciary*. It influences public policies in two ways, namely, (i) the power of judicial reviews, and (ii) the advisory power of the Supreme Court;

8. *Advisory Bodies and Consultative Committees, e*.g., Standing Labour Committee, Indian Labour Conference, Import and Export Advisory Committee and the Central Advisory Board of Education;

9. *Pressure Groups*, like trade unions, chambers of commerce, students' unions and women's conferences;

10. *Political Parties*. Political parties declare their policies through election manifestoes and strive to capture power with a view to implementing them;

11. *Professional Associations*, like Bar Associations, All India Medical Council, Teachers' Associations, etc;

12. *The Mass Media*. The role of the mass media in creating, moulding and expressing public opinion is well-known. It can very well bring to bear heavy pressure on policy-making.

DECISION-MAKING

Significance

Decision-making is a common everyday phenomenon. All of us are all the time making decisions whether on personal or public matters, in important or insignificant fields. Indeed, no organisation can be run without taking decisions; and if it is to be run on sound lines, decisions have to be, by and large, correct and reached in time. Similarly, decision-making is the essence of all management, public or private. The power to make decisions has been correctly identified with the power to manage. No one can ever aspire to be a successful executive if he is either incapable of taking decisions or is prone to make wrong decisions. A great leader, somehow, develops an uncanny judgement which usually results in correct decisions.

However, decision-making, though highly important, is equally difficult. People tend to shirk making decisions. It has perhaps been rightly observed that people would rather face a cannon than take a decision. Existence of an excess of problems to solve, too little time, fear of repercussions and not knowing what to decide are some of such difficulties. There are too many problems with too little time to solve them. It is generally the case of a backlog of decisions with busy and harassed executives running a race against time. It is virtually the problem of too much work chasing too little time. Then there exists the lurking fear of repercussions of decisions. No decision can possibly please everybody, and an administrator very often has the unpleasant duty of annoying more persons than he can possibly please. Again, he may just not know what to decide, that is, be just unable to see his way through various alternatives. In the words of March, "An executive existing in the complex environment of the business organisation has a three-stage decision problem—(i) to which of his many problems should he direct his attention; (ii) how much time, effort and expense should he invest in resolving uncertainty about that problem; and (iii) what solution to the problem should he use."

Meaning and Nature

Webster's Dictionary defines the term as "the act of determinating in one's own mind upon an opinion or course of action." In the words of Terry, it is "the selection of one behaviour alternative from two or more possible alternatives." In short, to decide means to come to a conclusion. "A decision is usually made within the guidelines established by policy. A policy is relatively extensive, affects many problems, and is used again and again. In contrast, a decision applies to a particular problem and has a non-continuous type of usage." Decision has been rightly described as "a moment in the process of policy-formation." However, the policy itself is the result of a decision. An important point to remember about a decision is that it is only a means to an end, never an end in itself. Again, decision-making is not a static process. Decisions are constantly being made and remade in response to changing requirements. There is nothing sacrosanct about a decision and nothing permanent about it. This is illustrated by the anecdote concerning Abraham Lincoln and a committee who were calling upon him to complain about the generalship of U.S. Grant. The committee Chairman said, "Why, Mr. President, certainly you know that General Grant is making a lot of decisions. He is making one right after another, and some of them are all wrong." Lincoln raised his head, was silent for a minute, and then replied: "Well, Mr. Chairman, I guess you are correct all right, but I reckon that if he makes a bad decision, he soon finds it out and changes it without delay. Gentlemen, I propose to keep right on with General Grant."

According to Millett, an examination of three aspects of decision-making is required to enable us to understand this process.

1. *Personal differences among individuals which make some decisive and others indecisive.* There are persons who delay, temporise, postpone and avoid decisions. They cannot be firm about a decision and always try to keep loopholes through which they could wriggle out later. On the other hand, there are persons who are resolute firm and prompt in taking decisions. What makes persons behave one way or the other, is a problem, beyond the scope of this study. Perhaps social and professional background may have something to do with it. Thus, judges may tend to be more decisive than lawyers. Similarly, intellectuals, who may have deep specialised knowledge, are generally supposed to lack the faculty of

taking decisions. "In matters of leadership, for example, they prove to be irresponsible (absent-minded, non-punctual), non-decisive (ultra-judicial, see so many sides they can never make up their minds), and non-persuasive (a little 'queer', not interested in people)."

2. *Role which knowledge plays in decision-making.* "The careful accumulation of detailed facts, their analysis and interpretation, the use of broad concepts of human and physical behaviour to predict future developments—all these elements in use of knowledge enter into decision-making in varying degrees." Statistics, work study, operations research and management survey can with advantage be utilised to collect data to build the decisions on.

3. *Limitations—personal and institutional—which circumscribe decision-making.* "On the one hand, decision-making must consider the aspirations, traditions, and attitudes of the agency administering work. On the other hand, there are personal predilections among administrators which also limit decision-making." We shall revert to this aspect at the close of this chapter.

Who Makes Decisions?

Decisions in an organisation are made by many persons, they are a co-operative venture. One person seldom decides questions which are subject to public scrutiny. In the words of Seckler-Hudson, "Decision-making in government is a plural activity. One individual may pronounce the decision, but many contribute to the process of reaching the decision. It is a part of the political system." In the last analysis, however, the manager or the chief executive of the organisation should make the final decision. No administrator, worth his name, can afford to shirk this responsibility; he must decide or quit. Of course, a busy and overworked executive needs assistance and staff help and he must not be denied any facilities on that count. While taking decisions the administrator would do well to acquaint himself with the necessary precedents bearing on the question and attempt to anticipate future conditions and events, and the effect of his decision on them.

Bases of Decision-Making

There seems to be no unanimity regarding the factors which help in decision-making. Perhaps there are no such fixed bases. A decision often depends on the criterion or basis believed to be important in the particular situation. The means of arriving at a decision may be rational, deliberate, emotional, impulsive or habitual. Intuition, facts, experience and authority are among the most common bases used in arriving at a decision. Seckler-Hudson enumerates twelve factors which must be considered in decision-making—legal limitations, budget, mores, facts, history, internal morale, future as anticipated, superior, pressure groups, staff, nature of programme and subordinates. One thing that must be insisted upon in decision-making is that decision should be based not on objective but objective considerations. A frequent complaint against administration that one comes across in our country, unfortunately is that decisions are taken on grounds other than merit, that is to say, considerations of caste, religion, politics, etc., tend to gain the upper hand. In other words, decisions are biased.

How to make a Decision?

Nobody can perhaps give a fool-proof answer to this question. No technique can probably suit all occasions. However, one thing that can help in this process is practice in decision-making. It has been truly said that one cannot learn swimming by studying the literature on it or by observing others swim: the only way to learn to swim is by getting into the water and doing it. This analogy holds true in the case of decisions too. Administrators should, therefore, be encouraged to take decisions. Terry lays down the following sequence of steps which, when followed, will assist greatly in the making of a decision:

1. Determine what the problem is;
2. Acquire general background information and different view-points about the problem;
3. State what appears to be the best course of action;
4. Investigate the proposition and tentative decisions;

5. Evaluate the tentative decisions;
6. Make the decision and put it into effect; and
7. Institute follow-up and, if necessary, modify decision in the light of results obtained.

Problems of Decision-Making

From the above discussion, it should have been clear that decision-making is a highly complex process. An attempt is made now to focus attention on four of the difficult problems facing it:

1. *Involvement in Routine*. A study of decision-making in public or business organisation reveals that day-to-day routine problems tend to dominate with the result that long-term decisions are either avoided or postponed. A person with responsibility for both routine activities and long-term planning is likely to find the routine taking the much greater share of his time. Prof. March calls this proposition 'Gresham's Law of Planning'. Prof. March, of he Carnegie Institute of Technology, has been engaged in research work on 'Business Decision-making' for the last six years or so, and here is reproduced, in his own words, the result of the laboratory experiment in this field.

"We have attempted to reproduce in the laboratory some of the critical characteristics or the executive's decision problem. In the preliminary experiment, subjects were asked to handle a relatively simple administrative job. The job involved three kinds of activities:

(i) *Routine Communication*. They were to communicate to relevant clerks information on the current inventory levels in various warehouses;

(ii) *Intermediate Planning*. They were to make any necessary reassignments of warehouses to groups of clerks so as to maintain an approximately equal work-load in each group;

(iii) *General Planning*. They were to suggest any other changes in procedure that might be appropriate.

"The subjects were told that each of the three jobs was equally important and should be given equal attention. After a training period to allow the 'executive' to become accustomed to the task, the work-load (the rate at which information on warehouse was received) was varied systematically. As the workload varied, we observed the proportion of communications dealing with routine activities as opposed to planning activities by the subject".

"Two results of this experiment are significant here. First, despite instructions to spend only one-third of the time on routine matters, subjects spent a good deal more than that even when the work-load was relatively light. Second, consistently as work-load increased, subjects spent a smaller proportion of their total time on planning activities. At peak loads, virtually no planning was evidenced."

2. *Which Problem to Solve*? Almost every adult has to face such a question frequently whether in personal or official life. So long as the problems are few and simple, the administrator can solve all of them. But as the number of problems increases and as they become more complicated, the administrator is faced with the question which of the many problems to solve. Thus, at any given time, he may have a long-range budget to approve, a letter to another government agency to dictate, speech inaugurating a conference to prepare, a telephone to answer. There are other occasions, however, when problems are more difficult and of greater moment. One such problem arises in the case of determining priorities in preparing plans for the country. There are competing demands and conflicting pressures, too many demands chasing too few resources. To have more schools or more hospitals, to introduce free and compulsory education or to develop higher education, to have more roads or additional rail links, to have more steel plants or fertilizer plants, etc., are a perennial source of worry to the planner.

3. *What is a Right Decision*? Should the emphasis be on observing the form or carrying out the spirit? "It would be difficult in a large-scale organisation to point to a single decision of some consequence that is reached without being

part of a specified operating method, pinned down by checks and balances, reviews and concurrences, supporting fields and staff papers." The procedural approach becomes self-defeating when it is used as a criterion for determining the rightness of the decision. Procedure through proper channels, efficiency and economy are undoubtedly important in evaluating a decision. But "the right decision must meet a higher test. It must accord with the general interest, the constitutional spirit, and the moral principle. Nothing short of this will do."

4. *Bias*. Perhaps the greatest difficulty in decision-making process is the element of bias introduced in it. This element is so important as to need a little detailed treatment.

Elimination of bias is a part of the general problem of rationality in administration. The public official, including the political chief at all levels and all jurisdictions, is responsive to and, to a degree commensurate with his office, determinant of the ethics of the community. As a public official, he is continuously responsible for retaining the public confidence. He is responsible too for the development and maintenance of the integrity and confidence of his own organisation. The public official does not lose his personal identity by virtue of responsibilities as public official. Indeed, it is his task to reconcile his personal views and activities with the duties and responsibilities of his public office. The growing significance of government makes it all the more necessary. The government is now so huge and affects our lives so directly that there is need to give the citizens better protection against the ever-expanding administrative powers. The public has a right to expect that a government agency is acting on an independent and objective footing and thereby maintain confidence in and respect for administrative decisions. The aspect of official conduct with which we are concerned here, is that of bias.

5. *What is Bias*? Bias is rather a vague term difficult to define precisely. Literally, bias is something oblique or slanting. Used in a figurative sense, it means a swaying influence or undue leaning to one side. It may take the form of prejudice or predilection. Prejudice is an unfavourable opinion or feeling formed beforehand or without knowledge, thought or

reason. Predilection, on the other hand, is a mental preference or partiality; it is a favourable predisposition. A bias, thus, may be favourable or unfavourable. Bias exists where an occurrence is due to a real cause besides chance. For example, an unbiased coin is one that, when tossed, gives equal number of heads and tails. If it behaves differently, it is said to be a biased coin. Bias may, thus, be defined as an extraneous factor which is not relevant to the issue. There is an element of unreasoning or irrationality about bias. It may, however, be unconscious. It is just there as a built-in part of the individual's personality, a part of psychological and cultural make-up. Bias may also be cultivated or acquired. But in no case it is deliberate.

To realise the exact significance of bias it may be necessary to understand its features. First, bias should not be confused with unethical conduct. Favouritism, nepotism, venality and other forms of corruption are the result of deliberate and conscious acts on the part of the public official. Bias, as stated earlier, is often unconscious or sub-conscious. Secondly, the distinction between 'official bias' and 'personal bias' should be carefully noted. 'Official bias' of an authority is inherent in the duty imposed on it. It becomes personal when it is used in favour of, or against some individuals or groups of individuals. Thirdly, there may be departmental, institutional, or professional bias. It is quite common for an agency to be under the obligation to follow a certain policy in its decision. Lastly, bias is connected with values and traditions which differ from time to time and place to place. It is, thus, relative to time and place.

6. *Location of Bias.* Location depends upon the person judging and the norms he has set down for himself. The first way of locating bias is whether a particular decision has been taken in accordance with established rules, procedures, norms, and traditions. In the second place, it should be found out whether a decision has been taken on objective grounds or on subjective basis. Lastly, the test should be whether an act of an official can be justified before an impartial and independent authority. A word of caution may be added here,

viz., the tendency to locate bias should not become so exacting as to demoralise administration and take away all initiative from public officials. It must be recognised that our civil servants, by and large, take decision on objective basis.

7. *Causes of Bias*. First, it has to be admitted that administrative action often involves discretion and it is in this field that the probability of bias manifesting itself is more. Secondly, insufficient awareness on the part of the public servant of what is public interest, or what is required of him, may lead to bias. Thirdly, strict adherence to rules and procedures may create a bias for red tape. This is often called the administrator's bias. Fourthly, as indicated earlier, bias may be the result of inheritance. Fifthly, bias may arise out of the influence of the environment, i.e., out of the forces external to the individual as person. Many such forces are inculcated in the individual by education and training, while others accrue through absorption from the environment. Sixthly, bias may be the result of the fear on the part of the public servant of the consequences of his actions. Such a fear may drive the officer to reckon the reaction of his boss as an important factor on his decision-making, which means a fettered judgment. Seventhly, 'caste consciousness' in the official hierarchy is also regarded as a cause of bias. However, this is evident largely in recruitment and promotion cases, and does not affect the general public at large. In brief, bias in administration may be the result of preferences, either personal or of the superiors, caste, class, community, religion, language, profession, region, value, attitudes, ideology, pressure groups etc.

8. *Elimination of Bias*. The problem really is not so much how to eliminate bias as how to utilise it, how to reconcile conflicting attitudes, how to strike a balance between different types of bias, and how to sublimate it. Bias should not be condemned *per se* out of hand. Not all bias is undesirable. Not merely the officials but the people too are biased. For example, there exists a popular bias in India against police. There exists, therefore, the problem not only of official bias

but also of popular bias. The issue before us is twofold: How to build healthy and constructive types of bias in administration, and how to eradicate undesirable types? As regards discouraging unhealthy bias, attempts should be made to protect the individual from his own bias by avoiding situations where bias bill begin to operate. There already exist numerous provisions and safeguards to achieve this need. We may discuss problem in the fields of policy-making, adjudication and administration.

A policy, being a deliberate act of choice and preference, is bound to have a slant or bias. Take for instance, policies like abolition of zamindari, planned development, socialistic pattern of society, ceiling on land, prohibition, concessions for schedules castes and tribes, etc. All such policies are openly and avowedly prejudiced against certain classes of persons and predilected towards others. The same may be said of such of social legislation which is often enacted without adequate objective research and analysis. The persons responsible for policy-making are the legislators and ministers. Now the only safeguards against the bias of policy-makers are that no person can become a member of legislature or remain so if he holds an office of profit under the government, is a government official, or/and is involved in a contract with any governmental agency. Such safeguards, however, leave many loopholes. Thus, there is no safeguard against ministers taking decisions regarding business or industrial enterprises in which they have shares or in which their close relatives occupy vantage positions. Similarly, there is no legal bar for any political party to receive donations from business and industrial concerns subject to the recent amendment to the Company Law. In our country, we have yet to adopt in full the well-known American 'conflict of interest' clause which prevents public officials including ministers from taking decision on matters in which they have interest.

In the field of law, the proper significance of bias is to denote a departure from the standard of even-handed justice which the law requires from those who occupy judicial or quasi-judicial office. Such a person, when adjudicating as between two or more parties, must come to his adjudication with an independent mind without any inclination towards one side or the other in the dispute. A judge ought to be indifferent or unbiased between the parties. The principles governing 'doctrine of bias' vis-a-vis judicial tribunals are well-settled, and they are two: (i) no man shall be a judge in his own case; and (ii) justice should not be done but manifestly and undoubtedly seem to have been done. The two maxims yield the result that if a member of a judicial body is subject to a bias in favour of, or against any party to a dispute, or is in such a position that a bias must be assumed to exist, he ought not to take part in the decision or 'sit on the tribunal' and that 'any direct pecuniary' interest, however small, in the subject-matter of inquiry will disqualify a judge, and any interest, though not pecuniary, will have the same effect, if it be sufficiently substantial to create a reasonable suspicion of bias. These principles are equally applicable to authorities who are empowered to discharge quasi-judicial functions like administrative tribunals.

The above principles could with profit be extended to administrative officials. Thus, pecuniary or personal interests in the decision should make an official incompetent to deal with the case. The same should hold good or any other connection with the parties or the matter at issue which is apt to reduce the confidence in his ability to act without prejudice. Incompetence of a superior officer should also extend to his subordinates insofar as they will be precluded from making a decision or taking part in the preparation of a case unless and until a substitute is named. And it goes without saying that one of the subordinates cannot be named as substitute. If, for instance, a Minister or the head of a department is actuated by bias, he cannot leave the decision to one of the chiefs of divisions in the department, but another Minister has to act in his place.

Another field in which good work in the direction of elimination of bias is being done in our country is the Psychological Research Wing of the Defence Research and Development Organisation. The wing has been working on the developing techniques to eliminate bias in different types of assessment of the qualities in recruiting personnel in the army. The wing has evolved intelligence tests which will not be biased in favour of any particular group. To avoid certain types of bias all the examinees are asked to put on a uniform dress, and numbers are given for identification. It is for the same reasons that in all public examinations candidates are identified by roll numbers and no person is appointed as examiner, any of whose relations is appearing at that particular examination. Some Universities go too far in this direction. To quote from the regulations of one such university, "No person shall be appointed as paper-setter in any paper for an examination, if any of his or her close relations intends to appear at that examination in that paper—the term 'close relations' includes wife, husband, son, daughter, grandson, grand-daughter, brother, sister, nephew, niece, grand-nephew, grand-niece, uncle, aunt, first cousin, son-in-law, daughter-in-law, brother-in-law and sister-in-law. Before setting the paper, the paper-setter should inform the Registrar by name, if he is the author of a book or booklet on the subject and the standard for which the book can be utilised." Similarly, an amendment to the All-India Service (Conduct) Rules, 1954 provides that "No member of the services shall, except with the previous sanction of the Government, permit his son, daughter or dependent to accept employment with private firms, with which he has official dealings, or with other firms having official dealings with Government." It is for the same reason that High Court Judges are prevented after retirement from practising before the same court, or Supreme Court Judges, from practising before any court, or the Auditor General from accepting any government post after retirement. Lastly, the Madras Government has prohibited its officers from getting streets, localities, institutions, halls, etc., named after them.

There is another side of the problem of bias which is equally, if not more, important, namely, the need to build up healthy and constructive types of bias in administration. Thus, one of the most pressing needs of our country today is how to create administrative leadership which will be dynamic, plan-conscious and democratically oriented. No plans can be effectively implemented by a 'neutral' and 'indifferent' public official. If the great experiment in democratic decentralisation is to succeed, our officials have to develop a positive and constructive bias towards it. Proper recruitment, training and discipline may go a long way in inculcating such attitudes in the Civil Service. In the United States, much emphasis is given to executive development programmes. In India, too, Government has embarked on a large-scale training programme. The use of case studies in training may help in fostering the desired type of bias. Another aspect of the training programme should aim at developing individual insight into his own bias. The psychological techniques of bringing the subconscious bias into the conscious and then eliminating it may be tried with advantage.

DECISION-MAKING AND HERBERT SIMON

Decision-making is a subject that has come to the forefront in administrative thinking and administrative theory only recently. While the modern decision-making is compounded of contribution of two groups of social scientists—philosophers and economists, the philosophers were the ones who set the ball rolling.

There are mainly three important components of decision-making. What exactly does a man do when he makes a decision? He is faced with a problem, or, for that matter, recognises a problem. In the second step, he has a number of alternatives. He himself seeks them out or they are presented to him and looks at the alternatives. And the third step is the choosing of one alternative out of the whole lot—that one alternative, which, according to him, gives the best results. It was left to Herbert Simon to take a large bit of economic theory and add to it philosophical theory to lay the foundation of modern theory of decision-making. Herbert Simon was the first to blend the two—the philosophical with the economic thought.

The first point which Simon makes in his book, *Administrative Behaviour*, is that every decision consists of a logical combination of fact and value propositions. A fact is a statement indicating what the product is, was, or has been. A statement of fact may be proved or disproved. Some examples of fact are offered here: A table is made of wood; the room is warmed by central heating; or the number of people in a class is 20 or 22.

These are all statements of facts; they are either true or false statements. On the other hand, value is an expression of preference. When one says he likes a morning walk, it is a statement of preference; it is a value proposition. When one says that a national day like 26th January is a good occasion, it is a statement of preference. Every decision, as Simon explains, is made up of several fact statements and one or more value statements or usually a decision is compounded of one value statement and several fact statements. To cite Simon's own example, suppose a commander wants to decide on the method of attack. The value proposition with which he starts, is: I should attack; to attack the enemy one must do it successfully. This is a value statement. The "fact' statement is: An attack is successful only when carried out under conditions of surprise. This is a fact verified by earlier experience. Secondly, there is another fact statement—the conditions of surprise are concealment of the time and place of attack. Combine these two fact statements about concealment and about the necessity and the use of surprise with the value statement—attack successfully. Combine all these logical statements and you get a decision: Set the time and place of attack: Value statement: Attack successfully—is a value statement of the first order. Decision on time and place is a value statement of the second order. Similarly, every decision can be shown to be compounded of several fact statements and value statements. A value statement which one begins with, is a value statement of the first order, and the subsequent one is of the second order. Simon himself held the view that this particular mode of explaining decision-making is only of theoretical value and it does not come in handy in natural decision-making situations. But this is not wholly, correct. Simon undervalued his own contribution in this regard. It has been proved that this is very important in understanding decision-making.

Secondly, Simon explains that a decision is a choice between several alternatives. This idea is derived from the economists. When one is faced with a problem, he has a number of alternatives and he has to choose between them in order to maximise profit or whatever one wants to achieve. Further, every alternative entails consequence. According to economists, one is called upon to choose out of the various consequences of an alternative in order to maximise his profits. Thus viewed, a rational decision should have three components. First of all, one is aware of all the alternatives, *i.e.*, when one is faced with a problem, unless he knows all the alternatives, he does not know which one to choose. This is a condition—knowing of alternatives—which precedes decision-making. Secondly, he must know every consequence of an alternative. Each alternative has some good consequences as well as some bad consequences. (Your preference for that alternative may not be misplaced with the second condition of a perfectly rational choice.) And, thirdly, there should be a perfectly rational choice, i.e., he may be able to project himself into the future. A particular consequence may seem to be good today, it may not be the same good tomorrow and even bad the day after. So a certain amount of projection into the future is necessary to visualise a consequence. If the choice is to be rational, it goes without saying, all these three conditions should be fulfilled. But no choice can be strictly 100 per cent rational. So what exactly can be achieved in a situation is what is called *subjective rationality*. An objective rationality which fulfils all the three above-mentioned conditions is impossible in a world in which we live. The subjective rationality is a condition in which when one knows a *few* alternatives of which he knows a *few* of the consequences, and he chooses out of these alternatives. So, this sort of subjective rationality is all that human beings can hope to command. Herbert Simon pointed out—in fact he was the first to point this out in an emphatic manner, when the idea of maximisation was canvassed by economists—the constraint imposed by the time factor. In one situation or in one organisation, when one wants to maximise, the element of time comes in. A person has got to make a decision, and a good decision today may well turn out to be a bad decision tomorrow, and a bad decision may emerge as a good decision later. It is also true that a human being is capable of achieving a higher subjective rationality on which he can base his choice. This requires a certain minimum condition which he has to fulfill and then he can look at all the alternatives in a particular order and then choose that alternative which satisfies such minimum conditions.

The behaviour of human beings depends upon a certain amount of *satisfising*. A human being will choose an alternative which fulfils certain *satisfising* conditions. Satisfising would depend heavily on certain conditions. Or, if a person looks at the alternatives, his choice may fall on an alternative which satisfies in order to achieve as much maximisation as possible. So, this element of choice in looking at the alternatives is ever present in human situations. In fact, quite often we find in life that there are certain conditions which should be present before we make a choice. This means that the way in which we *scan* the alternatives, would depend upon certain conditions—certain limitations. The first limitation on human beings is that objective rationality is impossible as already discussed. Secondly, there is the important element of choice, in the matter of *satisfising*. There is the third limitation imposed on us in the matter of rational choice, this is the element of sunk cost. If we have already made a decision, this decision prevents us from taking another decision. For example, if one is already married, he is prevented by law from marrying a second time. Similarly, if a person has got an engineering degree and he wants to become a doctor, he cannot apply for a medical position. Or, what he has done already, this is a decision which prevents him from taking other decisions.

Actual behaviour of human organism has been observed in the matter of decision-making. Studies reveal that three steps are necessary in rational decision-making. First, recognise the problem that needs to be solved. The second part is the search behaviour. Once a person has recognised a problem he goes on searching for various alternatives. This is search behaviour. After search behaviour has gone on for a while, each organism decides on one of the alternatives. Some organisms can go on collecting; others will stop at a particular point. This search behaviour continues till he gets at an alternative which satisfies the minimum conditions that he has got for himself in regard to the problem. Suppose the standards are pretty low, then the second or even third alternative may satisfy. In this case, the intelligent organism would immediately raise its own standard and go on waiting for further alternatives. When a person goes on searching for alternatives but none of the alternatives satisfies the minimum conditions that he has laid down for years, then the next step towards rationalisation is to lower the standard until he could look whether any one of them would satisfy the lower standards. As he goes on lowering the standard there comes a point where we cannot lower the standard any further.

The third point which Simon makes in regard to decision-making is important from the point of view of organisation. How are decisions to be classified? The word "decision" can be applied to all possible situations wherever there is a choice element. How do we distinguish between the various types of decisions? In common parlance, the decisions are made at different moments and at different levels of gravity. Simon employs two terms—programmed decisions and unprogrammed decisions. A programmed decision is one in which a certain programme exists in our mind or on paper which automatically gives us the solution once we work out the programme. Every bureaucratic rule or regulation is a programme and every application of a programme gives us a programmed decision. Suppose a rule or regulation tells us if an application for a licence satisfies certain conditions, give him the licence. All we do in decision-making in this case is whether the applicant should be given a licence or not, and this depends on whether the conditions prescribed in the regulation are fulfilled or not. Once they are fulfilled, we issue a licence. This type of a decision is called programmed decision. Yet this kind of a programme itself may be so complicated that the decision-making, too, becomes complicated. The regulation, for example, may not tell very clearly what to do; it leaves a lot of discretion. It is, thus, not a simple programmed decision. An unprogrammed decision is one for which we do not have any precedence or rules and regulations to direct us. The decision is to be worked out personally. Indeed, a programmed and an unprogrammed decision are the two ends of a long spectrum. No decision exists in human life which is completely unprogrammed. We have accumulated certain knowledge and experience. A certain vague programme does exist in our mind even for the most unforeseen situations. Similarly, there is no completely programmed decision-making.

Even in the case of choosing oranges, as between big and small, there is discretion as regards the precise diameter.

Decisions have been classified into several levels, but for the sake of simplicity they can be broadly classified into two levels. One is the simplest level in which rules and regulations or precedence tell us how to recognise the problem and take a decision. The rule may, for example, say what exactly is a completed application and what exactly is not; then it will tell how to study the problem and also give its solution. It is the example of a simple programme. But this is not always the case. Suppose in a programme, there are possibilities of three types of situations. For situation A give remedy X, and for a situation B the solution is Y, and for a situation C inject a dose of Z. This is a slightly higher level of decision-making. It does not simply define one situation; it defines three possible situations and provides different solutions for these. A complicated programmed decision is verily as difficult as a simple unprogrammed decision. As between a programmed and an unprogrammed decision, there is a very important point which applies to the Indian situation. When we are faced with a situation in which precedence exists but there is no absolutely fool-proof precedence, we are faced with a situation in which we have got to make an unprogrammed decision. For example, development or economic growth is a subject on which a lot of literature has been published; but there is no simple formula for economic growth. In spite of all that has been written, no theory tells us when we are getting to the take-off stage. Nor does any theory give us practical guidance as to what we have to do. The progress of science and the progress of organisations in other countries have made more and more decisions, programmed and mechanised. For example, a lot of clerical work which was done by human beings can now be done through a programmed computer. We even get a situation in which bulk of the clerical work is done—can be done—by a computer with a suitable set of programmes. Even in India there is an important difference between commercial organisations and government organisations. For example, public administration maintains large sections in every office to prepare salary bills. Practically, all this work in most of the big business concerns is now handled by computers. Similarly, more and more routine decisions can be programmed. In fact one may say that the regulation or the rule book was an invention to enable less intelligent human beings to make programmed decisions; that the rule book in democracy has a programme for less intelligent beings who must be enabled to make programmed decisions from time to time. But—and here is one—they then apply the same programme time and again, even when the society has overgrown these programmes. (So, in an industrialised society, the tendency has been more and more to take unprogrammed decisions of greater and greater flexibility.) We get more and more programmed decisions being relegated to the computer. This phenomenon gives rise to two problems. First, it gives rise to enormous demand for skilled men who do not exist in sufficiently large numbers in any society. Secondly, it also creates the problem of unemployment—of what to do with less intelligent human beings who are not wanted any more because of the computer. And the society is called upon to provide for a programme of leisure or employment for all these people. Further, even the most modern programme which a computer does, is no better than the human being who designs the programme. The order of intelligence is somewhat lower in the case of a computer than the skilled human being who sets the programme for the computer, but the computer is more intelligent than the less intelligent human being who cannot carry a particular programme. That is, a computer can learn only that much what it has been designed to learn and it can learn this only when one plays on it.

Something may also be said about the recent advances in decision-making theory and decision-making studies. First of all, important advances have been made over the last 40 years in the matter of the degree of rationality in decisions. The rationality of a decision is important in several ways. To put this in a perspective, when an organisation is faced with a decision, it is faced with a risk also, i.e., it has got to take a risk. Such a situation entails some alternatives. One alternative is mass group, that is, large group. (This may lead to what may be called incremental decision-making.) Rationality is promoted by increasing the knowledge by gathering more facts and by evaluating the probabilities. Twenty years ago, a good manager was distinguished from a bad enthusiasm. Now, an element of inherited enthusiasm is being slowly driven out of the manager by presentation of more facts and more information about the consequences of the alternatives. This is being done by not only the computer which is capable of sorting out the alternatives and presenting the facts but also by human beings. An attempt is, thus, made to reduce the area of risk and uncertainty. But, we cannot make everything certain and risk-proof. This calls for more skilled and even detailed management.

The second path along which studies have progressed is of the study on *human irrationality*. Why is it that human beings who want to live a certain way, cannot live? Also obvious is the element of uncertainty about human beings. There is a basic irrationality in human subconscious which is being explored by the psychologists. Part of human irrationality is certainly due to lack of our knowledge. Studies have disclosed that many entrepreneurs do not want to maximise profit; what they seek is to maximise sales. It has been revealed that human organism loses the capacity to get satisfaction out of the profit; it wants to get satisfaction out of Bigness—the megalomania. An increasing volume of such analyses does help to reduce the element of irrationality.

The third along which progress has been made is in regard to making decisions *accepted*. It may be given to draftsmen to make a decision but these decisions have got to be carried out. To get the decisions carried out, we must make them sound, rational and acceptable to those who are required to carry them out. Acceptability can be secured in three ways. One is, of course, force. Second is the recourse to emotional empathy and hypnotism. Both these methods of getting decisions accepted are, however, fraught with risks. The third method is to produce the same appreciation of the decision in our colleagues. This appreciation is secured by making them see the facts, as, for example, I see them. Then, the other persons get imbued with all the values which led me to the decision so that they make the same decision without my telling them of my decision. This may be promoted by what may be called *consultation* and in-service training. A boss must consult his subordinates. He may completely overrule them. Also the decision he takes may be different with the opinions given, but consultation is absolutely necessary in decision-making. Once the chief executive has consulted his subordinates, it invests him with moral strength and gives the subordinate a sense of satisfaction. Nothing else is more damaging in regard to getting decisions carried out than lack of consultation.

One more important point is in regard to collective decision-making. It should be safely asserted that decision-making is essentially an individual act. Collective decision is a contradiction in terms of an organisation. The examples of collective decisions are expressions, such as, "Government of India have decided" or "the Government of Uttar Pradesh have decided"...What exactly is the Government of Uttar Pradesh? It is collectivity. The term has some meaning. This problem has been explored by economic theorists as well as by decision theorists and most of the literature on the subject is clothed with highly mathematical jargon. Two important ideas have emerged from the mathematical investigation. A distinction is drawn between the two types of collectivity. This distinction, to be sure, is not quite correct but occupies two ends of the spectrum—team and coalition. In a team it is only one person who makes the decision—the captain—and other members of the team accept the decision. When a person joints an organisation he swears: "I promise to serve my organisation lawfully." Automatically, a decision made by his superiors becomes valid for him; it is, indeed, everybody's decision. It gains acceptance by contract; by hypnotism or force; finally, through consultation. It may, however, be emphasised that consultation does not automatically generate acceptance of the decision; consultation *plus* contact does.

This is team work. The other end of the spectrum is one in which every person in the team nurtures his own value or preference and has his own appreciation of the problem. This type of collectivity is called *coalition*. Each one bargains with everyone else. Ultimately, a common decision emerges which is not exactly equal to each person's expectations. Each person has sacrificed something. A person is bargaining for a common goal as well as for a goal of his own. He is prepared to give up a bit of his own goal to accept the common goal. He may get something in return—it may not be necessarily money. Also, in return for this, in regard to own the goal he has to agree to sacrifice some of his own goal. In the process, we get mathematically, a collective decision. Indeed, a new branch of mathematics, called game theory, has sprung up to explain this. Game theory is not of very great practical use as yet. It essentially applies to a situation in which there are two or more rivals in a completely bargaining situation.

It may finally be asked: How does the theory of decision-making help in a study and administration of the human phenomenon? It is certainly not true that a study of the decision-making theory will automatically lead to better decisions being made by an administrator. When one studies about the physical activity in a book, he does not benefit straightaway but such a study does deepen an interest in the physical activity. Similarly, it may make one more physically apt when he gets to know more about decision-making literature. This itself is an achievement. The most important method of learning, of course, is to observe, analyse and police one's own behaviour. Secondly, it is commonly believed in India and to a lesser extent outside India that by looking at other people's decisions one can learn to make decisions himself. It is this belief that prompts the compilation of case studies. It is partly true that one can, in this way, improve his decision-making capacity. This is at least true in two ways. It is true to the extent that he is made aware of the decision-making process and thereby to observe his own decision-making behaviour. Secondly, it is true in the sense that theory imparts life and meaning to an individual situation. Thus viewed, a study of others' decisions provides a theory to an individual situation and also makes the theory instinct with life. In these two senses it is useful but in another sense it is useless. Since this method of study is becoming a bit too popular in this country, it is necessary to be aware of its limitations. In the first place, reliving another man's life through case studies never succeeds. The most significant part of a decision is the agony of it. One cannot relive the agony and anxiety and put himself in another man's position.

In regard to decision-making, there are two basic weaknesses in Indian character which militate against rational decision-making and the earlier we recognise it, the better. Choice-making, according to us, acquires meaning and significance only when a clear distinction exists between God and Devil, so to say. Unless one says one alternative is better than the other, he is not faced, so do we generally believe, with a true decision situation. That is the first weakness of the Indian character. The second weakness lies in the execution of decisions. This is so dramatically highlighted by a statement, like a policy being good but carrying out of the decision being imperfect. Let us be absolutely clear that when we talk of a decision, we automatically imply that we have taken into account all the difficulties. Otherwise, a decision degenerates into a mere pious resolution. When we talk about our plans being good and execution being bad, we are doing violence to the English language.

5

Public Relations and Publicity

During recent years of plethora of government information and publicity agencies have come into existence, and their number is constantly on the increase. Good public relations has come to be regarded as an important attribute of the preset-day leadership, and its significance can hardly be overstressed. Some of the important factors, that have contributed to this importance, may be stated as follows:

1. *Vast increase in government functions.* The modern Welfare State, with its philosophy of looking after the citizens from 'the cradle to the grave', is rendering innumerable services to the public. The very size and complexity of these services render communication with the public imperative. The public has to be made aware of the various facilities offered to it by the government. This mere informational aspect of public relations is assuming vast proportions;
2. *Urgent attention paid to public and private iniquity.* The government is under a constant pressure to defend itself against public criticism. The public is highly sensitive to wrongs and mistakes of public authorities, while turning a deaf ear to worse iniquities of private organisations. Thus, the Mundhra Deal would hardly have attracted any publicity if Life Insurance Corporation were a private business concern. Government work, thus, has not only to be well done, but the public has to be convinced that it is being well done. Government in a free society must function in the glare of publicity;

3. *The civil servant today occupies a changed role.* It is not enough for a career official to implement policies; he has to explain government policies to the people and build up popular support for them. To use an American phrase, he has to 'sell' policies and programmes of his agency. This gives 'political' orientation to his tasks.

MEANING AND NATURE OF PUBLIC RELATIONS

What is Public?

The term 'public relations' stands for governmental relations with the public. The term 'public', though frequently in use, is not easy to define. The general public is really not one but a collection of many 'publics'. The general public is a vague, unidentifiable and amorphous entity. We hardly feel its presence except at the election times or times of civil commotion. However, the ordinary citizen, who is the unit of public, is identifiable, and comes in daily and constant contact with the administration or some aspects of it. He needs information on many points; he needs help in filling up the ever-growing number of forms; he requires assistance in getting acquainted with procedures; he expects expeditious disposal of his case; and he rightly demands polite and courteous behaviour on the part of government officials. How to determine administration's relations with him, is the main crux of public relations. Generally, the governmental organisations have to deal with particular public, that is, organised groups of public, like trade unions, chambers of commerce, students' unions, teachers' associations, political parties, religious or caste groups, press, women's councils, etc. Each agency of the government, thus, has to direct its public relations to that part of the public with which it is directly concerned, that is, its clientele, for example, the agriculture department's clientele is the farmer, the labour department's labour, and so on. However, there are wider publics too with which administration has to deal, the most important of these being the legislature, the press and the political parties.

The legislature, under a democratic system of the parliamentary or presidential variety, constitutes an important segment of public. It is true that it is the ministers, as political executives, who come in direct contact with the legislature; the contact of civil servants at best is indirect. Nevertheless, there are important points of contact between the legislature and public officials, particularly of the higher echelons. One such important point of contact is the committees of the legislature which summon officials to explain matters or answer objections. The estimates and the public accounts committees are good examples of such contact. In the U.S.A., committee hearings sometimcs are a gruelling experience for the officials appearing at such hearings. Then there are requests, enquiries and complaints from individual members of the legislature, and officials concerned have to deal with these in as courteous and expeditious a manner as possible.

Administration's relations with the press in a free society may well be regarded as top priority in the field of public relations, and these tax the ingenuity of the press officers. It is not for nothing that the press is called the fourth estate. Its power is tremendous. No government ever desires and cherishes a hostile and irresponsible press. The public, on the other hand, has no use for a captive press. A balance between the two extremes is needed. What we need is a fair, impartial, independent and responsible press. Every Government, therefore, has arrangements to keep the press people fully informed and briefed. The pressmen have a press-gallery in the legislative chambers; there are press enclosures in public functions; they are invited to all governmental functions; they are also taken on public expense to sites of big dams, industrial establishments and agricultural farms, etc., etc. The newsmen certainly for a privileged group of the public. Of course, such facilities are necessary to enable the press to discharge its duties satisfactorily. The government also possesses enormous patronage in the form of government advertisements which are ever increasing with the rapid growth of public enterprises. Then there are the press conferences at which the top leaders meet the press. In the U.S.A., the President holds a press conference every week. In India, the Prime Minister meets the press once a month. Finally, there is the Press Information Bureau. Information regarding the policy, plans, achievements and other activities of the Government of India is made available to the press in English and 12 Indian languages by this Bureau. During 1959, textual services were received about 3,378 Indian newspapers and periodicals, photographic service by 953 and photographs in the form of ebonoid blocks by 746. Indian and foreign correspondents accredited to the Government of India at headquarters numbered 174 in 1959. The Bureau's Information Services in Hindi and Urdu are issued from the head office in New Delhi and those in other Indian languages from the nine regional offices. In addition, information centres have been opened at a number of State capitals.

One of the most difficult problems in democracy is the relations of the administrative officials with the leaders and office-bearers of the political parties, particularly, of the ruling party. There are frequent complaints in India of political interference in official work by the members of the political parties. "It is related of a certain Collector that a member of a local Legislature appeared before him and made a request. The Collector said that he would let him have an answer after two days. Two days later, he explained to the M.L.A., very politely, why his request could not be accepted, and how, if it was, various other people would be detrimentally affected. The M.L.A., with equal politeness, asked if he could use his telephone. Permission being given, he phoned up the Minister and said that he had made this request and had been given this answer, that he was naturally very disappointed and trusted the Minister would take necessary action. He then handed over the telephone to the Collector saying the Minister wished to speak to him. The Minister said that he knew the facts of the case and desired that what the M.L.A. asked should be done. The Collector hesitated, suggested sending him the papers for consideration and attempted to argue. The minister was adamant and ended the conversation by saying, "Well, you know my views. You can do what I want or..." The Collector in this case decided to do what the Minister wanted and passed orders accordingly. The story came out through the M.L.A., who used it to let his friends and constituents know how Collectors should be dealt with. Such interferences have given rise to the 'slick officer' who attempts to ingratiate himself with the legislator by doing him favour and anticipating his wishes in order to use him, that is, his influence with the Minister for his own advancement. This is, undoubtedly, a delicate and difficult aspect of public relations. Every democratic country has had to fact it. We can confidently hope that as the politicians become more mature with responsibility and more understanding of their role with experience, healthy relationship would be established between them and the public officials.

What Public Relations Is

Public relations has existed in its present form for such a relatively short period that there is little general agreement on its precise definition or its proper scope, or its practical responsibilities. Every expert has his own definition, and no two definitions agree. A student of public opinion has collected more than fifty definitions from fifty experts in the field. The term has been defined by the *Encyclopaedia American* as "the art of analysing, influencing and interpreting a person, idea, group or business so that he, or it, will be recognised as serving the public interest, and will benefit from so doing." It operates in many different and constantly changing ways to meet the need of the client, the problem and the objective. According to Millett, public relations of management have four primary aspects; (1) learning about public desires and aspirations, (2) advising the public about what it should desire, (3) ensuring satisfactory contact between public and government officials, and (4) informing the public about what an agency is doing. It is in similar sense that the term has been used by Bernays. Public relations to him has three meanings: (1) information given to the public, (2) persuasion directed at the public to modify attitudes and actions, (3) efforts to integrate attitudes and actions of an institution with its public and of its public with that institution.

What Public Relations is Not

To make the understanding of the term complete, we should also know what public relations is not. Public relations usually is distinguished from general informational activities of the government, internal communications and publicity. One of the important functions of government is to collect a great deal of general information and publish it for the use of the general public. Many departments of the government are engaged in such an activity. Instances of such general information are census reports, weather forecasts, crop reports, food statistics, labour statistics, industrial and commercial statistics, employment figures, etc., etc. Such information is not a part of public relations; it is just the function of certain units of government. Secondly, public relations ought to be distinguished from internal communication within an agency. Internal communication aims at creating an understanding of the objectives, policies and decisions of the agency among its employees. The better such a system of communication, the healthier shall be the working of the agency. Hierarchy, procedure through proper channel, conferences, meetings, informal gatherings and conversations at luncheons and teas are some of the media of such communication. All this, however, is quite different from public relations. Finally, a confusion often arises between public relations and publicity because the two are closely related. As one writer has put it, "Public relations deal with the individual's publicity with the people in mass." Publicity is the often misunderstood and misused function or phase of public relations, primarily due to its being confused with propaganda. It operates mainly by getting its client (in this case the government) well presented in the channels of communications available—newspapers, magazines, radio, television, and others. It can work best only when it is viewed in its proper perspective—as a tool of, but as no substitute for, a public relations programme. Publicity works right as a tool only when it comes after all the other steps have been taken or adequately considered, for example, research analysis, recommendation, and so forth.

TOOLS AND TECHNIQUES OF PUBLIC RELATIONS

There can possibly be no exhaustive list of tools, instrumentalities and techniques of maintaining good public relations. Time, place and person always make a difference. There are times when gimmicks work wonders, and there are persons who, with their original approach and imaginative devices, win spectacular success in the field of public relations. Such tings, however, are bound to be infrequent. Among the normal tools may be listed publicity, advertising, personal contact, public speech and direct mail.

Publicity

It is the most important aspect of public relations, and has become a must for every large organisation, including the government. There is hardly a government today without a Department of Information or Publicity. Both democratic and totalitarian regimes make full use of this powerful weapon of influencing and moulding public opinion. Publicity means to make public or to disseminate knowledge of facts. It has been defined as "the art of dealing with the people in the mass." In practice, however, publicity shades off into propaganda. The two terms can certainly be distinguished but the difference is rather too thin. Perhaps the best example of publicity degenerating into propaganda was Hitler's Ministry of Enlightenment under the notorious Dr. Goebbels. Publicity is open, free and factual, while propaganda may be sinister, secretive and based on falsehood. The Nazi belief in the 'big lie' was almost pathological. Constant and high pressure propaganda may well enslave and pervert the public mind. It is for this reason that governmental publicity is often looked upon with disfavour and suspicion.

The principal media of modern publicity are of three types—visual (advertisement, publications, silent movies, demonstrations); auditory (radio broadcasts and lectures); and audio-visual (films and telecasts). All these methods are made full use of by modern governments in their publicity drives. Of these, radio and television are obviously the most powerful media. Television played a very important role in the last presidential elections in the U.S.A. Discussions and debates between the two presidential candidates seen on the television screens by millions of Americans went a long way in determining the popular choice. In India, with the television age yet to come and radio being still beyond the reach of the majority of the people, public speaking still plays an important role as evidenced by the people gathering in thousands to listen to their leaders. Public speeches are not only well attended but are also well reported in the press.

The publicity work of the Government of India has been entrusted to the Ministry of Information and Broadcasting. This

Ministry was created in October 1941, and is charged with the responsibility for publicity and broadcasting activities of the Government of India and the general conduct of government relations with the press. The various activities of the Ministry and the important services rendered by it can be briefly described under the following heads:

1. All India Radio
2. Press Information Bureau
3. Publications Division
4. Directorate of Advertising and Visual Publicity
5. Films Division
6. Research and Reference Division
7. Directorate of Field Publicity.

1. *All India Radio*. It comprises the entire broadcasting system of the country, and also includes the experimental television service. At the end of 1977, there were 82 full-fledged radio stations, as against only 6 in 1947, with studios, transmitters, receiving centres and other facilities in addition to four auxiliary studio centres and a television studio centre covering all the important linguistic areas. There were 59 medium and short-wave transmitters in regular operation, a television transmitter, and frequency modulating lings between transmitters and studios at three locations. The stations are grouped into four regions—North, West, South and East. In addition, Radio Kashmir has two stations. There has been a simultaneous growth in the number of radio-set owners since the inauguration of broadcasting in 1927. Thus, as against 3,954 sets in 1927 there were, in 1977-78, nearly 1.74 crore domestic receiver sets. In addition, there were 1,09,625 community receiver sets.

   The first television centre was set up in Delhi in September 1959. At present there are 200 T.V. stations in the country.

2. *Press Information Bureau*. The Press Information Bureau serves the Indian press and correspondents of the foreign

press stationed in India with news material and photographs concerning the activities of the Government of India. The Bureau acts as a link between the Government and the public through the Press—informing the public about Government activities and policies and keeping the Government in touch with the main trends of public opinion as reflected in the Press. The Bureau's services are made available in 13 languages, including English and Hindi. To serve newspapers in all parts of the country, the Bureau has a network of regional offices which are connected with headquarters by teleprinter circuits.

In addition to daily news releases, the Bureau provides feature articles, background material, and reference and record material in the form of texts of communiques, policy statements, printed reports, etc. Bureau officers in charge of publicity for the activities of the various Ministries, discuss subjects of current interest with correspondents, answer their queries, and arrange interviews for them with authoritative policy sources. The Bureau also arranges Press Conferences for Ministers and high officials to explain to the Press the scope and purpose of important Government decisions or policy statements. During 1960-61, 156 such Press Conferences were held. Press liaison services are also provided by the Bureau for official meetings and international conferences held in India.

Bureau officers also co-ordinate publicity through other media in the case of certain Ministries. The Bureau is also responsible for arranging the accreditation of newspaper correspondents and cameramen at Delhi.

The Bureau is also responsible for publicity for and to the Armed Forces. This is handled by the Defence Wing of the Bureau. In addition to the normal press services, the Wing produces pamphlets, organises advertisement and poster campaigns and produces feature shots. Thus, it helped in the production of a documentary film on the Rashtriya Military College.

The Bureau has at present 16 regional or branch offices. Two more branch offices are shortly to be set up at Ahmedabad and

Bhopal. These offices distribute press material received from Delhi to newspapers in their area in the regional languages. They also ensure better co-ordination with State Publicity Departments. In addition to these, there are 15 Information Centres and proposals to set up two more Centres at Delhi and Bangalore are under consideration. Most of these Centres are run by the State Governments concerned in collaboration with the Government of India on the basis of 50-50 cost sharing. Each Centre has a reference library and reading room, containing important newspapers in various languages, literature and charts on the Five Year Plans and publications of the Central and State Governments. Documentary film shows are also held occasionally.

3. *Publications Division*. The Publications Division in the Ministry of Information and Broadcasting is responsible for the compilation, production, distribution and sale of popular pamphlets, books, journals, albums, etc. for providing authentic information about the country's cultural heritage, the activities of the Government, the progress of development programmes and places of tourist interest. It also advises the various Ministries and Departments of the Government on the preparation and production of publicity literature relating to their specific activities. Publications are brought out in English, Hindi and regional languages. A similar role is performed in the State by the Departments of Information and Publicity.

The Division publishes 18 magazines, including general and cultural magazines, such as *March of India* and *Aj Kal* (in Hindi and Urdu), a children's magazine, *Bal Bharati* (in Hindi), journals devoted to community development, *Kurukshetra* and *Gram Sevak* (in English and Hindi), and the 'Plan' (*Yojana* in English and Hindi), besides the programme journals of All India Radio. Four journals, namely, *Indian Information, Bharatiya Samachar, Metric Measures* and *Metric Map Tol*, were started during 1958. Story books for children in Hindi and regional languages are also being brought out.

During the decade 1950-60, the Division released a total of 239 books, pamphlets etc., for general, tourist and Five Year Plan publicity in the various languages. Some of the important publications were: *Women of India, Nuclear Explosions and Their Effects* (Revised), *Maulana Azad—A Homage, Indian Birds* (Hindi), *Jawaharlal Nehru's Speeches*—Volume III, *Speeches of President Rajendra Prasad*, 1952-1956 (Second Series), *Community Development in India,* and *India* (A Souvenir).

The Photo Unit of the Division helps in setting up exhibitions on the activities of the various Ministries. During 1958, the Unit assisted in the display of photographic enlargements in various pavilions of the 'India 1958' Exhibition.

4. *Directorate of Advertising and Visual Publicity.* While in the States, advertising and visual publicity is undertaken by the Department of Information and Publicity, at the Centre this responsibility rests with the Directorate of Advertising and Visual Publicity. The Directorate functions as the central organisation of the Government of India for the execution of its advertising and visual publicity requirements. It is responsible for the planning, production and release of display advertisements to newspapers and periodicals, the designing and production of printed publicity materials and the issue of classified advertisements on behalf of the various Ministries and Departments. For visual and outdoor publicity, the Directorate utilises various media, like posters, folders, broad sheets, pamphlets, handbills, calendars, hoardings, display panels, cinema slides, neon signs, models and charts, and also organises exhibitions.

During 1960, the tempo of publicity through this Directorate reached the highest levels so far and appropriately marked the final phase of the second Five Year Plan. There was intensification of publicity both for the Plan and for other important campaigns. With two additional field exhibition units and three mobile exhibition vans fully in operation during the year, exhibitions were carried to a larger number of people, especially in non-urban areas.

To prepare the public and secure their co-operation for the 1961 Census, an extensive campaign was launched, utilising the media of Press and visual publicity material. Wide publicity was also given to the Government of India Prize Bond Scheme. The educative campaign for Posts and Telegraphs was also intensified.

To facilitate speedier distribution of publicity material produced by the Directorate and to economise on transport, it was decided to arrange for regional distribution from Bombay, Calcutta and Madras (along with similar arrangements for the distribution of publications). Distribution from Madras has already started; similar arrangements are being made at the other two centres.

5. *Films Division*. The Films Division is responsible for the production and distribution of Government of India news-reels and documentary films for the general information and education of the public. The subjects for documentaries are selected at the beginning of each financial year in consultation with the Ministries of the Government of India, State Governments, the Film Federation of India, the Film Advisory Board and other organisations, especially interested in documentary films. While the Films Division undertakes the bulk of this production programme through its own units, a number of Films are assigned each year to approved private producers; these films are produced under the guidance and supervision of the Films Division. A list of approved producers, for this purpose, is prepared every year on the recommendation of a committee consisting of officials of the Government and representatives of the industry.

For production of weekly news-reels, the Films Division arranges coverage of important and topical news items depicting the life and progress of the country, and its international relations through its staff camera-men stationed at important centres in the country. Besides, items covered by State Film Units, as also foreign news items received under exchange arrangements, are included in the news-reels.

The documentaries and news-reels are distributed all over India for commercial and non-commercial exhibition through the distribution offices of the Division. In addition, wide publicity abroad is secured for important events in India through films screened in cinemas and on television under exchange or other arrangements in foreign countries.

6. *Research and Reference Division.* This Division functions as the central pool of current and background information for the media units of the Ministry. Its functions are: (i) to undertake basic research on matters of publicity; (ii) to provide guidance and background notes on current and other topics; (iii) to build up a compendium of knowledge on important subjects, and to prepare publicity material for the use of various media units of the Ministry. In addition, the Division undertakes investigations on various topics referred to it from time to time by the Information Ministry or other Ministries.

Since 1953, the Division has been compiling annually a standard authoritative work of reference on India under the title "India—A Reference Annual", which provides information on the diverse aspects of national life and activities. Since 1955, the Division has been issuing the bi-weekly service, "Background to the News", with the object of providing the background to select news items of current and continuous interest. The Division has also maintained a library which at the end of 1960 had 17,500 books, and bound volumes of reports, periodicals, etc. A number of standard journals, periodicals, and magazines were also available in the library. Lastly, the Division undertakes surveys and investigations. Thus, it conducted survey, through a mail questionnaire to assess public reactions to programmes of publicity for the plan undertaken by the various media of the Ministry. A proposal for entrusting the Division with the work of continuing evaluation of programmes in respect of all media under the Ministry during the Third Plan is under consideration.

7. *Directorate of Field Publicity.* For purposes of Plan publicity, the country has been divided into 14 regions with 76 mobile (field) units spread over the country. Each unit has to look after a number of districts. As detailed coverage of such a large area is not possible, the activities of the field units are concentrated primarily in large fairs, festivals, and on special occasions and central places at which large number of people collect. In addition, in the rural areas, regular publicity activities are organised in collaboration with the district and

the block authorities. Publicity is carried on through all media, viz., film-shows, camps, exhibitions, talks, discussions, debates, etc. Full co-operation is extended to the State Governments in their Plan publicity efforts. Besides providing general information on the Plan, attention is also given to special aspects of the Plan, e.g., Small Savings, Family Planning, Metric System of Weights and Measures, Panchayats and Co-operatives.

Personal Contact

Public relations, in the ultimate analysis, are nothing but personal contacts between public officials and individual members of the public. The average citizen judges the quality of administration by his contact with the petty officials. Hence, he emphasis on smart-looking receptionists, a broad smile on the face, habitual use of phrases like 'Thank you', 'May I help you', and 'Any service for me', etc. Courtesy weeks, so often celebrated in our country, aim at similar results. One of the great demands on public officials in free India is meeting the constant stream of visitors everyday in the week. Political executives have to carry even a heavier burden on this score.

Direct Mail

In a democracy, the political executives in particular receive a heavy mail. Our Prime Minister, for instance, receives thousands of letters every month from persons and organisations of different types, and each person expects at least an acknowledgement. It is a stupendous task but any minister can afford to neglect it or be indifferent to it only at his peril. Prompt and courteous replies to letters go a long way in establishing good public relations. "I remember Paul Hoffman telling once in staff meeting," writes Cleveland, "that we should answer every letter the day it comes in, even all we could say was that we would reply in detail later on." "When I ran a filling station (petrol pump)," he went on, "I found that a man would not wait for gas (petrol) more than two or three minutes if nobody paid any attention to him. But if you gave him a big "hello' and explained that there were several cars ahead of him, he would sit there quite happily for a quarter of an hour."

WHO SHOULD BE IN CHARGE OF PUBLIC RELATIONS WORK?

Public relations is fast approaching the status of a profession. There are universities in the United States which award degrees and diplomas in public relations. Almost every big organisation, governmental or business or otherwise, now maintains a separate public relations department staffed largely by the experts or professionals in the field. In our own country, every State Government has an Information or Publicity Department with a separate service of that name. The same is true of the Union Government. In brief, there are 'public relations men' all around us in this age of high pressure democracy. But are the relations of the public susceptible to treatment at the hands of these professionals? All too often people regard public relations men with the same jaundiced eye which they flash at the mention of terms like 'propagandist', 'press agent' or 'lobbyist'. Nothing can be more damaging to public relations than its being identified with propaganda. Therefore, it is in the interest of the organisation that public relations must start at the top. It fact, public relations can be only as good as the continuing conduct of the chief person presiding over it. One reason the businessmen got into trouble in Government is that many of them are accustomed to delegating to others the task of dealing with the public. In January 1953, toward the end of two long days of a Senatorial hearing on his General Motors stockholding, Charles E. Wilson revealed how much he had learned about public relations at the age of 62. "The thing that perhaps I overlooked myself," he mused, "was that not only did I have to operate honestly and fairly without prejudice, but all the people should also think that was the way I was operating, and that part of it I did not quite appraise." Where had he been? Presumably producing cars and trucks while somebody else worried about what the public would think. The contrasting case is of course that of Paul Hoffman. By handling his own public relations from the start, he sold the Marshall Plan and himself in the same package: "To millions of people in the easy days of that singular project, he was the Marshall Plan."

Throughout history, certain leaders seem to have been their own best public relations men. In recent years, President Franklin

D. Roosevelt perhaps capitalised upon this trait more adroitly than many other leaders of men. He had the remarkable ability of sensing the public wants, needs, fears, likes or dislikes, and of acting accordingly. Similarly, during the War years, Prime Ministers Wintson Churchill seemed to have the same ability and power over his people. He epitomised the average Britisher's will and determination to fight and defeat the Nazi aggression and tyranny. Our Prime Minister Nehru belonged to the same distinguished company. He was the most effective public relations man on behalf of the Government and the greatest vote-getter for the Congress party. The Prime Minister was not indulging in exaggeration when he said that he was himself a great tourist attraction in India.

6

Effective and Responsive Management

The Government, both at the Centre and the State, share the concern for ensuring responsive, accountable, transparent, decentralised and people-friendly administration at all levels. There is, however, considerable frustration and dissatisfaction amongst the people, especially the weaker sections of society, about the apathy, irresponsiveness and lack of accountability of public servants, even as the expenditure on staff continuous to increase. There is increasing anxiety about growing instances of corruption and criminalisation in public life and administration. The people, particularly the vulnerable groups, are also greatly concerned about the deterioration in the performance of agencies concerned with law and order and the investigation of offences. Their faith in the registration of offences, their timely investigation and the delivery of prompt justice has been eroded.

Time has come for a strong message to be conveyed that administration is for the people and not for the public servants themselves. There has to be a change of attitudes, and public servants should realise that efficiency will be measured not in terms of what the services purport to offer, but in terms of public satisfaction. Simultaneously, there has also to be a cleansing of the services and codification of the ethics, value systems and the interface with the politicians.

Necessary corrective steps must taken to arrest the present drift in Government and public services, and take urgent measures to restore the faith of the people in the fairness and capacity of administration. With this objective, the Prime Minister had inaugurated a Conference of Chief Secretaries in November, 1996 on 'An Agenda for an Effective and Responsive Administration'. In the Conference, a number of issues were raised which emphasised the need for bringing about a transformation in the public services to make them more efficient, clean, accountable and citizen-friendly. The conclusions of the Conference, which were sent to the State Governments for implementation, are given in *Annexure I*.

Following the Conference, a national debate has been generated throughout the country to elicit views from a wide crossection of people. Responses have been received from retreats organised in Mussoorie and Hyderabad, and a number of leading academic institutions in Delhi and other places. Written communications have been received from officials, experts, voluntary agencies, citizens groups, media, etc. Follow up action has been initiated on some of the priority areas to demonstrate the determination of the Government of India for implementing these reforms and to provide models for adoption by the State Governments.

The focus of these discussions has been to evolve a concrete Action Plan, for gearing up the Government machinery to provide a responsive, transparent and clean administration to the people and to address issues of reform and morale in the civil services. The Action Plan proposed to be discussed in the Conference includes initiatives in the following areas:

1. Making administration accountable and citizen-friendly;
2. Ensuring transparency and the right to information; and
3. Taking measures to cleanse and motivate Civil Services.

The adoption and implementation of the proposed Action Plan for an effective and responsive administration would require a strong political will, and reiteration from both the Central and the State Governments of their commitment to provide an accountable and responsive administration. Instances of responsive administration and initiatives taken by the Central and State Governments already are described in the supplementary notes given in *Annexure XI*.

ACCOUNTABLE AND CITIZEN-FRIENDLY GOVERNMENT

The citizen's perception of the State and its functionaries is primarily based on its role as a service provider, law enforcer and regulator. Improving the quality of administration and providing a responsive interface between the citizen and the public services require initiatives in following areas:

1. Citizens' Charter

The State Governments and the Ministries/Departments at the Centre are all involved in some manner or the other, in providing public services. Apart from an overall lack of transparency and accountability in the System, most delivery systems suffer from ad-hocism and delay. It is, therefore, important to identify and publicise the standards of services and time-limits that the public can reasonably expect, particularly in critical activities with a public interface. Government of India has directed Ministries/Departments and other agencies with public interface to formulate a Citizens' Charter, lay down time-limits and standards for services, avenues of grievance redressal, and put in place monitoring systems and independent scrutiny to ensure implementation of the Charter. A number of Departments have already formulated such Charters. Though the Charter is not proposed to be made justiciable, it would carry a moral commitment of the Government and would provide a framework under which public services can be evaluated. The principles of the Citizens' Charter have been enunciated at *Annexure II* which the State Governments can use to formulate their own charter according to their needs. Some model Citizens' Charters are given in Annexure II for information.

2. Redressal of Public Grievances

The poor record of most public agencies in the area of prompt and effective redressal of public grievances is a major cause of public dissatisfaction and a subject of criticism by the elected representatives. Public grievances primarily arise out of the inaccessibility of officials, failure to even acknowledge applications, non-enforcement of any kind of time-limits, and unsympathetic attitude of officials at various levels. A note highlighting the areas of action is given in *Annexure III* to enable Central and State Governments to review their existing system of redressal of public grievances, and institute measures not only for streamlining these, but also to monitor the steps taken to improve their efficacy.

3. Decentralisation and Devolution of Powers

Responsive Government would also require complete decentralisation of delivery of services through fully empowered elected local Government bodies, both in rural and urban areas, consistent with the spirit of the 73rd and 74th Constitutional Amendments. The Central/State Government need to take steps to strengthen the financial and administrative capacity of the local bodies and vest them with adequate resources and powers. A note on the subject is given in *Annexure IV*.

4. Review of Laws, Regulations and Procedures

In the changing administrative scenario, particularly in the context of economic liberalisation a number of existing laws and regulations have lost their relevance. The laws and regulations militating against the interest of the weaker sections of the society and the poor are required to be urgently amended. Similarly, existing procedures also need to be changed to make the whole process of approvals, sanctions, etc., simpler and transparent. Government of India has initiated a comprehensive exercise for amending the Civil Procedure Code, Company law and a number of other laws, as well as to reduce the time taken in disposal of cases in civil and criminal courts. It is necessary the State Governments undertake similar exercises in this regard and effect necessary changes in the laws and regulations. A note on the need to review and effect necessary changes in the laws and regulations. A note on the need to review existing laws, regulations and procedures is given in *Annexure V*.

TRANSPARENCY AND RIGHT TO INFORMATION

It has been noticed that secrecy and lack of openness in transactions in responsible for corruption in official dealings, apart from being contrary to the spirit of an accountable and democratic Government. Consequently, there is a demand for introducing greater transparency in the functioning of Government departments and public bodies. There is also a need to ensure to the people an easy access to all information relating to Government operations and Government decisions, as well as that on the performance of the Government, except to the extent specifically excluded by law. It is increasingly realised that, more the effort at secrecy, the greater the chances of abuse of authority by the pubic functionaries. Therefore, the following two areas/issues need to be addressed in this regard.

1. Transparency in Government and Right to Information

There is a widespread consensus on the need to assure freedom of information to the public and to amend such laws that stipulate unnecessary restrictions on free access of the public to information. Government decisions need not be clouded in secrecy, except in the interest of national security. Based on the discussion of an Inter-Ministerial Working Group, a statutory scheme to ensure freedom of information subject to certain safeguards, and to amend a number of central legislations, has been formulated. Details of these are given in the *Annexure VI.* State Governments could undertake a similar legal exercise, while endorsing the Central initiative, and ensure greater openness in the working of the Government departments, public agencies and elected local bodies, and provide information on procedures for various statutory approvals.

2. Access to Information

It is also important to improve the access of the public to information from public offices, through streamlining of internal procedures, computerisation, and by setting up public facilitation counters in offices. It is proposed that all the offices under the Government of India and the Public Sector undertakings will have computerised facilitation/information counter so that information and assistances is available to the public on various essential services and approvals. The State Governments may consider setting up of similar facilitation counters not only at the municipal and district levels, but also in the various State Directorates. A note on the subject is given in *Annexure VII.*

IMPROVING THE PERFORMANCE OF THE PUBLIC SERVICES

The civil services in India have played a significant, indeed a critical, role in maintaining the integrity of the country and in bringing about major developments in post-independent India. However, in recent times, the services have been facing a grave crisis of identity and role definition. People now believe that public services are meant to benefit government servants and politicians and not the public. The emphasis here is on all public services which substime all technical, professional law enforcement and administrative personnel. Though issues relating to efficiency and effectiveness of the administrative machinery have been discussed from time to time, the reforms initiated have only dealt with minor procedural changes, without really addressing the issue of improvement in the quality of services. The Government had initiated an exercise to discuss the specific reforms that could be undertaken to improve the image of the services enhance their effectiveness. The following proposals had emerged in this regard:

1. Code of Ethics

Adoption of the Code of Ethics of public services based on Constitutional principles and values, with appropriate amendments in the existing codes of conduct. Such a code, given in *Annexure VIII,* not only seeks to regulate the role of the civil servants, but also specifies the relationship between employees in public services and politicians, so that the basic commitment of the civil servants towards the welfare of the public and the principles enshrined in the Constitution is reiterated.

2. Cleansing the Administration

Though the rationale for the civil service in promoting the progress and integrity of the country is as valid today as before, there is an urgent need to tackle corruption and the increasing erosion of moral values in public life. The recommendations which have emerged in this regard have been collated in the note given in *Annexure IX.* These measures, once adopted, would need to be widely publicised to instill public confidence, both in the probity of all political and administrative functionaries, and in prosecution of the corrupt without exception.

3. Stability of Tenures and Constitution of Civil Services Board

Frequent and arbitrary transfers of public servants affect the ability of the system to deliver services effectively to the people. It has been seen that implementation of area development programmes and poverty alleviation schemes suffer where the officials are shifted frequently. Since the success of such schemes depends on having officials, with sufficient local knowledge and understanding to execute the schemes. Hence, it is felt that arbitrary transfers really operate against the interest of the people.

FUTURE ACTION

The above-mentioned package of measures, proposed as a part of the Action Plan on a responsive and accountable administration, would include both a number of one-time actions for immediate consideration, such as the Freedom of Information Act, Citizens' Charter, measures to tackle corruption and grievances redressal; as well as long term and ongoing reforms, such as inculcation of ethical values, objective criteria for transfers and placements, judicial and legal reforms, computerisation, building employees morale and orientation of public functionaries. However, there can be little doubt that any Action Plan is only as good and credible as its level of implementation and monitoring. It is proposed that the Plan itself can be elaborated and operationalised in concrete terms, and then pursued individually by the Central and State Governments. The progress, under various items of Action plan, would continuously be monitored by the Cabinet Secretary in close consultation with the Chief Secretaries of the various States and Union territories. The Action Plan would need to be well publicised, not only to secure widespread acceptance and feedback from all the stakeholders, but also to enlist the cooperation of the people in the implementation of the plan and in its evaluation.

ACTION PLAN

1. Citizens' Charter and an accountable administration
2. Effective and speedy public grievance redressal system
3. Empowering elected local bodies in rural and urban areas and decentralised delivery of services

4. Review of laws, regulations and procedures
5. Transparency and Right to Information
6. Access of the public to information from public offices and creation of facilitation counters
7. Code of Ethics for public services
8. Tackling corruption and cleansing the administration
9. Stability of tenure and a scheme for Civil Services Boards.

Annexure I

OPERATIVE RECOMMENDATIONS OF THE CONFERENCE OF CHIEF SECRETARIES

The Recommendations of the Conference grouped under three headings: (1) *responsive administration,* (2) *cleansing civil services,* and (3) *commitment to principles in the Constitution* are given in the following paras:

RESPONSIVE ADMINISTRATION

1. The crisis in administration calls for a redefinition of the role of government and its function and its real focus to serve the public effectively as much as to ensure efficient and cost-effective administration. Accountability, transparency and cleansing public service are all interconnected issues for ensuring a clean and responsive administration. It is necessary to converge the efforts of various public agencies for delivery of basic services in rural and urban areas and for single-level dealings with the public. This calls for steps to reorganise work procedures, for delegation down the line and an effective management information system accessible to all. Simultaneous steps to address the right-sizing of public services, value for money on public expenditure, restoring, effective audit, monitoring and evaluation, good financial management systems, etc., are needed.

2. It is necessary to introduce greater transparency and openness in the functioning of Government and public bodies. This would cover, for example, movement towards a Right to

Information Act, Transparent and well-publicised procedures for approvals by the general public and entrepreneurs under various statutes and regulations for allotment of land and immovable property; systems of assessment, levy and collection of various taxes and charges; award of work tenders for construction and provision of Services; procurement of goods and services; and various arrangements for involvement of private sector in contracting of services; and infrastructure projects by suitable amendment of relevant laws. The aim should be to move towards a citizen-centred administration.

3. The citizens in urban and rural areas should be provided with widespread and easy access—through the media, posters and various forms of neighbourhood-level communications—to all information relating to Government operations and reverse the undue emphasis on secrecy, details of various Government and local schemes, information on award of tenders and procurement, procedures for identification of beneficiaries under various Government schemes, and for receipt of benefits thereunder, publication of scores for all cases of admission to colleges and for recruitment, delivery of various civil services, etc. The progressive computerisation of information on public operations and work procedures will be of benefit to the government and the people.

4. Accountability should be interpreted in a larger sense in relation to public satisfaction and responsive delivery of services. We may consider the phased introduction of Citizens' Charter for as many service institutions as possible by way of citizens' entitlement to public services, collaboration of consumer organisation and citizen groups—wise publicity to standards of performance, quality, timeliness, cost, etc., for public services, and the provision for periodic and independent scrutiny of performance of the agencies as per set standards.

5. Immediate measures are needed for strengthening the machinery for grievance redressal at all levels, increased thrust on the needs of disadvantaged and vulnerable sections,

attention to systemic reforms, meaningful efforts to reach the unserved public-spirited citizen panels to assess service organisations, gender sensitive approach at all levels, and well-understood systems of filing complaints relating to poor services and malfeasance and prompt action thereon, accompanied by close monitoring of delays and punishment of the delinquent while devising ways to filter frivolous complaints. The good examples in different states should be widely publicised and scaled up along with due recognition for innovation and citizen-friendly attitudes.

6. The fullest possible decentralisation of service delivery and the administration of income support schemes, and effective utilisation of available resources, through the elected urban and rural local bodies, accompanies by the required devolution of powers and resources.

7. Encouragement to the widest possible awareness and participation of citizens and various representative groups in local decision-making, and the implementation of schemes affecting their livelihood and quality of life. The media has an important role to play in this regard.

8. Urgent steps for legal reform, for access of the citizens to quick and cheap justice, while initiating steps for amendment and simplification of the concern laws and obsolete legislations for introducing simple and speedy procedures. A number of laws and regulations militating against the interest of the poor need to be quickly amended.

CLEANSING THE CIVIL SERVICE

1. It is recognised that responsive administration depends on reforms in civil service at all levels, adherence to ethical standards, and basic principles of the Constitution, and a clear understanding of the relationship regulating the civil servants and the politicians. It has to be clearly appreciated that the political executive should concentrate on policy formulation while implementation is left to public services at various levels.

2. The approach to eliminate corruption in public service needs to address prevention, surveillance and deterrent prosecution,

and deal ruthlessly with the nexus between criminals and unscrupulous elements. It requires concerted efforts of politicians, public services and all stakeholders in civil society. The existing procedures for departmental enquiries and vigilance proceeding should be revamped. Rules and legal provisions should be amended to enable immediate and exemplary prosecution and removal of corrupt officers without giving them recourse to any political protection. It is necessary to remove the scope for any interference in the prompt prosecution and punishment of, corrupt officials. It is necessary to devise systems to break the nexus between politicians, bureaucrats and criminals which has developed in a number of places.

3. The numerous service and conduct rules should be reviewed in order to arrange for the review of the integrity and efficiency of officers at any stage during the career, and the compulsory retirement of officers of doubtful integrity.

4. Simultaneous with the measures given above, the preventive steps would include not only regulatory reforms to reduce scope for discretion and secrecy at all levels, developmental schemes and approvals.

5. Other in-built steps should include improvement in service conditions and right-sizing public services, improving the system of performance appraisal and promotions through transparent procedures, recognised systems of rewards and penalties, consistent action of senior management to support the subordinates in sincere performance of duty according to law and procedures, and in resisting illegal directions.

COMMITMENT TO PRINCIPLES OF THE CONSTITUTION

1. The Government of India and State Governments should draw up a Charter of Ethics and Civil Service Code for the civil service, based on fundamental principles of the Indian Constitution such as secularism, equality, impartiality, social justice, attention to the needs of the weaker sections, rule of law, etc. This code would regulate the role of the legislators and the relationship between civil servants and politicians.

2. It should be agreed that the loyalty of public servants should be only to the service for the public and the rule of law. This is particularly relevant in the context of the permanent character of civil service.

3. State Governments will be requested to devise suitable mechanisms, including a high-powered Civil Service Board, and amend relevant rules for transparent decisions on postings, promotions and transfers of senior officials on the lines of Central Government. Similar Boards should be set up to govern functionaries at lower levels and in elected local bodies. These boards could be strengthened in their apolitical functioning by the appointment of Civil Services Ombudsman to deal with grievances of officials. It should be recognised that the public suffer equally from frequent transfers of heads of departments. Appropriate legislations may be considered to incorporate some of these suggestions.

Annexure II

CITIZENS' CHARTER AND ACCOUNTABLE ADMINISTRATION

Scheme

One of the important means of ensuring accountability and transparency in the agencies engaged in providing services to the people, or enforcing laws and regulations, is to organise their actions around the concept of Citizens' Charter. This part of a national movement in countries, like the UK and Malaysia, where it lays out the citizen's entitlement to public services and responsive administration of regulations. It places the citizen at the centre of administration instead of making him a passive recipient of services rendered indifferently with no concern for quality, timeliness or cost. It is to be seen as a visible symbol of accountable government. The Government of India has directed all Ministries, Departments, and agencies under them, with a public interface to publish Citizens' Charter, starting with services. The object is to bring all the service rendered by these agencies under the charter over a period of two years.

Citizens' Charter is based on the principles of: (1) wide publicity of standards of performance of public agencies and local bodies; (2) assured quality of service; (3) access to information and courtesy and helpfulness of staff; (4) choice and consultation with the citizens; (5) simplified and convenient procedure for receipt and acknowledgement of complaints, and time-bound redressal of grievances; and (6) the provision for independent scrutiny of performance with the involvement of citizen groups.

While it is not justiciable, it represents the moral and democratic commitment of the government to service of the public.

In order to accomplish this task, it has been directed that each Central Government Department and its public agencies should work out its own Citizens' Charter and related actions in terms of the nature of work and, more importantly, the groups of clients or members of the public, geographical concept, nature of regulatory function and paid-for services. It should also evolve a plan containing both long-term and short-term/moving targets for improved public satisfaction and efficient performance through systems improvement, technological and information inputs, staff orientation, work place changes, use of alternate providers, partnership with citizen groups, voluntary agencies and the corporate sector, etc. An in-built machinery will be set up in each Ministry/Department for independent system auditing and periodic monitoring of performance with reference to the Charter principles and to attend to the capacity-building and orientation of the staff. It is envisaged that consumer organisations, citizen groups, experts, retired public servants, elected representatives and others are involved in this process of formulation and scrutiny of performance so as to ensure that the commitments made actually meet the needs of the people. Once the areas of activities sought to be improved are streamlined, adequate publicity will be given so that the people are made aware of the proposed changes. The entire process will be monitored periodically by a core group under the Cabinet Secretary.

Many Central agencies, such as the Railways, Post, Health, Central Board of Direct Taxes, Central Board of Excise and Customs, Petroleum, Industry, Delhi Development Authority and Passport Office and others have announced a series of citizen-friendly initiatives. The Ministry of Home Affairs have set up a Task Force to formulate specific steps for a citizen-friendly law enforcement system and crime prevention. It has also announced setting up of a Police Complaints Authority for Delhi. The Central Health Ministry has requested all the State Governments to set up emergency care services in bigger hospitals on the pattern of what has been considered for Delhi, as also a system of registration and rating of nursing homes. State Governments, like Himachal Pradesh, have announced a Citizens' Charter for revenue functionaries.

PROPOSED ACTION

The State Governments could consider formulation of Citizens' Charter on the lines indicated above of services provided by various State and local agencies with public interface, such as the Offices of the Collector, Superintendent of Police, Municipal bodies, Zilla Panchayat, Tehsil and Block Office, Transport Department, electricity offices, water supply and sanitation services, etc. Monitoring systems similar to those proposed in Government India could be installed to ensure availability of sustained benefits to citizens. The concept of the model office based on computerised counter services will be an important means of implementing the Charter. The close association of citizen groups, elected representatives and media could be considered for success of the venture and for continuous feedback on performance through independent citizens' panels.

Annexure III

EFFECTIVE AND SPEEDY PUBLIC GRIEVANCE REDRESSAL SYSTEM

The poor record of most public agencies in the area of prompt and effective redressal of public grievances is a major cause of public dissatisfaction and the subject of criticism by elected representatives. It is noticed that many of the Government Departments and their subordinate offices, which have substantial public interface and where large numbers of public are required to go daily, do not display the required orientation to the needs and circumstances of the public, especially the weaker section of society, women and the handicapped.

It is also found that adequate facilities are often not available in the public offices for reception of the public seeking various types of information or with various queries and demands of services, and arrangements for seating and waiting of the public, water supply and sanitation, protection from rain, sun, etc., are insufficient or non-existent in police stations and other public offices which the citizens are required to visit. There are often no display boards relating to information generally desired by the public on the location of offices and facilities, various procedures involved, fees, submission of forms, time taken in disposal, etc. The names of grievance redressal officers are not often widely published, and these officers are also not accessible as stipulated to meet the public.

Apart from lack of facilities and friendly reception, the public grievances primarily arise out of inaccessibility of officials, failure to even acknowledge applications, unwarranted delays and non-enforcement of time limits, lack of information, harassment and activities of middlemen, demand for speed money, ignorance of procedures and forms, and the unsympathetic attitudes of officials at all levels. In big cities, citizens are often required to travel long distances to visit different offices due to lack of decentralised locations at the ward level for providing information on dealing with complaints. The methods for payments of various taxes and service charges are often inconvenient, not suited to the working hours of such members of the public who do not have access to servants. As regards the villagers in dispersed villages throughout the district, they face great problems in approaching the tehsil and district offices for getting copies of records, licences, payments, applications under various Government schemes, etc.

State Governments have instituted systems of time-bound redressal of citizens' grievances, which are often monitored through computers and programmes like Administration to the People in Andhra Pradesh. The district officials are required in many States, like Tripura to visit villages and blocks together periodically in order to listen to the grievances of the people, and redress them on the spot. Janta Darbars are also convened by Ministers.

The progress in respect of disposal of public grievances is being monitored in the Central Government by the Department of Administrative Reforms and Public Grievances. The Directorate of Public Grievances in the Cabinet Secretariat deals with cases of individual grievances for Central agencies with a large public interface, and has the power to call officials and the concerned files to give a binding order. Central Ministries like Railways, Posts and Telecommunications have set up Lok Adalats to deal with complaints in the presence of the consumers. There are social audit panels of imminent citizens which look into the quality of services of the Postal and Telecommunications Department. There is an Ombudsman for the commercial banks. The Central Manual of Office Procedure provides for the fixation of time limits for dealing with public grievances, while the Code of Conduct Rules provide for disciplinary action in case of discourteous behaviour or negligence in grievance redressal.

Similar arrangements can be considered at the state level. Apart from cells located in the office of Chief Ministers, as in fact is being done in states like Tamil Nadu, Karnataka and Haryana. This will help in high-level attention to systemic causes of grievances through delegation, decentralisation, flexible norms, simplified procedures, review of forms, etc. The performance review of officials could incorporate attention to grievance redressal and public perception of the services of the agency.

A number of measures could be considered for immediate improvement in the situation. The language and tone of various application forms should be user-friendly, and the forms be widely available in various outlets, including post offices. Every office should display at a prominent place its organisational structure, indicating names of officers and their functions, and location of their rooms. Every public servant should normally be available during working hours to respond to the public in person or on phone. Every application or petition should be acknowledge through standards acknowledgement slips. Every application should also carry such a slip for future response. Time-limits should be fixed for approval or rejection of applications for permits, quotas, certificates and approvals, on the basis of well-publicise and uniformly applied criteria. This should be accompanied by delegation of financial and administrative powers at the operational, level and well-enforced standards of accountability. The District Administration should set up mechanisms to contact the people at the local level periodically, specially for remote and inaccessible areas. Senior officials, like Collector and Superintendent of Police, should not get so overloaded with work or committees that they are unable to devote enough time to meet people regularly and deal with their problems.

The number and periodicity of contact for the people and Government offices would be minimised, and the officers should allow for the flexible needs of the working population. Every department should choose a few priority areas from the citizen's newpoint for computerisation and allow free access of the citizens to this information in this computer. Finally, every public body should have a well-defined mission statement spelling out standards of service provided to the public, such as garbage removal, water supply to power supply. The officials responsible for good work should be given recognition and reward, and the innovative practices should be widely disseminated.

The real issue, however, is the need to bring about a total change in the attitude of public servants towards redressal of public grievances at all levels and to pin-point responsibility for action on grievance of the people. This is dependent internally on measures to improve their levels of motivation and morale through rewards for good work and punishment for deliberate negligence and through awards for suggestions. The senior officers should constantly supervise the staff at the cutting edge level in police stations, sub-division, etc. Every official in public offices should wear name badge.

A demonstrable and effective way of ensuring prompt redressal of public grievances would be through establishment of independent Public Grievances Committees, consisting of eminent citizens. Such Committees can be authorised to inspect the adequacy and functioning of grievance redressal systems in various public offices, and report to the Cabinet Secretary (for Central Government) and Chief Secretary of State Government on actions to remedy the system, and to take firm steps against negligent officials. It is also possible to set up independent watch dog committees at district level to report to State Government on the working of grievance redressal systems. The Himachal Pradesh Specific corrupt Practices Act makes the omission on the Part of an officer to discharge his statutory or *bona fide* duty a corrupt practice. Similar enactments or the provisions of draft Karnataka Administrative Procedure Bill could be considered to oblige officials to respond to requests of the public.

Proposed Action

The State Government could consider an urgent review of the system of redressal of public grievances at the State, district, city, block and village levels, and devise arrangements for their sensitive and prompt redressal, and ensure regular independent review of these systems. Steps could be taken to fix responsibility in each office for dealing with grievances, for attitudinal orientation of officials at all levels, and for continuous monitoring of the redressal system. This could be integrated with the overall package of measures for responsive administration. The State Government could consider dettong up independent watchdog committees at the district and city levels to report to high-powered cells in the State Government on the functioning of the local grievance redressal systems, as well as cases of negligence and delay.

Annexure IV

EMPOWERING ELECTED LOCAL BODIES IN RURAL AND URBAN AREAS AND DECENTRALISED DELIVERY OF SERVICES

Context

Responsive administration requires that service delivery and administration of income support schemes are decentralised through the elected local bodies in rural urban areas. This alone makes for meaningful democracy, as articulate in the 73rd and 74th

Constitutional Amendments. These Amendments contain the provisions for: regular elections, constituting District Planning Committees, drawing up illustrative list of functions, and establishment of State Finance Commission for assigning commensurate resources to local bodies. The Central and State Governments envisage implementation of all the poverty alleviation schemes and integrated rural development through the panchayats and nagarpalikas. States like Kerala and Andhra Pradesh have made a success of bottom-up planning by providing the help of resource persons to enable Gram Sabhas to prioritise their needs and prepare development plants. Examples abound of support to the widest possible participation of people, women and NGOs in the planning and delivery of services, which also eliminates the delay and costs of bureaucratic intermediation.

At the same time, the agenda of real empowerment of elected local bodies, has largely not gone beyond conforming legislation in most States. Centralised system for Planning and service delivery often through functional agencies, still persist, and the local self-government bodies and the elected functionaries are not enabled to function with adequate control over local functions and resources. The functions for each tier of Panchayati Raj need to be demarcated and commensurate resources provided on the basis of recommendations of State Finance Commission.

The transfer of local function to the elected local bodies will also help in the right-sizing of State Governments, pervaded the former are giving adequate personnel and administrative support. The constitution of District Planning Committees to prepare plans for economic development and social justice, as already done by Keralas, will help to consolidate village and city level plans, based on local priorities and people's contribution. The NDC has already recommended that 41 per cent of the plan resources be set apart for decentralised planning.

The Panchayati Raj Institutions and the Nagarpalikas would also provide an umbrella for the convergence of various sectoral, poverty alleviation and area development programmes at each tier, including schemes focused on women, for various welfare and income support schemes would help to cut down corruption and leakages in these schemes. Madhya Pradesh and Rajasthan provide examples of the benefits of transparency in public distribution system, development works, public hearing, etc., with the oversight of Panchayat bodies and local volunteers. As the Approach Paper for the Ninth Plan asserts social audit and transparency in the functioning of Panchayati raj Institutions in crucial for their growth.

Proposed Action

The Central and State Governments could move purposefully to ensure the effective empowerment of elected local bodies in urban and rural areas, as envisaged in the 73rd and 74th Amendments, through the assignment of all local functions and planning according to the illustrative Lists in the Constitution, accompanied by steps to strengthen their implementation and financial capacity, and the vesting of executive powers in these bodies. The State Government could also take early steps to devolve adequate resources, commensurate with the assigned tasks and decentralised delivery of services, based on the recommendations of State Finance Commissions. The central and State Governments could encourage and sustain unitary agencies and people's participation in all the schemes for the delivery of basic services identified in the Conference of Chief Ministers in July, 1996 and in all local development schemes. All village-level schemes could be reoriented and integrated under the Panchayati Raj, and bottom up participatory planning could be encouraged. Cooperatives and similar self-governing systems could be encouraged in all spheres of economy and resource management.

Annexure V

REVIEW OF LAWS, REGULATIONS AND PROCEDURES

Background

In the course of review of the experience with implementation of various policy changes announced by the Government in the context of economic reform and liberalisation of procedures for inflow of foreign investment, it has been found that foreign investors and small and big industrialists alike cite administrative red tape, requirement of multiple approvals, and cumbersome rule sand regulations causes of delays and cost escalation, and less than commensurate benefits flowing from policy initiatives of the Government. The effective delivery of services and benefits under various welfare schemes to the public are also frustrated by rigid procedures and archaic laws, apart from insensitive attitude of the officials and unwarranted transaction costs.

It has pointed out that many of the old laws, rules, regulations and procedures in the Central and State Governments have lost their relevance considerably. Many of them not only stand in the way of a responsive administration, but are found to be often operating against the interest of the poor and the marginalised groups. Laws on the subject operated by one or more departments often overlap or conflict with each other, leading to fruitless parallel proceedings. They also increase the cost of transactions and litigation tremendously for the average citizen and subject him to corruption at every stage. The opaqua regulations, however, allow the unscrupulous builders and middleman to break the rules with impunity, sometimes in collusion with the officials.

It is recognised that various State Governments have undertaken detailed exercises to simplify and liberalise various rules and regulations. Many Central Ministries have also been addressing the issue seriously and a major exercise for amending various laws affecting economic reform, industries and urban development is under way. The Law Ministry has taken up an exercise for legal reform, having regard to the recommendation of expert committees, to reduce the time taken for disposal of cases in courts, to provide for alternate systems of dispute resolution, to reduce the scope for unnecessary adjournments, facilitate pre-trial conciliation, etc. The Finance Minister has also announced a series of legal initiatives and review of present laws in the Budget speech.

Central and State Governments could review the regulatory and legal framework in different economic and social sectors to see whether the objectives for which the regulations were put in place are properly defined, after consultation with affected groups, whether these objectives could be better achieved in any other manner or made more citizen-friendly, whether it is necessary to continue the existing regulations at all, whether the machinery for their implementation is adequate and cost effective, and whether the presumed social and economic benefits of the regulations warrant their continuance. Where there are a number of orders of government on the subject, every Department should bring out a comprehensive government order on the subject, every five years. It should also bring out lists of Acts and Regulations implemented by it every five years, along with informative notes in the local language for wide dissemination.

The review by the States, in turn, could cover the multiplicity of forms and return, and the design of the forms itself, as well as the possibility of making transactions paper less, as have been tried out by the Central Excise Department in Delhi. It should be possible to receive the applications to various agencies required from an investor or the applicant at one point and help him to secure the clearance of all the agencies. The number of required clearances could be cut down, and the process of approval itself can based much more on self-regulation. Building commencement certificates could be issued by architects, and various certificates could be issued by accredited persons or agencies with severe penalties on the issuing persons for any violation.

Some of the suggested requirements for effective decision making included:

1. Reduction in number of levels and stages (including calling for a number of certificates) through which decision-making process goes through, so that the Government progressively reposes more faith in the citizens in matters like issue of licenses;
2. Delegation of financial powers should be in relation to the current price levels and should be reviewed every three years;
3. It is necessary to review the present provisions of audit and place more emphasis on systems audit to reduce enormous

delays due it fear of audit even in trivial matters, disproportionate to the expenditure involved.

4. All public officers should publish handouts in simple local language, the procedures to be followed, the method of filing forms, fees and other requirements, and make them available to the public on demand.

It is possible for the Central and State Governments to work together in this important exercise since it is the essence of more citizen-friendly administration, access to swift justice, reduced corruption, and success of the economic reform process. It will also help to effect savings in the huge time, manpower, and legal costs incurred by Central and state Governments, and their agencies, in pursuing litigation without any hope of a final result for many years.

Proposed Action

The Central and State Governments could draw upon agenda for priority reform of the legal system and procedures to facilitate economic reform, reduce obstacles to economic and social activity of the poor and marginalised groups, to enable speedy flow of services to target groups in various schemes, to facilitate early approvals under various statues, to provide the people access to swift and inexpensive justice, and to cut down the tendency of cases in criminal and civil courts. A core group of central and state officials and legal experts could be set up to review efforts already taken/under way in this regard, and suggest areas of legal and regulatory amendment/reform to the next meeting of the Chief Ministers after wide consultation. Meanwhile, the Central and State Governments could proceed expeditiously with amendments to restrictive laws and procedures, where the proposals are finalised.

Annexure VI

TRANSPARENCY AND RIGHT TO INFORMATION

Context

There is a political consensus and popular demand for introduction of greater transparency in the functioning of government and public bodies, and widespread and easy access of people to all information relating to Government operations and Government decisions, as well as performance of the Government, except to the extent specifically excluded by law. A new culture of information and helpful attitude, as opposed to secrecy and mystification, should pervade all government offices.

It is increasingly realised that, more the effort of secrecy, the greater the chances of abuse of authority by the public functionaries. At the same time, the provisions of Official Secrets Act, 1923, and the Code of Conduct Rules for Government employees prevent most of the information about affairs of Government from being disclosed to the public. The most damaging consequence of the legislation and the Code of Conduct is the generally secretive behaviour which it has encouraged in the civil service, and the denial of items of unclassified information, and the details of development expenditure, to the citizens. The Budget speech of the Chief Minister, Tamil Nadu, mentions that one major reason for occurrence of irregularities is that information leading to decision taken by the officers at various levels do not reach the public.

There have been efforts since 1990 to introduce legislation to ensure Freedom of Information, and to amend the Official Secrets Act. The call for greater transparency and Right it Information has been given in a number of States. Some States have issued circulars in ensure the availability to the people of details of development expenditure and inspection of revenue records in public offices, apart from the provision for public hearing. Chief Minister, Andhra Pradesh has announced that a White Paper will soon be issued on giving information to the people. Bilaspur, in Madhya Pradesh, is implementing a transparent public distribution system and recruitment for jobs. The budget speech of the Chief Minister, Tamil Nadu, refers to the proposal of the State Government to enact a law to provide the public Right to Information. According to the Chief Minister, this will enable the public to get details about the schemes of the Government, the works executed by various Departments, the essential commodities supplied to each of the shops under Public Distribution System and pave the way for the people to question the irregularities in the system.

The Government of India set up a working group under the Chairmanship of Shri H.D. Shourie to formulate a Bill for Freedom of Information, and amendments to relevant laws for this purpose. Based on the discussions of this Group, a statutory scheme has been formulated to ensure freedom of information subject to certain safeguards in public interest. These are outlined in the Appendix at the end of this Annexure.

Amendments to other Enactments and Rules

Simultaneous with the proposals for enactment of the Freedom of Information Bill, the Government of India is also formulating amendments to Section 5 to the Official Secrets Act, and Sections 123, 124 and 125 of the Indian Evidence Act to bring them in line with the provisions of the new legislation. It is also proposed to amend the relevant sections of the Central Code of Conduct Rules in order to enable Government employees to release information to the public consistent with the provisions of the new legislation. The rules relating to classification of official documents and records are also proposed to be amended suitably.

A detailed exercise could be carried out by an Expert Group to identify various Central and State Laws which contain provisions relating to release of information, and propose amendments to bring them in line with the Freedom of Information Act.

Pending action to pass these legislations, detailed instructions could be issued to all the Central Ministries/Departments, and agencies and PSUs under them, to introduce greater transparency in their operations, and to ensure widespread and easy access of the public to all unclassified information. This can be followed up by department, specific instructions to be issued and enforced by each department.

Proposed Action

The Central and State Governments could endorse immediate formulation of the Legislation for freedom of Information on the lines of the statutory scheme, amendments to the relevant provisions of the Official Secrets Act, 1923 and the Indian Evidence Act and other relevant laws. They could process consequential changes in Code of Conduct Rules, Classification of official records, etc. The legislation for Freedom of Information may be introduced in Parliament at the earliest. The administrative arrangements for its implementation may be worked out in three months by a group of Central and State officials and legal experts to be constituted by the Government of India.

In the meantime, the Central and State Government could issue instructions for greater openness in the working of Government departments, public agencies and elected local bodies, and providing information widely on procedures for various statutory approvals, details of allotment of land and property, criteria for assessment and levy of taxes, criteria for, and information on, award of work tenders and procurement of goods and services, criteria for the selected lists of, beneficiaries under various Government schemes, building approvals, development expenditure and works, etc. Counters could be set up in public offices of easy and prompt availability of such information to the public. The employees at all levels could be oriented and directed to be courteous and open in dealing with the public and in the provision of information not prohibited by law.

Appendix

A STATUTORY SCHEME FOR FREEDOM OF INFORMATION

Purpose

The statute may be called Freedom of Information Act. It may be enacted by Parliament and shall come into force from a date to be notified in the Gazette. Its purpose would be to progressively provide greater access to information under the control of Government of India, State Government, Union Territories and other governmental agencies and organisations substantially controlled or funded by the Government (hereafter referred to as public authorities), in order: (a) to promote openness and transparency in administration; (b) to enable fuller and more meaningful participation of the people in making and implementation of policies and programmes affecting the public; and (c) to promote accountability and responsibility in administration.

To fulfil these purposes, the right of access to information would be provided to citizens on the broad principles that; (a) access to information should be the rule and denial of access the exception; (b) the grounds for denial may be clearly and specifically defined; and (c) there should be a provision for an independent mechanism which provides remedy to applicants against decisions to withhold information.

Scope

The scheme should apply to all Ministries/Departments of Central/State Governments and their attached and subordinate offices and other bodies, including PSUs and autonomous bodies, substantially funded or controlled by the Government, and local bodies excepting bodies/organisations, such as intelligence services, that may be specifically exempted from it. So far as the judiciary, Tribunals and such other judicial/quasi-judicial bodies and Parliament/State Legislatures are concerned, the scheme would only cover their administrative/support services with the concurrence of the Chief Justice or the Speaker, as the case may be.

Obligations on Public Authorities

Each public authority should publish periodically, and keep updated information indicating: (1) particulars of its organisation, functions and responsibilities; (2) description of its decision making processes in terms of procedures and powers and responsibilities of its officers and employees; (3) Norms for performance of activities, such as prescribed periods for their processing and completion, physical and financial targets, etc., and the actual achievement with reference to such norm; (4) Classes of records under its control, including the rules, regulations, instructions and lists of manuals, etc., used by its employees for carrying out activities. (5) The facilities provided for access to information; and (6) The name, designation and other relevant particulars of the officer, to be called the Public Information Officer, to whom requests for information may be addressed.

It shall also be the duty of the concerned officers of a public authority to give reasons for decisions—whether administrative or adjudicative—to those affected and to disclose the relevant facts and analyses when major policies or decisions are announced.

Grounds for Refusal of Access in Certain Cases

Access to information may be refused where:

1. The request is too general or of such a nature, that having regard to the volume of information required to be retrieved or processed for fulfilling it, it would involve disproportionate diversion of the resources of a public authority or would adversely interfere with normal functioning of such authority; provided that, where access is being refused on the ground that the request is too general, it would be the duty of the Public Information Officer in a public authority, to help the requester as far as possible to reframeme his request in such a manner as would facilitate compliance with it;
2. The request relates to information that is required by law or convention to be published at a particular time; and
3. The request relates to information which is already contained in published material available for sale.

Procedure and Forms of Access

Each public authority shall appoint officers to be called Public Information officers in its offices, who should be vested with adequate administrative authority to obtain relevant information within their organisations. While appointing these officers, the public authority concerned shall keep in mind the overriding need to provide access to information as conveniently, cheaply and effectively and as close as possible to a citizen's place of residence or business.

It will be the responsibility of the Public Information Officers to deal with requests for access to information and to ensure timely compliance with such requests where the information being requested for is not being withheld or access is not being refused. The decision whether to accede to requests or not would also be taken by him.

A request under this Scheme should be made in writing and should, as clearly as possible, specify the particulars of the document or record to which access is being sought. Where a citizen cannot, for a valid reason, make a request in writing, the Public Information Officer may either accept an oral request or assist the requester in making a written request.

The Public Information officer shall endeavour to provide access as expeditiously as possible and a decision in the matter should be taken within the maximum period of 30 days from the date of receipt of the request. In case the decision is to refuse access, the grounds for refusal should be clearly indicated, along with a description of the review procedure open to the requester.

In the event it is not possible to respond to a request within the period of 30 days, the period may be extended up to a maximum of another 30 days for reasons to be recorded and communicated to the requester, in writing.

Lack of response from a public authority, within the above mentioned period, shall be deemed to amount to a refusal of request for access to information and the requester shall be entitled to seek recourse to the review procedure.

Access may be provided in one or more of the following forms: (1) A reasonable opportunity to inspect records/documents; (2) Supply of copies of documents; or (3) Where the information requested for is stored in computers, a provision of access through terminals or supply of print-outs, etc.

Access should ordinarily be provided in the form it is requested for unless: (1) it would disproportionately divert the resources of a public authority; or (2) would be detrimental to safety or preservation of the record document in question.

Fee

Fees may be charged for access to information and may include an application fee and an additional fee based on the cost of supplying the information, such as cost of research involved in compiling the information and cost of copying, etc. The fee may be waived in the cases where the disclosure can be said to be in the larger public interest.

Exemptions from Disclosure

Disclosure of information may be refused if the information is covered by any of the following categories:

1. Information disclosure of which would prejudicially affect the sovereignty and integrity of India, security of the State, conduct of international relations, including information received in confidence from foreign governments, their agencies or international organisation;
2. Information disclosure of which would prejudicially affect the conduct of Centre-State relations, including information received in confidences from a State Government or any of its authorities/agencies;
3. Information in the nature of Cabinet papers, including papers prepared for submission to Cabinet or submitted to Cabinet, other than the documents whereby such decision are published;
4. Information, other than exclusively factual information, in the nature of internal working papers, such as inter-departmental/ intra-departmental notes and correspondence, papers containing advice, opinion, or recommendation for the purpose of deliberative processes in a public authority;
5. Information, disclosure of which would prejudicially affect the enforcement of any law, including detection, prevention, investigation or suppression of crime or contravention of any law; or would lead to incitement to an offence; or would prejudicially affect the operations of any intelligence organisation to be specified by the Government, or would prejudicially affect public safety or the safety of an individual; or would prejudicially affect fair trial or adjudication of a pending case; or would reveal the existence or identify of a confidential record or source of information, or would

prejudice future supply of information relating to violation in or contravention of any law;

6. Information the disclosure of which would prejudicially affect the Government's ability to manage the economy or would prejudicially affect the legitimate economic and commercial interest of the public authority, or would cause unfair gain or loss to any individual or organisation;
7. Information, the disclosure of which would prejudicially affect the management of services under, and operations of public authorities;
8. Information in the nature of trade or commercial secrets or any information having a commercial value, which is likely to prejudicially affect the competitive position of a third party provided that, excepting in the case of trade or commercial secrets protected by law, disclosure may be allowed if public interest in such disclosure, outweighs in importance any possible harm or injury to the interest of any such third party;
9. Information, the disclosure of which would not subserve any public interest;
10. Information, the disclosure of which would cause unwarranted invasion of the privileges of an individual; and
11. Information, the disclosure of which may result in the breach of Parliamentary privilege or would amount to violation of an order of a Competent Court.

Severability

If a request for access to information is refused on the ground that it is in relation to information which is exempted from disclosure, then notwithstanding anything contained in this Act, access may be given to the part of the document which does not contain any information that is exempted from disclosure under this Act and which can reasonably be severed from any part that contains any such information.

Third Party Intervention

Where a public authority intends to disclose information has been supplied in confidence by a third party, or which might contain trade or commercial secrets of a third party, and such disclosure can reasonably be expected to harm the interest of such third party, a notice may be given to it of the intended disclosure and it may be permitted to make a representation within 14 days of the receipt of the above notice, stating reasons why the information should not be disclosed. The public authority shall take such representation into account while taking a decision on the request for information. In the case of information other than trade or commercial secrets protected by law, disclosure may be permitted if public interest outweighs in importance any possible harm or injury to the interest of the third party.

Internal Review

A requester, whose request for access to information has been rejected by an Information Facilitation Officer, may make an application for review of that decision, to the Head of Department having jurisdiction over the concerned office of the public authority to which the request had been addressed.

The review application shall be disposed of by the concerned Head of Department within 30 days of its receipt. In case the request relates to information in the nature of third party information, the disclosure of which can reasonably expected to cause harm to such third party, the Head of Department shall also send an appropriate notice to such third party affording it the opportunity to make a representation, and shall take into consideration any such representation, if made, while taking a final decision on the review application; provided that, excepting in case of trade or commercial secrets protected by law, disclosure may be permitted if public interest outweighs the expected harm or injury to the interests to any such third party.

A review application may also be made as regards the fee proposed to be charged by the Information Facilitation Officer.

Appeal

The Machinery under the Consumer Protection Act, 1986 may be used as an appellate mechanism with an appeal under the

Freedom of Information Act being dealt within the same manner as a complaint under the Consumer Protection Act.

Rules and Regulations

Rules and regulations may be made to carry out the purposes of the Act. They may deal with matters, such as fees and waiver of fees, forms of application for access, review and appeals against decisions to deny access, procedures for review, appeal and other similar matters.

Annual Reports of Public Authorities

All public authorities shall, in their annual reports, include a separate chapter detailing the operation of the Act. The reports may mention, *inter alia*, statistical data including the number of requests for access to information received during the year, the number of refusals along with broad reasons for refusals, the costs incurred in providing access and the fees recovered, details of review applications and appeals and their disposal, etc.

Council for Freedom of Information

Councils may be set up at National as well as State levels, under the chairmanship of the Ministers in charge of Department of Administrative Reforms with a suitable number of members representing such interests as may be specified, for reviewing the operation of the Act and to advise the Government on making the Act effective, including training and orientation of employees, streamlining procedures, etc.

Review of Other Laws and Rules/Regulations

There are a number of laws containing provisions which may impinge on disclosure of information which would need to be reviewed and amended to make them consistent with the proposed Freedom of Information Act. For example, the provision of Section 5 of the Official Secrets Act will have to be amended suitably, keeping in view the principles underlying the proposed Freedom of Information Act. Similarly, Sections 123, 124 and 125 of Indian Evidence act may need to be reviewed. Rule 11 of the Central Civil Services (Conduct) Rules, 1964, and its corresponding provision.

i.e., Rule 9 of the All-India Services (Conduct) Rules, 1968 would also need to be amended. Similar action would need to be taken in respect of the relevant rules for the State Civil Services. The Working Group on Right to Information and promotion of open and transparent government is looking into some of these aspects. However, a detailed study is required to identify all laws which may have to be revised.

Annexure VII

COMPUTERISED ACCESS OF THE PEOPLE TO INFORMATION FROM PUBLIC OFFICES AND FACILITATION COUNTERS

Scheme

An integral aspect of administrative reforms, both in the short term and in the longer perspective, is related to the speedy and easy access of information to the public on the services and activities of Government and the development of appropriate Management Information Systems in Government. There are considerable delays in redressal of grievances and securing access to information, since government department with a public service interface do not have a mechanism to provided information to the citizens across the counter or to deal with their queries and complaints at a single point.

This would necessarily involve two areas. The first is related to the development of an appropriate computerised network of information to internally link all offices of Central Government, Telecom or Railways, as well as to integrate Central or State offices for effective information sharing in the cause of services to investors and the public, and more intelligent government. The second aspect would be linked to the need to ensure widespread and easy access of citizens to information at various levels in the Government, and its agencies, as well as the issue of revenue records and certificates, simplified and speedy systems of securing approvals and permits, redressal of grievances, etc., with the help of computers.

The Expert Group set-up by the Government of India is examining these issues. Meanwhile, the Government is studying the legislative amendments or new laws necessary to ensure the legal and transactional acceptability of computerised data transfer and print outs.

It is evident that a significant infrastructure to create a computerised public interface is already available through National Informatics Centre (NIC), which is working closely with the state governments. The district NICNETs are fully operational, and district level NIC coordination Committees have been setup to supplement the Committees at the State Level. NIC has already setup 6,000 data bases and the GISTNIC is providing information on various aspects of the economy and functioning of Government, to which a new section on public services is now proposed to be added. All the districts are proposed to be computerised with NIC help over the next few years, to provide up-to-date information on judgements and the stage of cases, with 150 courts covered already. Many state governments are taking full advantage of the facilities provided by NIC, including the Central Assistance for the computerisation of land records, and have also devised their on systems to computerise procedure information to public, etc. States like Andhra Pradesh are monitoring the movement of files, and implementation of schemes through computers.

As part of the programme to disseminate information on public services to the pubic, it is proposed to set up citizen information centres on a pilot basis (starting with all State Capitals) through the efforts of the Department of Consumer Affairs and Public Distribution, and the involvement of state governments. These centres would be run by voluntary agencies with assistance from the Consumer Welfare Fund. However, the real help needed by the citizens in terms of securing various services or getting their complaints promptly attended to, besides information on procedures and forms, can be provided only through counters set up in public offices.

The Government of India has decided that all officers of the Government and agencies under it should have a computerise public interface, aimed at dissemination of information to the public for a fee or free of charge. The Central Government Ministries and their agencies would take steps to ensure provision of all unclassified information on procedures and decisions to the public through facilitation counters which should be set up near the reception hall of the Ministries or offices, similar to the Lakhima model in Maharashtra. These counters would be operated continuously during the day by trained officials with courteous approach, with the capacity to converse in English an the local language, and capable of using computers. The salient features of the facilitation centre are given at the end of this annexure. These counters can be provided with computer consoles to provide instant information on the status of pending cases, waiting lists, etc., and also print out permits and licences across the counter wherever possible.

The State Governance could consider similar steps to identify services most frequently required by the people, and set up people facilitation counters in all offices with a public interface in the districts and towns, State Departments, Directorate and Public Utilities. The Central Government could consider supporting the establishment of these counters through help from the NIC training of staff, etc., and ensure delegation of powers and procedural changes for this purpose. The Central and State Governments can jointly work towards providing the people of India in all tehsils, districts and towns so that, over the Ninth Plan period, all the public offices have at least one information and facilitation outlet for the harassed consumers or the applicant. The facility could be extended to the police stations at the same time.

Proposed Action

The State Governments could consider steps to promote widespread and easy access of the people in rural and urban areas to information on public services, details of Government schemes, status of applications, allotments and permits, etc. They could ensure this through a systematic and phased computerisation of administrative operations with the help of NIC, and the emphasis on providing quick information and assistance to the people across the counter for priority services in all offices with public interface. This could be linked with the scheme for public facilitation counters in all government offices.

Appendix

PUBLIC FACILITATION CENTRE: SALIENT FEATURES

- Provide information regarding services, schemes and procedures through brochures, booklets, reports etc.
- Provide information regarding position of waiting list and applications through computer, screens updated every day, and through computerised query to departmental data base.
- Provide information regarding matters, such as bill payment, registration, land/house allotment, payments, etc., or phone or personally to the public.
- Forms which are to be utilised for various procedures should be available at the Facilitation Centre, even if the Processing is to be done elsewhere.
- Receive complaints, issue acknowledgement slips, indication the section dealing with the complaints.
- A sufficiently senior officer is to man the Facilitation Centres with appropriate orientation, capable of speaking English and local language for handling customers, and knowledge of use of computers.
- Time limits and other details be notified through display boards at the Facilitation Centres for completion of various procedures and for disposal of cases.
- Ensure easy accessibility to Facilitation Centres for the customer and average citizen, and publicity regarding the location and hours of access.
- Utilising Interactive Voice System where feasible for enquiry response.
- Benches and fans for the waiting public, especially the old and the handicapped.

Annexure VIII

CODE OF ETHICS FOR PUBLIC SERVICES

Responsive and clean administration depends, *inter alia*, on adherence of the employees in public services to ethical standards and the basic principles of the Constitution, such as secularism, social justice, attention to the needs of weaker sections and vulnerable groups, equality and rule of law.

Both Central and State Governments no doubt have notified regulations governing the conduct of employees in various services which address these issues. However, they are more in the nature of formulations of do's and don'ts, and do not represent a positive statement of values and beliefs that should govern the public and private conduct of civil servants.

Nor do they provide clear directions to the employees on certain issues effecting their morals, motivation, sensitivity, and professional skills. This is relevant at the present juncture, when there is much confusion regarding the desirable service norms for these services, and the rewards from adherence to the highest standards of probity and integrity. There has been support for such a code from both officials and members of the public.

It is in this context that the enclosed Code of Ethics has been formulated. It spells out the employee's obligation to the Government and the Constitution, the right of public comment, conflict of interest, accountability to the public, concern for the value of public assets, release of information, integrative role, professionalism, and teamwork. It clearly brings out the expected behaviour of the employee in case of illegal directions of superiors, the need to refrain than seeking favour from politicians, the principles of responsive administration, supportive role of senior officers, and the role of public services in a secular Constitution wedded to the Rule of Law and Directive Principles of Policy. The Code would apply to all services, generalist and technical. The Government of India proposes to give a legal shape to this code by incorporation it in the Code of Conduct Rules for the All India Services and Central Government employees.

Proposed Action

This initiative of the Central Government for assuring values in the public services could be endorsed by the State Government and they could consider enforcing the Code of Ethics as an integral part of the Code of Conduct Regulations for State Services, after appropriate changes to suit local circumstances.

Appendix

CODE OF ETHICS FOR THE PUBLIC SERVICES IN INDIA

Objective

The objective of Code is to prescribe standards of integrity and conduct that are to apply in the public services. The principles stated below underlie and supplement the rules and laws regulation the public and private conduct of various public services.

Obligation to Government and the Constitution

The constitutional and administrative role of the public services is to assist the duly constituted Government, of whatever political colour, in formulating and implementing policies of the Government and in administering the public services under the Central of the Government in the most effective and efficient manner, within the framework of the Indian Constitution.

It is the obligation of every employee in the public services to uphold the Rule of Law and respect for human rights, and to act solely in the public interest while making recommendations or exercising administrative authority. He or she must maintain the highest standards of probity and integrity.

In relation to the general public, employees in the public services should conduct themselves in such a manner that the public feels that the decisions taken or the recommendations made by them are objective and transparent, and are not calculated to promote improper gains for the political party in power, for themselves or for any third party.

Employees in the public services should not seek to frustrate or undermine the policies, decisions and actions taken in the public interest by a duly constituted Government, be declining or abstaining from action which flows from ministerial decision or statutory obligations. Where, following the instruction of the superior authority implementation of such decisions or action would appear to conflict with the exercise of impartial professional judgement, or affect the efficient administration of the department or undertaking, the employee should set out the points of disagreement clearly and courteously in writing to the superior authority, and seek explicit written instruction thereon.

Where an employee in public services has reasonable grounds to believe that he or she is being required by the superior authority to act in a manner which is illegal or against prescribed rules and regulations, or if any legal infringement comes to his or her notice, he or she should decline to implement the instruction. He or she would also have a right to bring the facts to the notice of the Head of Department or the Chief Secretary (Cabinet Secretary in the Central Government) or the Minister. It shall be incumbent on the Chief Secretary (Cabinet Secretary in the case of Central Government) to examine the issue carefully and advise the Chief Minister) Prime Minister in the case of Central Government) appropriately.

Right of Public Comment

Generally, employees in public services have the same rights of free speech and independence in the conduct of their private affairs as other members of the public. However, they also have a duty not to compromise the Government by public criticism of, or comment on, policies. They should, therefore, ensure that their contribution to any public debate or discussion on such matters maintains the discretion appropriate to the position they hold, and is compatible with the need to maintain a politically neutral Public Service.

Conflict of Interest and Peer Pressure

Employees in public services should refrain from decision in respect of which they have reason to believe that they are calculated to benefit any particular person or party at the expense of the public interest.

Every employee in the public services shall disclose any clash of interest when there is conflict between public interest and private interest, or he or she is likely to benefit from any act of omission or commission while discharging his or her functions.

Employees in public services should be alert to any actual or potential conflict of interest, financial or otherwise, and should disclose this to their superiors, whether the conflict covers them or their family members.

Employees in public services should maintain their independence, dignity and impartiality by not approaching politicians and outsiders in respect of service matters or private benefit, and exercise peer pressure to dissuade those within their own cadre who do so, and to set in motion disciplinary proceedings against such persons. Any such approach on his or her behalf in such matters would be deemed to be at the instance of the employee.

Accountability and Responsiveness to the Public

Consistent with accountability to the superior officers and the Ministers in accordance with Constitutional provisions, employees in the public services should be accessible to the people and practice accountability to them in terms of quality of service, timeliness, courtesy, people orientation, and readiness to encourage participation of, and from partnerships with, citizen groups, for responsive Government.

Employees in the public services should be consistent, equitable and honest in their treatment of the members of the public, with particular care for the weaker sections of society, and should not ever be, or appear to be, unfair or discriminatory. Decisions in pursuit of discretionary powers should be justifiable on the basis of non-arbitrary and objective criteria.

Employees in the public services should accept the obligation to recognise and enforce the citizen's right for speedy redressal of grievances and commit themselves to provide service of declared quality and standards to the citizens.

Employees in public services should respect the right of the public to information on all Government activities and transactions except where they are debarred from releasing information by provisions of law or valid instructions.

Concern for Value of Public Assets and Funds

Employees in public services should avoid wastage and extravagance, ensure effective and efficient use of public money within their control, and endeavour that the benefits of schemes for disadvantaged and poor sections of society are not wasted or diverted for the benefit of others. They should avoid ostentation and set examples of austerity for others.

Non-Abuse of Official Position

Since employees in public services have a responsibility to take decisions on merits, and they are in a position of trust, they must not use their official position to influence any person to enter into financial or other arrangements with them, or with anyone else. They must not abuse official position to obtain a benefit for themselves or for someone else, in financial or other forms.

Safeguards in Release of Information

Employees in the public services should not unauthorisedly release information which is not permitted by law, or compromise private or business interests, or the privacy of an individual when such information has been received in confidence. They should not take improper advantage of official information acquired in the course of their work, for unwarranted gain themselves or others.

Integrative Role

Every employee in public services should recognise the integrative role of public services in national development, and resist internal and external attempts to fragment public services and society on caste, communal or religious lines. He or she should cultivate national outlook to rise above sectarian, service, cadre or departmental loyalties.

Continuous Improvement Through Professionalism and Teamwork

It shall be the duty of every employee in the public services to continuously upgrade his or her skills and knowledge, strive for creativity and innovation and nurture values of team working and harmony.

All employees in public services should promote and exhibit public and private conduct in keeping with the appropriate behaviour and standards of excellent and integrity. They should support the juniors in the latter's efforts to resist wrong or illegal directives and in abiding by the Code of Ethics. At the same time, they should reward good work and punish any dereliction of duty or obligations, based on objective and transparent criteria.

Annexure IX

TACKLING CORRUPTION AND CLEANSING ADMINISTRATION

The Context and Consequence

It is not an exaggeration to talk about corruption in terms of a crisis or a cancer endangering India's society, polity and economy. There has been a distinct increase in transactions in Central and State Governments, where the presence of corruption has been substantiated. Evidence points to an increase of corruption in higher bureaucracy and elected political functionaries, often in collusion or in nexus with criminal elements. Corruption is rampant in administration of welfare schemes, public distribution system, police, revenue and irrigation departments, and several other sectors where people come into contact daily with administration. Corruption at lower levels takes the form of speed money for expediting approvals providing legitimate services, or bribes for twisting rules. A matter of grave concern is the vertical integration of corruption at various levels of government between officials and politicians and the inability of top functionaries to check the prevalence and growth of corruption. Corruption in public life is of course part of the malaise of black money and erosion of the moral fibre of Indian Society.

The effect of corruption on the economy and public administration in terms of waste, distorted resource allocation, reduced revenues, unfavourable perceptions of foreign investors, etc., is obvious. More insidious from the point of view of responsive government and the welfare of the poor, is diluted standards of goods, services and construction, hazards to life and safety of the public from spurious goods, leakage of benefits and subsidies meant for the poor and the denial of fair treatment and justice to people other than those able to access money and influence. That is why there is a strong demand by the public for effective punitive and corrective measures to tackle the problem. This concern is reflected in the manifestoes of all political parties in the 1996 General Election.

The Scheme

The Government of India is committed to integrity and impartiality in public life and clean administration, and to take effective steps to eradicate the evil of corruption. It is determined to pass the legislation for Lok Pal in the current Session of Parliament. Along with similar statutory steps by the States, it should be possible to proceed vigorously in cases of allegations against ministers and public functionaries through an independent institution with credibility and assured powers.

Along with this following steps can be considered for investigation and prosecuting quickly all cases of corruption and misconduct of officials at all levels and for ensuring swift and exemplary punishment of the guilty:

1. Elimination of corruption in public services should address preventive, surveillance and deterrent punishment, and deal ruthlessly with the nexus of officials with criminal elements and venal political functionaries.

2. Rules and legal provision should be amended to enable immediate and exemplary prosecution and removal of corrupt officials without recourse to any political protection.

3. There should be no scope in the rules for any interference in prompt prosecution and punishment of corrupt public servants, and permission for such prosecution should be given within a prescribed period to investigating agencies, like the CBI, where prior approval has been stipulated. At the same time clear norms should be laid down to prevent demoralisation of public servants on account of frivolous complaints or inquiries.

4. The Investigating agencies and vigilance machinery should be strengthened by provision of adequate staff, powers, resources and independence, accompanied by proper accountability for results. The Preventive aspect of corruption in government or the public sector depends on an independent and well-staffed vigilance set-up.

5. Amendments should be formulated to the relevant rules on the lines of those proposed in the rules relating to All India and Central services to provide for the premature retirement of officials at a reasonably early stage of employees' careers to weed out elements which are either inefficient or of doubtful integrity. It is further necessary to amend the relevant Service Rules to enable the review of integrity and efficiency of officials at any stage during their career, and to provide for premature retirement of officers of doubtful integrity in public interest.

6. The existing procedures for departmental enquiries and vigilance proceedings for Central and State Government employees should be revamped in order to ensure their completion within a year. The proposed steps in Central Government include:

   (a) Prescribing firm time limits for all the stages from preliminary investigation to issue of chargesheet, to actual enquiry and the issue of final orders of exoneration or punishment;

   (b) Ensuring, through training, compliance with all legal requirements of enquiry and opportunity to the defendant so as to avoid procedural infirmities that lead to legal challenge;

   (c) Agreeing with Public Service Commission and Chief Vigilance Commissioner on time limits for consultation and advice;

   (d) Ensuring adequate number of full-time or part-time inquiry officers, and providing them with adequate incentive and training;

(e) Suspending or transferring to non-sensitive posts those personnel who are being prosecuted or proceeded against departmentally on charges of corruption;

(f) Providing for summary procedures in cases where charges relate to penalties other than removal, dismissal and reduction in rank;

(g) Dealing with deficiencies pointed out by the Courts of Law; and

(h) Making a careful distinction between petty procedural irregularities and substantive misconduct to eliminate the former from detailed inquiries and close such case after recording adverse remarks in the CR, issue of warning or counselling the officer.

7. Attachment and forfeiture of properties (movable or immovable) acquired by public servants by corrupt or illegal means not only in their own names but also in the names of their relatives and others under their control can be considered, through provision modelled on the Smugglers and Foreign Exchange Manipulators (Forfeiture of Property Act, 1976); and prompt penal action in respect of proven holding of assets disproportionate to known sources of income.

8. Areas of discretion available to various levels of administration should be curtained to the minimum, along with steps to prevent their arbitrary use. Equally urgent are steps for deregulation, procedural simplification, elimination of unnecessary controls, decentralisation and delegation, monitoring of service delivery through citizen groups, greater transparency in all areas of public interface and corruption prove agencies, and the review of the rules and procedures governing procurements, contracts and extortion, as these would bring down the incidence of speed money on the one hand and extrusions at the decision-making level.

9. Objective and transparent criteria for the transfer and promotion of officials in order to insulate them from political influence in action taken according to law and in public interest.

10. Strengthening role and powers of Audit in the identification of financial and procedural irregularities to be followed by investigation for possible corruption.

11. Close networking of different agencies like Lokpal/Lok Ayukta, CBI/CVO, Income Tax authorities, Enforcement Directorate and CAG in terms of sharing of information and intelligence, and coordinated investigations.

12. Encouraging adoption of code of Ethics not only by civil servants but also all public functionaries, media, professionals, and the corporate sector based on constitutional principles and moral values.

13. Assuring adequate remuneration, congenial working conditions and access to housing and health care for the employees.

14. Mobilising public opinion against corruption, increasing awareness of avenues of complaints and investigation, and supporting efforts of citizen groups, media and NGOs in this respect.

15. Encouraging officials at all levels to bring irregularities or suspected corruption to the notice of the Chief Secretary, and to reward such officials in cases where the fraud reported by them are established.

Points for Decision

The Central and State Governments could draw up, adopt and implement the measures suggested above consistently and effectively, with an agenda of long-term and short-term actions, and based on total coordination of Central and State agencies and the CAG. The Lok Ayuktas could be adequately empowered and resourced to deal effectively with all cases or allegation of corruption. The efforts could be centred on immediate and exemplary prosecution and removal of corrupt officials without any political protection, while supporting honest and competent employees. The agenda could be monitored regularly by the Prime Minister/Chief Minister, Cabinet Secretary/Chief Secretary and the results would be widely publicised so as to instill public confidence in the probity of all political and administrative functionaries.

Annexure X

STABILITY OF TENURE AND A SCHEME FOR CIVIL SERVICES BOARDS

Background

It is not sufficiently realised that the effective and people-friendly administration of various policies and schemes of the Government, and the responsive delivery of services, depend critically on the stability of tenure of senior officials incharge of the programmes, and enforcement of laws. The responsiveness of a civil servant, and his capacity for evenhanded treatment of all sections of the public, depends to a substantial extent, on the degree to which he or she has a sense of continuity in the official position and does not feel threatened by the risk of premature transfer or any punishment for even-handed administration. The effectiveness of public administration in the States suffers from the ease with which tenures of officials serving in the field either in the regulatory or development field are cut short, leaving the officials demoralised, the public dissatisfied, and with the credibility of the Government seriously eroded. The public in fact perceives such actions as reflective of an unholy nexus between undesirable elements among politicians and civil servants. To impart stability to tenures of officers at the cutting edge of field administration, like District Magistrates, Superintendents of Police, Heads of Departments, etc., would not only help the officers to deepen their knowledge and experience, but also help the public to receive the services expected of the civil services with expedition and efficiency. The consequences of irrational and abrupt transfers are manifold. Most importantly, they result in unstable, short tenures, leading to frustration and demoralisation; the 'partiality' and 'objectivity' of the officer comes under strain; building up of experience-based expertise is prevented; and ultimately, the task or the job is prevented from being performed and thereby the Government's objectivities are to that extent, not attained. Different individuals react differently to the situation described above. A few resist firmly and pay the price; some offer passive resistance and try to do their best; what is worrisome is that an increasingly large number give in and reap the rewards of compliance. The major casualty is, of course, the total system.

While the conduct Rules provide for various opportunities to the officials in respect of proceedings of suspension, demotion, dismissal and minor penalties, they do not enjoy such safeguards as regards unjustified transfers. It is quite common place in several States to see mass transfers of senior officials at the district and secretarial level wherever there is a change of Government or leadership. It is often the case that the legitimate hierarchy for effecting the transfer and promotion of various officials is marginalised in favour of extra Constitutional systems based on extraneous influences. Consequently, not only is the ability and authority of the superior officials in enforcing complaint action in the public interest by subordinate officials eroded, they become incapable of ensuring effective and responsive administration through lower level functionaries. At the same time, the system should provide for weeding out the non-performers on the basis of objective criteria.

The demand for stability of tenure and objective criteria for transfers and promotions is not only an element of motivation and efficient performance of civil servants, but is a matter of great concern for the public at large. It is seen that, when an official with sufficient knowledge of the district or city or the department is available for a sufficiently long time to formulate policies, and implement schemes of poverty alleviation and the seven basic services in response to people's needs, effective governance is visible, especially in the context of the decentralisation of powers at the local level. This is seen from examples of excellent initiatives in this regard in districts or cities from officers with a long tenure and rapport with the citizens and their representatives, and the low level of development and utilisation of funds in districts or cities witnessing frequent rotation of officers. Further, the people can expect to receive fair, equitable treatment, unaffected by considerations of speed money or other benefits, only if the official is encouraged to have the courage and confidence to take decisions without fear or favour, or the penalty of premature transfer. These considerations are equally valid for the police and law enforcement agencies.

There has been a long-felt need for creation of an institutional arrangement for better personnel management at the State level. The Administrative Reform Commission in its report on State Administration in November 1969 had also felt the need for setting up an Establishment Board in each State for proper management of selection and posting for posts of the level of Under Secretary and above in the State Secretariats and field organisation. The matter has also been taken up in the Conference of Chief Secretaries held on the November 20, 1996. It had been concluded that the State Government could be requested to devise suitable mechanisms, including establishment of a high powered civil services Board, and amend relevant rules for enabling transparent decisions on postings, promotions and transfers of senior officials on the lines of Central Government.

Such an institutional arrangement already exists in Government of India in the form of the Central Staffing Scheme. Under the Central Staffing Scheme of the Government of India, the Appointments Committee of the Cabinet (ACC) is empowered to take decision in respect of selection and appointments of officers to Secretarial posts of and above the rank of Under Secretary to Government of India and certain important non-secretarial posts as also on various other related issue of personnel management. In this respect, ACC is assisted and advised by the Civil Services Board and the Central Establishment Board constituted therefore.

Though a complete transplant of the Central Staffing Scheme to the States is neither feasible nor desirable, it is suggested that the State Governments could consider initiating similar institutional arrangements. The true potential of the senior officials can be properly utilised for better management and development of the State. In this respect, guidelines for setting up the proposed Civil Services Board and its functions are enclosed herewith as Appendix.

These guidelines can become truly operative and generate credibility and morale in the civil services and the public only if Government employees are not permitted to bring political or other extraneous pressure to bear on the Government or on the transferring authorities for transfers and promotions. This issue is addressed in the Code of Ethics. Any employee, who brings such pressures should be liable for disciplinary action and in such cases strict punishment should be awarded. Such action should be initiated also in cases where references are received by Heads of Departments from outside agencies including political functionaries and members of the public as well as bureaucrats for effecting transfers. It could be ensured that these guidelines are seen as carrying the authority of the Chief Minister so that a proper message goes down the entire system.

Proposed Action

The State Governments could consider adoption of the above mentioned scheme for setting up Civil Services Board with the proposed functions, for recommending to the Chief Minister proposals on the transfer, promotion and placement of senior officials other than the Chief Secretary, DG of Police, and Chief Conservator of Forests, and for recommending action on grievances of officers, such as premature transfers or undue political pressure.

Appendix

SCHEME FOR CIVIL SERVICES BOARD

The proposed scheme will not apply to top functionaries like the Chief Secretary, Director General of Police and Chief Conservator of Forests who shall be appointed by the Chief Minister as at present.

The State Government may set up a Civil Services Board, charged with the responsibility of recommending to the Government transfers and postings of all officers of and above the rank of Joint Secretary in the State Secretariat, apart from Heads of Departments, Additional Heads of departments, Divisional Commissioners, Financial Commissioners, Collectors/District Magistrates and District Superintendents of Police. The Board could comprise the following: (1) Chief Secretary—Chairman; (2) One officer of the rank and status of Additional Chief Secretary (preferably the senior-most) or Chairman of the Board of Revenue or the senior-most Financial Commissioner, as the case may be in a State—Member; and (3) Secretary DOPT or Secretary, Appointments, GAD, as the case may be in State—Member-Secretary.

The Home Secretary and DG of Police could be associated while considering matters relating to appointments at the level of DIG and above in the Home Department. The Secretary, Forest Department and the Principal CCF could be associated in connection with matters relating to the Conservator of Forests and above. Similarly, the Secretary of the Administrative Department concerned could be associated, as a special invitee, when a proposal concerning the Head of the Department or an Additional Head of that Department is being considered by the Board.

The Board's functions could be as under: (1) To recommend a panel of names for appointment to all posts mentioned in second paragraph above; (2) To recommend All India Services officers and State service officers for their promotions as well as short and long-term training within and outside the country; (3) To advise the Government on personnel policy, especially career management of AIS officers and other State Civil Service officers; (4) To make proposals on transfers of such officers; and (5) To entertain appeals of officers against premature transfers and other grievances and submit the same with the Board's views to the Chief Minister.

The Board should meet on a pre-determined day of the week

The merits of the suggested system would be: (1) Ensure more responsive and citizen-friendly administration, and effective execution of development schemes and programmes of poverty alleviation and welfare of weaker sections; (2) Appointments and promotions would be made after due consideration of all relevant factors and would be governed by the collective wisdom of the Board, while leaving the final decision to the political executive; (3) It would, over a period of time, make possible much greater accountability of officers in terms of performance and service to the people as, in the envisaged system, minimum tenures, say of two to five years or as per the norm prescribed by the Government; (4) Over time, with experience of the working of this system, more attention would begin to be paid to cadré management and career planning; and (5) The civil service and the public would benefit from the presence of officials who are impartial and committed to be values enshrined in the Constitution.

Any premature transfer before completion of prescribed tenure should be based on sound administrative grounds to be spelt out in the transfer order itself. Such premature transfer may be deemed to be a minor penalty, so that the officers have a right to appeal against such orders if they feel aggrieved, and summary procedures can deal with the situation.

In view of the importance of ensuring public confidence in the integrity and impartiality of the process of recruitment of candidates for public service, the selection of Chairman/Members of Public Service Commissions and Service Selection Boards should be done on the basis of recommendations of a similar committee.

Above all, there needs to be an agreement at the level of both the political executive and the top officials that the instrument of transfer should not be allowed to be misused by the civil servants or the politicians in power; nor should the power be vested in persons other than the constituted authorities of Government. As a matter of policy, extension of service should not be given to any employee.

With the increasing number of district development and municipal cadres, institutionalised and transparent systems of placement and career planning appear to be necessary to supplement this. The Government should continue the present practice of rotation in sensitive posts. Consideration for posting at the place of posting of the spouse, attention to the needs of women and the handicapped, etc.

Annexure XI

SUPPLEMENTARY NOTES ON INITIATIVES TAKEN ON ACTION PLAN AND RESPONSIVE ADMINISTRATION GOVERNMENT OF INDIA IN ACTION PLAN

The government of India has taken following initiatives on Action Plan:

1. Constitution of Working Group on Right to Information and Transparency to draft legislative proposals;
2. Steps to initiate formulation of Citizen's Charter by a number of Central Ministries and Departments with public interface, and introduction of various citizen-friendly procedures and decentralised services by Railways, Posts, Telecom, Petroleum Ministry, Customs and Excise, Income Tax, etc;
3. Constitution of an Expert Group for Drawing up short-term and long-term plans for computerisation of Government operations and provision of services to the public, and steps already taken for computerisation in many Ministries;
4. Central scheme for computerisation for land records, digitisation of village cadastral maps, and consolidation of land holdings, with substantial benefits to cultivators, revenue administration, agricultural operations, etc;
5. Announcement of constitution of an independent Public Grievance Commission, as well as Police Complaints Authority for Delhi, speedy redressal of grievances relating to the Police on the one hand, and all the public utilities and departments of the Government of National Capital Territory of Delhi on the other. The Ministry of Home Affairs has set up a High-Level Committee with state representatives to examine various aspects relating to a more responsive administration citizen awareness of their rights, modification to existing laws, etc., and to make recommendations in three months;
6. Operation of the Directorate of Public Grievances in the Cabinet Secretariat to entertain and decide finally on grievances relating to Central departments and agencies with a large public interface, such as telecommunications, passports, and insurance;
7. Introduction of a pilot scheme by the Department of Consumer Affairs and PDS to set up citizen information centres in selected cities, to be run by voluntary agencies, with links to the Public Services menu on the GISTNIC;

8. Support to national and state training institutions for training of officials at various levels in the emerging areas of economic reform, decentralisation, delivery of basic services, gender development, health care, primary education, AIDS control, nutrition, etc;

9. Operation of Staff Adalats in Railways, Posts and Telecom for continuous attention to the problems and grievances of the staff;

10. Operation of Lok Adalats in Telecom, Posts, etc., for satisfactory settlement of the problems of the people and consumers by face-to-face interaction; and working of Social Audit panels, composed of eminent citizens, to listen to people's views and suggest improvements in the Posts and Telecom;

11. Approval for the use of the Local Development Fund with M.P.'s for the installation of citizen Radio in Village Panchayats, public transport, etc., to provide emergency communication and two-way messages to the public;

12. Initiatives of the Ministry of Health and Family Welfare for upgradation of emergency facilities in major Central Government Hospitals in Delhi, a system for regulation of private nursing homes through peer groups; the mobilisation of community participation and consumer awareness for safe food and drugs; and linkage of PHC's to extend secondary health-care services to the people in rural areas;

13. Formulation of a Code of Ethics for employees in public services;

14. Formulation of specific steps for streamlining the system of departmental enquiries and vigilance proceedings;

15. Steps for strict action against corruption and for integrity in public servants at all levels as, signified by the introduction of Lok Pal Bill in Parliament;

16. Constitution of an Efficiency Unit in the Cabinet Secretariat to undertake continuous exercise for delineation of

Government functions, departmental re-structuring, procedural reforms, etc.

Initiatives on Responsive Administration

A number of initiatives have been taken by the State Governments and Central Government agencies in respect of responsive administration in recent years. These deserve to be studied and scaled up in the Central and State Governments as a whole, utilising wherever possible available funds in sectoral programmes. These need to be linked to the decentralised delivery of services through elected local bodies on the following lines:

1. Improved sanitation and garbage collection with people's involvement in a number of cities like Surat, Pune and Chennai;
2. Taking grievance redressal to the people through mass contact and Lok Adalats at the village and neighbourhood levels;
3. Mass mobilisation schemes, such as *Janmabhoomi* and "Administration Going to the People's in Andhra Pradesh, bottom-up planning in Kerala, mass literacy campaigns etc.;
4. Computerisation of land records and other information, and people-friendly revenue administration in a number of districts;
5. Giving one life-time certificate to the people as done in Andhra Pradesh by incorporating birth, nativity and caste certificates;
6. Setting up service counters for instant information and relief to the citizens in a number of Central Government Departments, like the Passport, Railways, Posts as well as the offices of Collectors;
7. Ensuring transparency and Right to Information to the people including making a provision for public hearings as done in States like Rajasthan and Madhya Pradesh, association of neighbourhood groups and citizen bodies in the planning and implementation of welfare schemes, planning and implementation of poverty alleviation and housing schemes,

and empowerment of resident welfare groups as done in cities like Bangalore and Pune;

8. Establishing partnerships with voluntary agencies for health, nutrition and other schemes, and setting examples of inducting support from corporate sector;
9. Developing an innovative role of the AIR for grievance redressal as done in UP.

The Central and State Governments may take concerted measures for improved quality of administration and responsive services and schemes for the citizens through a package of multifaceted initiatives all which will together help to promote accountable and people-friendly government. These may include the following:

1. Wider accountability of all public servants for people-satisfaction and delivery of services according to a Citizens' Charter similar public statement of departmental goals;
2. Fullest possible decentralisation of service delivery, income support schemes and welfare activities through empowerment of elected rural and urban local bodies, accompanied by appropriate devolution of powers and resources in terms of the spirit and provisions of the 73rd and 74th Constitutional Amendments;
3. Encouragement to the widest possible awareness and participation of citizens and representative groups and voluntary agencies in the formation and implementation of schemes as already envisaged in ongoing sectoral schemes and in the Five Years Plan document;
4. Simplification and clarity in forms and procedures, with arrangements for setting up citizen information centres in all the districts and towns;
5. Transparent procedures and criteria for beneficial identification in the provision of services and subsidies, the operation of the public distribution system, etc., to ensure that the benefits fully reach the poor and the disadvantaged,

alongwith a system of public hearings to facilitate consultation by the public at the local level;

6. Giving the citizens widespread and easy access to all information relating to Government operations and laws, and reversing and undue emphasis on secrecy surrounding award of tenders and procurement, identification of beneficiaries, allotment of various assets, admission to colleges and schools, recruitment for jobs, etc;
7. Steps to enact legislation for Freedom of Information, amendments to the Official Secrets Act, Codes of Conduct, rules for classification of records, etc;
8. Training and orientation of both officials and elected representatives at all levels, steps to upgrade their skills, access to technological and computerised aids for information processing and storage, top-level support by delegation of powers and workplace improvement and rewards for good performance;
9. Equipping and orienting all public offices and delivery centres to provide quick and responsive delivery of public services, grievance redressal and information to the public, alongwith convergent services for target groups in areas of basic services identified by the Conference of Chief Ministers in July, 1996.

7

Co-ordination, Delegation, Communication and Supervision

Co-ordination is the first principle of organisation; it is also the first principle of management. It is thus, a very important problem in modern administration. Some writers go to the extent of substituting the term 'co-ordinator' for 'manager'. It should, however, be kept in mind that co-ordination is only a means to an end and not an end in itself. In the words of Newman, *"It is not a separate activity but a condition that should permeate all phases of administration."* Need for co-ordination arises due to three main factors.

1. to avoid or resolve conflicts or overlapping in the work of the employees or units of an organisation;
2. to prevent or discourage too much concentration on one aspect of work to the exclusion of the other aspects; and
3. to curb the growing tendency towards empire-building or greed for power prevalent in the different units of agency.

Meaning

In a negative sense, co ordination aims at removing conflicts and overlapping from administration. Positively. it attempts to bring about co operation and team-work among the employees of an organisation. A few definitions of the term by well-known authorities on Administration are given below:

Co-ordination is "the orderly synchronisation of efforts to provide the proper amount, timing and directing of execution resulting in harmonious and unified actions to a stated objective."

Co-ordination is "the adjustment of the parts of each other and of the movement and operation of parts in time so that each can make its maximum contribution to the product of the whole."

Co-ordination is "a process causing disjunct elements to a concentration on a complex of forces and influence which cause the mutually independent elements to act together."

Co-ordination is "the integration of the several parts into an orderly whole to achieve the purpose of the undertaking."

Mary Parker Follett defines co-ordination as the "reciprocal relating of all factors in a situation" and goes on to amplify it as "you cannot envisage the process accurately by thinking of 'A' adjusting himself to 'B' and to 'C' and to 'D'. 'A' adjusts himself to 'B' and also to a 'B' influenced by 'C' and to a 'B' influenced by 'D' and to a 'B' influenced by 'A' himself...and so on and so on. This sort of reciprocal relating, this interpretation of every part by every other part, and again by every other part as it has been permeated by all should be the goal of all attempts at co-ordination."

A simple and brief definition of co-ordination has been given by Seckler-Hudson as "the all-important duty of interrelating the various parts of the work." In general, co-ordination means making arrangements so that all parts of an organisation pull together towards defined goals, without duplication, without gaps and conflicts and on time. Some good examples of high class co-ordination are the assembling of a watch and the rowing of a boat. An orchestra represents perhaps the nearest perfection of co-ordination.

Co-ordination is sometimes confused with co-operation, but they do not mean the same thing. In the words of Terry, co-operation is *"the collective action of one person with another or others toward a common goal."* Co-ordination is much more than collective action and means "synchronisation of efforts". Terry gives a very interesting story to dramatise the difference: "Consider the story of the boy who wished to take an early morning train and accordingly set his watch ahead one-half hour before going to bed so that he would be sure to arise in plenty of time. Placing the watch on the table alongside his bed, the boy retired early to get sufficient rest. His father, knowing of his son's desire to take the early train, went to his son's bedroom and turned the lad's watch up one-half hour, believing this would give the boy extra time to get up and dressed. Likewise, the mother just before retiring went in the lad's bedroom and turned his watch forward one-half hour so that he would not be rushed in the morning. As a result the lad arose one and one-half hour early instead of one-half hour losing an hour of needed sleep. Co-operation among the actions of son, father and mother had been present but no co-ordination."

Co-ordination may be internal (functional) or external (structural). Internal co-ordination is concerned with co-ordinating the individual duties of persons working in an organisation. External co-ordination, on the other hand, is concerned with co-ordinatinig the activities of different organisational units. In the words of Appleby: "It (hierarchy) functions both perpendicularly and horizontally. The horizontal relationship is between units and between agencies commonly regarded as co-ordination in an effort to distinguish between co-ordination and administration. Co-ordination effected between units responsible to a single executive is co-ordination at the level of units, administration at the level of the executive to whom they are responsible, whereas he in turn participates in co-ordination with other agencies at his level."

How to Co-ordinate?

Means of co-ordination are many and varied. Planning, for instance, is a co-ordinating device par excellence. Planning involves the maximum utilisation of all the available resources in men, money and materials with a view to achieving the planned targets and goals within a limited period, and this is nothing but an exercise in co-ordination on a national scale. Secondly, there are organisational devices or institutionalisation of co-ordination techniques. These may take the form of conferences, panels, committees, symposia, interdepartmental meetings, staff units, co-ordinating officers, etc. Hierarchy in an organisation is a co-ordinating agency inasmuch as its main purpose is to evolve a consensus with the agency. As a matter of fact, organisation itself is a co-ordinating device. In India, there are numerous organisational devices to bring about co-ordination. The Union Government itself is above all a co-ordinating agency. The Central Secretariat, Cabinet Committees, Planning Commission, Zonal Councils, the National Development Council and the Prime Minister are all engaged in the same process. At the district level, the Collector is, above all a co-ordinator. This role will secure increasing emphasis with the introduction of democratic decentralisation. Then, there are Boards and Commissions helping in the same direction like the University Grants Commission, the Inter-University Boards, and the Indian Historical Records Commission. The institution of Conferences is also freely used towards the same end. These Conferences attempt co-ordination between the Centre and the States for expeditious disposal of schemes and for finding practical solutions of difficulties. They serve as forums for the exchange of ideas and the formulation of definite policy in the light of the discussions. They help in evolving common programmes and enable the review of the progress of implementation of such programmes. Such conferences are held at political, official, and professional levels. The conferences of Governors, Chief Ministers and Ministers of different departments are examples of conferences at the political level. At the official level are the conferences of Secretaries to Government and Heads of the Departments. Then, there are conferences of professionals like the Vice-Chancellors' Conference and the Irrigation and Power Seminar which is attended by the Chief Engineers of different States and the Heads of the River Valley Projects.

Standardisation of procedures and methods is the third medium of co-ordination. Procedures, which concern a large number of people and which are repetitive in nature, are generally standardised. Forms are a good example of standardisation of procedures. Manuals, regulations and rules are other examples of such standardisation.

Centralised house keeping is the fourth device to promote co-ordination. "In administration, house-keeping problems usually include supply, warehousing, the cleaning and maintenance of buildings, printing and duplicating equipment control, central mailing, transportation, and food and telephone service." The first Hoover Commission recommended, in 1949, the creation of an office of General Service to be in charge of such house-keeping services. The recommendation was accepted and the General Services Administration was set up the same year. In India, there are many agencies of centralised house-keeping like the accounting and auditing under the Auditor-General; construction, maintenance and repair of building under the Public Works Departments; supplies under the Directorate-General of Supplies, etc. The Union Public Service Commission serves the same purpose for recruitment and selection of public services.

Fifthly, the Finance Ministry (Department) is a great co-ordinator. The annual budget itself is an essay in co-ordinating the resources, expenditures and programmes of the government concerned, and it is the Finance Ministry that co-ordinates and reconciles the claims, demands and programmes of the different Ministries in order to evolve an agreed plan of action, that is, the budget. The Finance Ministry's role does not end with the passing of the budget and the allocation of funds among the Ministries; its sanction or approval is needed for the implementation of any programme by the operating departments.

Lastly, co-ordination is largely dependent upon the effectiveness of verbal and written communications which channel information and ideas down, up and across the chain of command.

In addition to the formal means discussed above, there are informal media of co-ordination which are not less effective for being informal. Personal contacts are perhaps the most important of these. They help free exchange of ideas, frank discussion and agreement by compromise. Committees and conferences furnish opportunities for such informal consultations. Dinners, lunches and cocktail parties have become recognised media of informal communication. Perhaps, by far, the important medium of 'unofficial' co-ordination is a disciplined party system. In our country, the fact of the Congress party being in power in all the States and the Centre is greatly responsible for co-ordination of policies, plans and programmes on countrywide basis. Lastly, the role of good leadership as co-ordinating factor cannot be over emphasised. In this respect, the impact of the Prime Minister Nehru on the administrative and political unity of the country was a great national asset.

Hindrances to Co-ordination

There are limits to the degree of co-ordination that an agency can achieve. The path of co-ordination is beset with difficulties. According to Gulick, some of these difficulties arise from (i) the uncertainty of the future—as to the behaviour of individuals and of people; (ii) the lack of knowledge, experience, wisdom and character among leaders and their confused and conflicting ideas and objectives; (iii) the lack of administrative skill and technique; (iv) the vast number of variables involved and the incompleteness of human knowledge, particularly with regard to men and life; and (v) the lack of orderly methods developing, considering, perfecting and adopting new ideas and programmes. To these, Seckler-Hudson adds four more, namely, "size and complexity, personalities and political factors, the lack of leaders with wisdom and knowledge pertaining to public administration and the accelerated expansion of public administration of international dimensions." In short, the hindrances to co-ordination are the enormous growth in the size of public ministration, the growing trend toward creating new agencies to administer to new needs and demands, thinning out of the span of control, the tendency on the part of the subordinates to pass the buck up, lack of delegation on the part of 'boss', etc., etc.

There are, however, thinkers who do not deplore the lack of co-ordination they, in fact, welcome it. Thus, Harlan Cleveland, till recently Dean of the Maxwell School at Syracuse University (U.S.A.), has challenged the desirability of structuring an organisation for full co-ordinated smoothness in function. His 'tension theory' suggests that there should be deliberate planning so that conflicts in jurisdiction and programme will arise among various bureaus and agencies, served better by having these conflicts within the administration to focus the issue clearly. A smooth organisation may override the public interest too early.

DELEGATION

Need for Delegation

In a one-man organisation all decisions are made by one individual. The smaller the organisation the lesser is the need for division of authority. It is when an organisation grows that the need for delegation arises, because one person or a group of persons can no longer make all the decisions. Authority and responsibility along with duties must, therefore, be divided. Delegation is one of the main ways for dividing and distributing authority. The extent of delegation of authority, however, is inversely related to the size and complexity of the organisation. Among the advantages of a sound system of delegation are the following:

1. The various levels of the organisation are used more appropriately. Thus, the chief administrator is able to devote his attention to more important questions and need not take time with decisions on operational details, which may suitably be dealt with further down the line. It has become a recognised principle of modern administration that the topman or the manager must not waste his time and energy over minute details and should deal only with top-level or exceptional problems of his organisation. Authority to make decision on day-to-day work should be allowed to make their own decision and answer for them.

2. A sound system of delegation tends to develop an increased sense of responsibility and an enhanced potential work capacity of individual employees. One of the duties of a manger is to build up his subordinates, and the best way to do it is to entrust them with responsibility and authority. If decisions are taken at too high a level, there is danger of undermining the authority of the person at the lower level, who, if they are to work effectively, must answerable for the actions and must carry a commensurate amount of authority.

3. The activities rendered by the organisation are improved and are discharged efficiently, economically and expeditiously by centering action points as far down the line as possible and as close to the scene where action is to be taken.

4. Proper delegation of authority is conductive to an effective control over operations due to clear definition of responsibility and of action at each level of organisation.
5. Delegation also minimizes delay when decisions have no longer to be referred up the line.

While sums up succinctly the reasons for delegation in these words: "Circumstances of magnitude and volume, however, require some delegation of authority and the settlement of much business at the point where it arises. The convenience of citizens alone compels most matters to be handled outside Washington. The avoidance of delay in administrative bottlenecks requires decisions at a hundred or a thousand field offices rater than a single headquarters establishment. In some cases, proper adjustment of policy and programme to local conditions requires discretionary field decisions. Certainly, the delegation of authority means greater energy, a higher sense of responsibility and better morale among field agents. They are not content to be mere messengers and reporters of their Washington superiors.

What is Delegation?

According to Mooney, delegation means conferring of specified authority by a higher to a lower authority. It is the devolution of authority by a person to his agent or subordinate subject to his right of supervision and control. Terry does not agree with this interpretation. To him "delegation means conferring authority from one executive or organisation unit to another." It is not necessarily devolution from a higher to a lower level; it may as well be from a higher to a lower level or between equal levels. Delegation may, thus, be "downward, upward or sideward". Downward delegation of authority is illustrated by a sales manager to his salesmen; upward delegation by stockholders to their board of directors; sideward delegation by certain African tribal chiefs and their Central Tribal Authority.

Delegation, it should be remembered, is not abdication of responsibility and does not connote the transfer of final authority. The person delegating authority does not surrender his overall responsibility and retains the power of inspection, supervision, control and review. He can even revoke his delegation and take back all the authority. On the other hand, "delegation of authority means more than simply assigning duties to others in more or less detail. The essence of delegation is to confer discretion upon others, to use their judgment in meeting specific problems within the framework of their duties." Delegation has, thus, a dual characteristic inasmuch as both the delegates and the delegator have authority vested in them at the same time. Organisationally conceived, therefore, delegation is only a way for dividing and distributing authority.

What to Delegate?

The manager should delegate as much as his subordinates can reasonably be expected to do, and just a little bit more. The art of delegating boils down to a weighing of the chance and consequence of error against the necessities of getting work done and of developing morale and utilizing subordinates to the extent of their abilities. Delegation, thus, requires knowledge of people and of situations, and has to be continuously revised to meet changes in personnel, programme or pressure. It is often forgotten that there are limits to delegation of authority as follows:

1. *The extent to which authority may be delegated is restricted* by constitution, laws and political institutions;
2. *The calibre of staff at the lower level.* Delegation to an incompetent individual is clearly impracticable. However, the excuse of staff incompetence as a reason for not making delegations sometimes reflects upon the administrator rater than upon the staff;
3. *The extent to which special programme requirements necessitate centralisation.* There may be situations where even the routine work decisions may not be delegated. This may be true in the early stage of a new organisation or when a crisis situation has developed or is developing;
4. *The extent to which work is of a stable and repetitive type.* Delegation is made easier when guidelines can be established

for lower levels to take action directly. If the conditions of work are changed frequently, delegation may be more difficult;

5. *The size of organisation and its geographical location.* The larger the organisation and the broader its geographic coverage, the greater are the chances for delegating authority;
6. *Methods of internal communications in the organisation.* Delegation becomes difficult if there is a lack of effective procedural system in internal communications and work controls;
7. *The degree of co-ordination which is required throughout the organisation.* A manager must co-ordinate or fail. Delegation of this power will be tantamount to abdication of responsibility.

Hindrances to Delegation

Whatever be the need for delegation, it is often seen that superior officers fight shy of it, and are generally reluctant to delegate authority. This tendency is particularly noticeable in our country today. The causes for such failure to delegate may well be summed up as: "Highly developed egotism on the part of persons who rise to positions of hierarchical leadership; their apprehension that others are incapable of making proper decisions or carrying them out in the desired manner; their fear that disloyal or subversive power centre may develop among strong subordinates; their impatience with the slower pace and the indecisiveness of subordinates; absence of emotional maturity in the topman; the desire of leaders to be always in the limelight and to take credit for everything; lack of knowledge of what to delegate and how; and lastly, the accountability of the chief to those above him or the ligislature or the people.

How to Delegate?

Certain mechanics can, however, be suggested to solve partially the dilemma of delegation so as to retain the basic control in the hands of the executive head, while permitting the right kind and extent of delegation for the execution of details, for example:

1. Planned and regularised contacts with staff as a part of each executive's and supervisor's duties are essential. In this way, the official periodically can see how authority is being exercised, can discuss problems, can give guidance and can determine if there are questionable points of policy or operation.

2. A systematic plan for reporting and reviewing operational records and documents will facilitate control. This includes such material correspondence, financial documents and personnel documents. In most cases, it is not humanly possible to review all such documentation, and sampling must be used. This means careful definition of problems and determination of the kinds of work to be done by the administrator personally, that which can be completed without his personal attention.

3. All reports of subordinates which contain specific information about performance, progress, results, new questions enables a review of progress and reveals the problem areas that are developing. A systematic plan of reporting specifically for those purposes facilitates control. It is also possible to simplify, standardize and shorten such reporting so as to give information expeditiously and with minimum time required of the official as well as those reporting.

4. In large organisations, the administrator may use one or more special assistants or a staff unit to develop statistical and operational information through compilation of operational data, inspections, audits and surveys. Generally, these inspections and survey procedures are geared to uncover areas of weakness which require corrective action and show ways in which the functioning of the organisation may be improved.

As we have seen, a proper plan of delegation envisages constant scrutiny with a view to improvement. However, certain general principles can be laid down by means of which the effectiveness of a system of delegation of authority can be assessed. These criteria may be outlined as follows:

1. Delegation of authority should be specific and customarily be in written form;
2. Policies, regulations and procedures should be well defined to assure uniformity of interpretations in the organisation;
3. Authority which can be exercised competently and safely at lower levels should be delegated. The right to decide the form of response to an operational challenge or problem is best delegated to the lowest practicable level so as to be near the scene of actual action;
4. Delegation should follow the normal line of command and should be made to a post rather than to an individual. Authority should never be delegated to an individual if it had not been delegated to his superior except with his implied consent. Distribution of authority at comparable levels should be uniform;
5. All parts of the organisation be familiar with the repositories of responsibility and authority and the extent thereof;
6. Delegations should be planned in the sense that they are integrated with the systematic development of a competent and trained staff and conform to the other operational plans and policies.

COMMUNICATION

Significance

Communication has come to be recognised as the first principle of administration. Effective communication is vital to the successful achievement of agency objectives. Persons working for an organisation will show greater devotion to it, take more interest in their tasks and develop a larger measure of identification with it if they understand the objectives of organisation, its policies and circumstances. An effective way to evoke a person's enthusiastic and active co operation is for the head of the agency to take him into confidence. Millett is right in regarding communication as, "the blood stream of administration organisation". Pfiffner considers it "the heart of management".

This is an age of communication. The average man, today, is much closer to his government and his neighbours; he identifies himself more with the life around him. Even in the international field, we are moving toward "one world". Researches in group dynamics and human psychology have proved that the successful working of an organisation depends upon winning the co operation of the persons working in it. Democracy demands that the public must be increasingly associated with administration. Business and government alike, therefore, have felt the need for establishing better communication channels in their organisations. Management has recognised the part that communication plays in promoting participation, co-operation and team work on the part of the employees. There is ample evidence of the recognition. Almost all civilised governments today have set up information, publicity and public relations departments. The literature on management is full of articles on communication. Conferences, workshops and other training programmes are being organised to develop communication skills, particularly in the United States.

Meaning

Communication is often used in the sense of imparting knowledge or transmitting information. The term, as used here, however, has a wider connotation, and includes interchange of thoughts, partaking of ideas, and a sense of participation and sharing. The essence of communication, thus, is not information but understanding. Millett has aptly defined it as "shared understanding of a shared purpose." Tead expresses the same idea as, "The underlying aim of communication is a meeting of minds on common issues."

Communication in an organisation may be internal, external and interpersonal. The first deals with the relationship between the organisation and its employees. The second is concerned with the relations of the agency with the public and is called "public relations". The third is related to the relationship among the agency's employees *inter se*. Communication has also been classified as "up", "down" and "across". "Up" communication is achieved by such method as systematic, written and verbal reports of performance and progress, statistical and accounting reports concerning work, written verbal requests for guidance, suggestions and discussions. Means are, thus, provided for the higher level to obtain evidence about work problems. "Down" communication is achieved through devices, such as, directives, manuals, specific, written or verbal orders or instructions, staff conferences, budget sanctions and establishment authorisation. The higher level uses these devices not only for command and control, but to inform the lower echelons concerning its attitudes and ideas and to give advice, guidance and direction. "Across" communication is achieved through exchange of written or verbal information and reports, formal and informal and personal contacts, staff meetings and co-ordinating committees. The aim is to bring together different but related parts of the organisation.

Media

Communication is possible through numerous media which may be grouped into three main types—audio, visual and audio-visual; that is, hearing, seeing, and both. The examples of the audio medium are conferences, meetings, interviews, telephone calls, broadcasts, public meetings, etc. Visual medium includes written communications (circulars, manuals, reports, bulletins and hand-books), and pictorial forms (pictures, photographs, posters, cartoons, flags, insignia, slides, etc.). Sound-motion pictures, television and personal demonstration are examples of audio-visual medium. Each of these media has its merits and limitations, and it is for the manager or the executive to decide which medium should prove effective and when.

The conference method is coming more and more in vogue as a means of encouraging communication whether in a business or a governmental agency. It is supposed to avoid delay, minimize correspondence and cut down red tape. According to Millett the important uses of the conference method are—(1) to gain awareness of a problem, (2) to help in problem solving, (3) to gain acceptance and execution of decision, (4) to help promote a sense of unity among the officials working in the organisation, (5) to help in appraising personnel, and (6) to encourage an exchange of information among administrative personnel.

The objectives of a conference are to aid individuals to discharge their present responsibilities more effectively, co-ordinate their working relationship, profit from the experience of others, organise their own experience, appreciate the problems faced by others, broaden their viewpoint and formalise organisational communication. The conference method possesses the advantage of creating a high degree of interest, full and equal participation by group members, satisfaction through mutual achievement, acceptance of results by participants, inculcating habit of analysis and integration of thought, developing group morale, and possessing an informality.

The conference method, however, has its limitations. In the opinion of the Estimates Committee (Ninth Report): "The conferences have become so many and are sometimes so unwieldy that it is impossible for officers participating in them to do full justice to the subject-matter of the discussions and, in practice, instead of the meetings, shortening discussions, notings, etc., they sometimes lead to protracted correspondence, inasmuch as different viewpoints which are expressed have to be recorded, corrected and reconciled and delay occurs in framing agreed minutes and sometimes further conferences become necessary as a result of incomplete discussions. Sometimes, the same officer has to attend more than one conference the same day and cannot obviously be fully prepared for each conference. Consequently, he does not contribute fully to the discussions. In short, the conference system is proving more elaborate than the original procedure of noting on files."

To be useful, therefore, a conference has to be carefully managed. It should not open without any preliminary planning, without the service of experts, without any rules, and without adequate organisation for effective work. Preliminary planning for a conference is very essential. The persons responsible for it should give adequate time for planning, and tasks should be assigned to several qualified persons in advance of the conference. The organisation of a conference is equally important. Right size of room, movable and comfortable chairs, good lighting and ventilation, good acoustics, provision of aids like blackboards, recordings slides and projectors, arrangement of seats, timing, etc., may seem small matters but help make the conference successful. Similarly, the procedure adopted, and the personality of the chairman may help or mar a conference.

Difficulties and Barriers

The first great difficulty is the complexity of language. Communication is made difficult by the 'tyranny of words' which at best are only poor vehicles for the expression of ideas. Word differences are a big hindrance to mutual understanding. This is particularly true of intentional words. According to Terry, words may be classed as extensional and intentional. The former type of words denote objects that are definite, namely, persons, places and material, and are easily understood. "In contrast, intentional words do not refer to something that can be pointed out. They neither always connote an identical meaning to different persons nor the same meaning to the same person at all times." To illustrate, the word 'easy' is subject to different meanings. Words, phrases, and idioms in the same language may have different connotations in different countries, for instance, the use of English language in England, the U.S.A., and India. The same is true of the Hindi language in different parts of India. The problem becomes more complicated in a country like ours with fourteen officially recognised languages and numerous dialects. Besides, the jargons developed by different disciplines further add to the complexity. Specialists tend to develop a language which is beyond the ken of the average citizen. The specialisation characterising modern administration has developed its own jargon which inhibits communication.

Secondly, there are, in the words of Pfiffner, 'ideological barrier'. "Differences in background, education, and expectation result in different social and political views. These are probably the greatest handicaps to effective communication and probably the most difficult to overcome." To these barriers may be added the lack of common experience and common background. All these may lead to differences in the perception of a problem with the result that, like the fable of seven blind men describing an elephant, each individual gives his own interpretation of the problem, thus, making the meeting of minds difficult.

Thirdly, lack of a will or desire to communicate is not unknown. Some managers do not believe that administration is a co-operative endeavour and a group effort; they do not think it necessary to share their ideas with their subordinates. Their concept of the role of the subordinates, in the words of the poet, is "not to wonder why but to do and die." To such executives communication is the one-way process of giving and passing on instructions to those below. They do no relish or encourage communication from below. They do not relish or encourage communication from below. Participative management is not for them. The obverse side of this attitude is sycophancy among the subordinates. A common weakness of a subordinate is to report only that information to his superior as is palatable to him. This is a sure way of spoiling the boss; nothing can be worse for the morale of a boss than to be surrounded by yes-men.

Size and distance may be said to be the fourth barrier to communication. The bigger an organisation and larger the number of its employees, the greater is the difficulty of communication. Then there is the problem of too many hierarchical levels. "Information must percolate through levels, each of which may include empire-builders who consciously modify or subvert higher authority. In addition, individuals interpret facts differently and tend unconsciously to colour them in transmission." The problem of distance arises in the case of an agency having its field agencies scattered throughout the country. The department of Posts and Telegraphs is a good example of it.

Lastly, there may be lack of definite and recognised means of communication. Channels of communication may be formal or informal. Formal channels are established procedures by which information flows through an agency. Hierarchy helps the process. Noting on files and the flow of files up and down the line are recognised means of communication. "Procedure through proper channels" epitomizes this concept. All such procedures aim not only at disseminating information, but also at creating consensus of opinion and understanding in the agency. But, however detailed and comprehensive the formal channels, there is a tendency for informal channels to be set up. According to Appleby, a good deal of circumvention of formal procedures is essential to make the transaction of business possible. Pfiffner and Presthus echo the same idea by saying, "The ability to short-circuit formal channels is, thus, a necessary and valuable art." Interpersonal contacts and personal relationship inevitably lead to direct personal contacts which break through the formal channels.

Essentials of Communication

According to Millett, there are seven factors necessary to make the communication effective, namely—it should be clear, consistent with the expectation of the recipient, adequate, timely, uniform, and acceptable. Terry recommends eight practices to achieve the goal:

1. Inform yourself fully;
2. Establish a mutual trust in each other;
3. Find a common ground of experience;
4. Use mutually known words;
5. Have regard for context;
6. Secure and hold the receiver's attention;
7. Employ examples and visual aids; and
8. Practise delaying reactions.

SUPERVISION

Why Supervision?

"That, which is not inspected, is not done," is an old but wise saying. Inspection, overseeing and supervision arise in response to needs inherent in the functioning of an organisation. Policy-making, programming, budgeting and staffing, by themselves, may not necessarily lead to successful results unless there is someone to ensure that what has been programmed is actually being implemented. Moreover, the workers on the front line very often need guidance and advice. At times, they run into difficulties and need a helping hand to extricate them out of these. Every organisation, public or private, therefore, provides for supervision as one of its most important tasks. One out of every seven workers in American commercial and industrial organisations, is a supervisor. Moreover, supervision is inherent in the hierarchical nature of organisations, each level of which supervises the one below it and is, in turn, supervised by the one above it.

What is Supervision

It is a compound of two words 'super' and 'vision', meaning superior power of perceiving. It means overseeing or superintending the work of others. It has been defined as "the direction, accompanied by authority, of the work of others." However, the term does not always convey identical meaning to all persons.

Margaret Williamson gives a graphic story to explain the different aspects of supervision. Some new group workers were asked; "What came to their mind when they heard the term 'supervision'?" Replies ran somewhat as follows: "Being safeguarded from making mistakes. Being helped by a person who understands. Satisfaction in having a point of reference. Being made to feel inadequate and inferior because of the authority and power of the person over me. Being pushed around." She defines supervision as "a process by which workers are helped by a designated staff member to learn according to their needs, to make the best use of their knowledge and skills, and to improve their abilities so that they do their jobs more effectively and with increasing satisfaction to themselves and the agency." In brief, supervision means the observation of results.

Supervision is more than inspection and investigation; the latter are merely parts of the process of supervision. Indeed, supervision is more than superintendence as an administrative task. It has an educative aspect too. A supervisor is supposed to teach the workers under him the best way of doing their work. In addition, it has a consultative role inasmuch as the workers turn to their supervisor for advice and guidance. A supervisor's role, thus, is that of a leader.

Supervision, in brief, has many ingredients. It is 'selecting the right person for each job; arousing in each person an interest in his work and teaching him how to do it; measuring and rating performance to be sure that teaching has been fully effective, administering correction where this is found necessary and transferring to more suitable work or dismissing those for whom this proves ineffective; commending whenever praise is merited and rewarding for good work; and, finally, fitting each person harmoniously into the working group—all done fairly, patiently and tactfully so that each person is caused to do his work skillfully, accurately, intelligently, enthusiastically and completely." Millett distinguishes between "substantive supervision" and "technical supervision". The first is concerned with the actual work done by an agency while the second deals with the methods by which the work is done.

Who are Supervisors?

All persons in authority, who control the work of others, are supervisors irrespective of their high or low status in the hierarchy. Thus, the foreman, the head-constable, the head-clerk, the head-master, the collector are all supervisors. It is, sometimes, thought that a supervisor merely supervises and performs no line functions himself. It is, however, not always so. Supervisors generally perform both the "responsibility" and the "work" jobs, though their main function is the former type of job. Supervisors are of two kinds—line and functional. The line supervisor refers to the control exercised by the persons in line of command. For example, in the Police Department of a State in India, the Inspector General supervises the District Superintendents of Police who in turn control the Inspectors and so on till we come to the Headconstable who is the first line supervisor. Functional supervision, on the other hand, is exercised by subject-matter specialists like the auditors, the accountants, the O and M specialists, statisticians, etc. While line supervision is of direct and commanding type, the functional supervision is staff function, and influences rather than commands.

How to Supervise?

Millett suggests six methods or techniques of supervision: (i) prior approval of individual projects; (ii) the promulgation of service standard; (iii) budgetary limitation upon the magnitude of operations; (iv) approval of key-subordinate personnel; (v) a reporting system on work progress; and (vi) inspection of results. Let us, briefly, examine each one of these techniques.

Prior Approval. This is a common mode of exercising control by the superior over the subordinate units. The top authorities simply lay down the objectives and policy in broad terms, leaving the details of the individual projects to be finalised later. In India, the prior approval of the departmental heads is not enough; in addition, the Finance Ministry/Department has also to give its approval. This arrangement not only ensures detailed control but also provides the much-needed flexibility to change the general plans through making changes in the projects. There is scope too of removing misunderstanding and rectifying errors. On the other hand, the process almost always tends to interpose delays, increases redtape, means additional staff to cope with the increase in volume of work, and creates diffidence and indifference on the part of the operating heads, nothing to say about the friction between them and top management. Such a system cannot be observed in times of stress, emergency and crisis, and becomes a mere formality as the operating units gain the confidence of the central office.

Service Standard. The second technique of supervision is for the top management to lay down targets or standards for the operating units to achieve. This, in addition to furnishing guide-points, audits their performance. Service standards, thus, set up norms of administrative output. For instance, the standard for a school may well be the strength of students, the percentage of passes, the quality of performance of the students, general discipline among students, good morale among the teachers, proficiency in games and other extracurricular activities, and the number of hours of teaching—any one of them, a few of them, or all of them. The determination of such norms is a difficult process, and there is the difficulty of striking a balance between quantity and quality, the attaining of targets and the way it has been done.

Work Budget. Budget, it has been rightly said, is much more than an array of figures; it is a plan of work and is a powerful instrument of control over administration. Thus, budget allotments for a school determine how much money will be spent on recruiting additional teachers, constructing new rooms, providing mid-day lunch for students, etc. The operating units, thus, work within the budgetary allotments and are not free to spend money as and when they like.

Approval of Personnel. No agency of government is completely free to recruit its staff. The superior staff is invariably appointed by the chief executive. Even in the case of the subordinate personnel, the top management usually insists on its prior approval for all posts except the insignificant ones. In fact, this work is often entrusted to the central personnel department of the agency concerned.

Reports. It is a standard practice in administration that the operating units should submit an account of their activities to the central office. Such reports may be periodic—weekly, fortnightly, monthly, quarterly, half-yearly or annual. Report may also be special or *and hoc*, that is, be concerned with certain special matter. The term may be used in a broad sense to cover the entire field of communication. Thus, according to Seckler-Hudson, "It reaches not only upward, downward, outward, and around within a given organisation, it must reach across to other agencies doing similar work, and up and out to the government-wide agencies and the office of the President." However, we are here concerned only with a system of internal management reporting. "These reports may be narrative or statistical; they may embrace the broad scope of all major activities, or they may be confined to a few essentials; they may emphasise achievement or deficiencies in performance." A good system of reporting has obvious advantages. It conveys information to the superiors about what is going on. It enables the supervisors to evaluate the performance of their subordinates, to understand the situation faced by them; and above all, to control the operations within the organisation.

Inspection. Inspection of some kind or the other has been an integral part of public administration for as many centuries as government has emerged as an organised unit. In general, the purposes of inspection are: (i) to see that the existing rules, regulations and procedures are observed; (ii) a sort of performance audit; (iii) instructing and guiding the persons working in the organisation; and (iv) improvement of efficiency. Inspection, it must be remembered, is not a mere fault-finding process, and the effectiveness of an inspection system is to be judged in the light of the above four ingredients. For a proper understanding of the nature and scope of inspection, a distinction should be made between inspection on the one hand and investigation and supervision on the other. Inspection work and investigation work differ greatly from each other. In the words of Millett, "...the purpose of inspection is to acquire information. It helps to clarify management, purpose and intention. It helps acquaint top management with the operating problems facing subordinate levels of management. It helps build personal relationship of mental acquaintance and confidence. The purpose of investigation, on the other hand, is to inquire into some alleged or suspected incident of an abuse of management authority. It is concerned with the personal wrong-doing, often of a criminal nature." As regards the relationship between inspection and supervision, Millett, regards inspection not as a separate management function but as a part of the process of supervision. As shown earlier, supervision is certainly a more comprehensive term than inspection, though at times, the two terms are used in the same sense. It may be said that inspection work is *post facto* review and has in a way a negative role. Supervision, on the contrary, is more positive and is in operation both before an action and after it.

Inspections are carried out in many ways. In the first place, the head of an agency himself is responsible for the inspection of offices and establishments under him. In other words, each superior is expected to inspect the work of his subordinates. This may be called a built-in system of inspection. Secondly, the administrative agency of the next higher echelon has also a duty to inspect the working of offices under it. Thus, a Divisional Commissioner has to inspect the Collectorates under him, and the District Collector, in turn, has to inspect the Tahsils/Taluqas. The third system of inspection is to set up an external, separate and independent agency, with the Government, charged solely with inspection work. A good example of such an agency is the Inspectorate of Offices in U.P.

To the above list of techniques may be added a few more, namely, work plans, written procedures or manuals, written and oral instructions, staff meetings and administrative follow-up.

How to Get Supervisors?

Supervision has come to be identified as a separate and defined function. Everyone cannot be a good supervisor. Supervision now needs specified knowledge and skill in using it. In addition, a supervisor should have certain qualities. Pfiffner lists eight such qualities, namely, command of job content, that is, expert knowledge of the work to be done, personal qualifications, like integrity; teaching ability, that is, the ability to communicate his ideas to the workers and make them understand the management's point of view; general outlook, that is, the supervisor should love his job and be absorbed in it and inspire those under him; courage and fortitude, that is, the ability to take decisions and assume responsibility; ethical and moral considerations, that is, freedom from vices having social disapprobation; administrative technology, that is, the ability to manage; and curiosity and intellectual ability, that is, intellectual alertness and receptivity to new ideas.

According to Halsey, there must be an adequate and reasonably well-balanced development of the following six qualities in a supervisor:

1. *Thoroughness*. A supervisor should collect all the information relevant to the issue and take care of every necessary detail;
2. *Fairness*. It includes a sense of justice, consideration and truthfulness towards workers;
3. *Initiative*. It is a combination of the three qualities of courage, self-confidence and decisiveness;
4. *Tact*. It is "the ability to win the loyalty and support of others by saying and doing those things which give them a feeling that they are playing an important part in whatever is being done;"

5. *Enthusiasm*. It is "an intense and eager interest in and devotion to a cause, a pursuit, or an ideal." It includes interest, knowledge and achievement;
6. *Emotional Control*. It means not the elimination of emotions but rather to control and channel them in right direction.

But the quality which is perhaps most necessary is the human relations aspect of supervision. The success of a supervisor, more often than not, depends on his personal relations with employees, taken as individuals. It has been rightly said that the "pattern of leadership desirable in supervisory positions is based upon behaviour that emphasises co-operation, participation, consultation, and satisfaction for the egos of the rank and the file, though the strong leader may have in subdue his natural desire for self-assertion and self-display." The Harvard Group's (Elton Mayo) Western Electric Research Findings and the Michigan (Rensis Lekant) Studies have proved "employees can be most effectively motivated by people-centred and democratic leadership aided by favourable institutional environment. Studies by the Institute for Social Research at the University of Michigan have suggested the following conclusions:

1. There is a relationship between the closeness of supervision and the level of output by the workers, the latter being an inverse ratio to the former. In other words, workers tend to produce more under less exacting supervision, that is to say, the crack of the whip is not effective as it is made out to be;
2. A supervisor treats his subordinates in the way in which he is treated by his superiors;
3. Wherever the supervisors are "employee-centred", the output of the employees is more than where the supervisors are "production-centred";
4. Supervisors of highly productive groups spend more time on and devote more attention to supervisory duties and less time and attention to direct production work than supervisors of groups with low output. In other words, a successful manager devotes more attention to "responsibility" job than to "work" job;

5. Participative management tends to greater production. Supervisors, who encourage group participation in common tasks, and adopt a helpful, rather than a primitive attitude towards the delinquent worker, being to high production category;

6. Successful supervisors usually train their personnel for job advancement even at the risk of losing their services.

Two problems arise in the matter of selecting supervisors. The first is the question of job experience versus supervisory skill. To what extent is it necessary for a supervisor to be an accomplished performer in the jobs of those whom he supervises? In other words, should the principal of a college be the best teacher or the superintendent of a hospital a very successful medical practitioner? There can be no presumption that a great scholar would necessarily make a good administrator. Barnard would, in fact, say just the contrary. The point to note is that persons should not be chosen to become supervisors on the sole basis of proficiency as journeymen. Brilliance in individual work is no guarantee of ability to supervise other people. The skills, which makę an excellent worker, are often not the same skills useful to a good supervisor. The second problem is : Should supervisors be promoted from the ranks or recruited directly from outside? Here again there can be no final reply. But, since a good supervisor needs to possess certain qualities, it is better to promote persons known to possess them than recruit persons directly on the basis of qualifications, but whose qualities would always be a matter of guess.

Training Supervisors

The question is often asked : Is skill in human relations and supervisory leadership teachable? It is said that supervisors are born, not make, and that it is better to select a good supervisor than to try to make him good. Whatever the truth in the above saying, the fact remains that "nine-tenths of genius is sweat". Qualities of a supervisor may be inherent, but they can be developed by training. In the words of Halsey, "It has been demonstrated time and time again that almost any person of normal intelligence and sincere desire to be of service to people can acquire considerable skill in the art of supervising people, if he will study its principles and methods and apply them thoughtfully, conscientiously, and persistently. The personality of the successful supervisor of people is made up of a number of qualities, and these qualities are made effective through the use of certain definite techniques. I believe, too, that the qualities necessary to success in supervising people can be developed, and that the required techniques can be taught, and skill in their use made permanent by practice. I believe that because I have seen it done by both old and new supervisors, and seen their departments improve as they become better supervisors."

Training programmes for middle and lower level officials have been expanded massively in the United States since the end of World War II. Among the newer training programmes, "work simplification" is one of the larger and more popular. There are hundreds of business and government organisations which are not providing such training on a large scale. In the case of the U.S. Department of the Army, every new first line (bottom level) supervisor is required to take the 16 hour on-the-job training course within six months after he joins the supervisory staff. Nearly all of the thousands of supervisors have been so trained. In the financial year 1960, a total of 10,588 Departments of the Army employees received the training. A similar massive on-the-job training is necessary in India as an aid to the accomplishment of Plan objectives.

8

Aids to Efficiency

In every public or private institution, undertaking or service, whose aim is, undoubtedly, the achievement of success, the key-note is 'efficiency', by which is meant she securing of the maximum result with the minimum of labour and resources, fiscal and material in the least possible time.

Efficiency can be enhanced through various aids and devices which can be classified into two categories, subjective and objective. Subjective aids may be mental or emotional, while the objective category may relate to the person of the worker or appertain to external facilities.

Mental aids may take the form of:

(a) General and cultural study;

(b) Special study;

(c) Research;

(d) Refresher courses;

(e) Employee counselling;

(f) Attitude surveys;

(g) Employee participation in work improvement suggestion systems; and

(h) Attitude training and education.

(a) *General and Cultural study.* It is increasingly recognised that aid given to the staff and the workers for improving their intellectual knowledge and culture

by providing library facilities in subjects of general interest and enabling them to follow the day-to-day events of the world in the realm of politics, sociology, economics and the like through the supply of journals, newspapers and magazines, pays a good dividend in the long run.

(b) *Special Study.* Where the employee is in charge of a specialised branch, requiring a close technical knowledge of the subject, it is worthwhile giving him opportunities of learning the improved techniques, new methods and machinery of work, and the special economy involved in the changes brought about by discoveries in science and art. A fully equipped library, maintained up-to-date with the latest books and magazines, should be made available. Further, facilities like periodical deputation to institutions like the Indian School of Public Administration would prove useful.

(c) *Research.* At higher levels in an organisation, the affording of facilities for research greatly contributes to a broader outlook, a closer insight and all-around improvement and innovation in the technique of work and management. Many ministries in the Government of India have their own research units. The Indian Institute of Public Administration offers facilities for such research.

(d) *Refresher Courses.* Such courses in theory and practice of administration make up for the inevitable fading of memory through lapse of time. If the employees at the supervision and direction level are to be kept posted with accurate information their memories have necessarily to be refreshed periodically. The National Academy of Administration and India Institute of Public Administration organize such courses for the middle-level managers. The Administrative Staff College at Hyderabad provides facilities for syndicate studies and exchange of views and experiences for the top level executives from business and the Government.

(e) *Employee Counselling*. Long and arduous research in human relations has disclosed that 'employee counselling' greatly contributes to an increase in production. The expression does not merely mean what it literally signifies, namely, the giving of positive advice by someone to the employees. Stahl defines it as "a means of giving psychological support to a personality and a method of getting employees to understand the cause of any dissatisfaction they may have and to do something about it themselves wherever that is practicable." The method adopted savours of a psycho-analytical technique of eliciting what the real feeling of the worker is towards his work situation and enables a self-introspection as to why he feels in a a particular way. The 'listener or the interviewer', generally, is a specialist who is not in the supervisory line and cannot affect the employees' prospects in the organisation. Interviews are entirely confidential between the interviewee and the interviewer. The counselling interview is described by psychologists as 'non-directive'. It may also be advisory and may include some positive 'building-up' approaches if an employee's attitude suggests that they are desirable. For counselling purposes, many industries and large governmental establishments have employed specialists who spend full time in this listening role with employees.

(f) *Attitude Surveys*. The formal questionnaire or interview survey of employee attitudes was greatly stimulated by the researches at the Hawthorne plant. Attitude surveys are a device to find out what employees are thinking about, what is motivating them, what they get the most satisfaction out of, in their jobs. The attitude survey is 'a diagnostic tool of the personel man to lay the ground work for improving human relations, and thereby production, in a working organisation". It has been used extensively in the U.S.A., in large industrial and government enterprises, and in the armed forces. A number of other federal agencies have also conducted surveys from time to time. There are no theoretical limits to the subject-matter scope of a survey except that it has to do with the individual and the organisation involved. Survey may be on specific areas of question, such as, physical working conditions or, on the whole, range to the employment relationships, covering pay, supervision, advancement, health, safety, quality or workmanship and product, equipment, hours, vacations, and everything that might affect the employees' attitude towards his job and the organisation, — Where this tool is used continuously and seriously for evaluating the effectiveness of administrative practices, and where positive action is taken over a period of years to meet the needs shown, employee attitudes can be improved to the benefit of the organisation, the public, and the employees themselves. In World War II this type of survey proved highly useful. A team of psychologists was engaged by the U.S. Government to survey and interpret to the higher staff the attitudes of the common soldier towards all that concerned him in the military service like discipline, uniform, sport, recreation, medical attention, food and residential accommodation.

(g) *Employee Participation in Work Improvement.* In any fair sized working force it has been found advisable to adopt some systematic method whereby workers are encouraged to express their ideas and gain recognition. A number of business concerns in western countries have long had recourse to suggestion system for this purpose. For example, the Departments of the Army and the Navy in the U.S.A., have for many years, sponsored extensive suggestion system, with full time staffs devoting their energies to the stimulation and processing of suggestions. The experience goes to prove that a reservoir of ideas may be tapped by this method—ideas that are often of real value for improving both work processes and working conditions. Such contributions, when adopted and given due recognition, obviously add to the workers' sense of partnership and personal worth.

Initially, suggestion plans were characterised by suggestion boxes placed at convenient places in the office and by emphasis on anonymity. Later, management committees were set up to pass on the feasibility of suggestion, both in industry and Government. In more recent years increasing attention has been paid to getting suggestions processed through regular supervisory channels so that full participation of all concerns in the U.S.A., have established production or suggestion committees composed of representatives of both management and employees' unions, which in various ways participate in the stimulation, consideration and adoption of ideas on work improvement. Of course, the final decision as to the adoption of a particular suggestion must rest with the departmental head or someone even higher up. The task of review committees and the supervisory line is to weed out the worthless suggestion, evaluate those remaining, make appropriate recommendations regarding the credit which the employee is to receive and report on the apparent applicability of the suggestions. Between 1943 and 1954 the Tennessee Valley Authority in the U.S.A accepted 76 per cent of 6,723 suggestions made.

Personnel administration is a matter of proper human relations and the operation of suggestion system offers unique opportunities for developing such relations. It is, however, only one such avenue and should be viewed in perspective with other aspects of employee participation.

(h) *Attitude Training*. Another factor which contributes to efficiency is a sustained training in attitudes. Training is a concept distinct from education. It means "any process by which the attitudes, skills and abilities of employees to perform specific jobs are increased," while the term education connotes the process of "increasing the knowledge, understanding attitude of employees, so that they are better adjusted to their working environment." For example, teaching a trainee how to operate a baling machine is called 'training', while the course in the economics of the process falls under 'education'.

Before training operative employees, its justification should be taken into account, and cost is the main criterion. Though all employees should undergo training, all need not be trained to the same degree and at the same time. There are several types of training (a) On the job training, (2) Apprenticeship, (3) Internship, (4) Learned training, (5) Vestibule training, and (6) Outside courses. In evaluation of a training programme, the data providing improvements and savings will relate to increase in output, decrease in unit time and unit cost, reduction in machine requirements, fall in labour turnover, decrease in accidents, and betterment of employee morale.

Given below are some of the hints for such training:

1. Take the new employee around the office to acquaint him with the people with whom he will work. Show him his work place and the equipment he will use. Make him acquainted as soon as possible with rules, privileges, hours of work, leave, pay days, etc.

2. Quickly familiarize him with some of the history and general objectives of his unit and its relation to the rest of the Department/Ministry. This can be done through orientation or induction meetings.

3. Prepare and make available to the new person a list of published material and reference that he will use to become familiar with his job. A moderate reading assignment may be made from this.

4. Explain to the new employee the organisational structure of his office with its lines of authority in order that he may know to whom he is to report, from whom he is to take directions and the limits of his responsibility.

5. Help the new employee to analyse his position. The analysis should include a list of the various duties of the position, why each is important, how to do it and some measure to know how well it has been done. The new employee should be convinced of the trainee's own desire to see himself become a first class employee.

6. Develop in the employee the habit of taking his requests for information, his problems and his difficulties to the immediate supervisor for solution. Show him how profitable this practice is to himself. No superior should neglect to explain to an employee that any time he becomes firmly convinced that he is not getting fair treatment from his supervisor, he should feel free to carry grievance to the supervisor's chief or personnel officer.

Attitude Education. By 'education' is meant the general increase in ability to adjust to one's environment, in contrast to the training referred to above, which means the performance of specific tasks.

Emotional Factors. Emotional factors are perhaps, the greatest contributories to the making or breaking of efficiency. While some traits make a direct positive addition to efficiency, others make an indirect contribution by barring descent into inefficiency. Fear of punishment, in any form, tends to maintain the level of efficiency. In institutions where standards of turnover are available, a close and continual watch can be kept on the quantum and quality of work turned out and penalizing lapses has often a salutary effect. Punishments may range from a mere disapproval to the drastic step of dismissal. But in inflicting punishments, great caution has to be exercised. Not only the susceptibilities of the employees and their mental and emotional reactions have to be gauged, but the effect on the morale of the rest of workers has also to be taken into account. Tact, imagination, sympathy and practical sagacity have to govern the superior's action in meeting out punishments. Fear of punishment can, at best, keep up the machinery of work and out-turn at the normal level, but can hardly serve as an incentive to increase efficiency, for which motives and impulses of an altogether different type make a contribution. Such are the pleasures of emulation, the thrill of excelling in competition with co-workers, the exhilaration at winning the compliments and appreciation of the powers that be and the hope or prospects of a rise in rank, status and salary.

So far, the mental and emotional aids, which are of a subjective type, have been considered. We now proceed to discuss the objective categories, which fall under two heads: (1) personal, and (2) external.

Personal Factors The factors, which contribute to the maintenance of efficiency are personal cleanliness, good health, wholesome food, regular habits, rest and recreation for all of which the affording of facilities by the management is extremely desirable. The innumerable external aids given to the worker take the form of:

(i) liberal conditions of employment;

(ii) fringe benefits;

(iii) service programmes;

(iv) equipment aid;

(v) supervision; and

(vi) Incentives and awards.

(i) *Conditions of Employment.* It is hardly necessary to state that among conditions of service, the most telling factor is the wage or salary and allowances. In Government service or a private concern the exigencies of administration or management require a hierarchy of officials and employees, who fall under defined categories or fixed or elastic pay scale and increments. The other conditions of service relate to promotions, leave holidays, hours or work, security of tenure, transfers travel facilities, retirement benefits, provident fund schemes, compulsory insurance etc. Much of

unrest among Government servants, particularly the "non-gazetted" services and among workmen in the private sector, is traceable to the disparity between the salary grades and wage rates on the one hand, and the inflationary spiral of price on the other. The recurring strikes, the disorganisation of industry and the threatened disruption of essential Government services are, after all, the symptoms of a deep-seated malady which has its roots in the maladjustment of economic policies to the basic needs of the workers in general. The reports of the Pay Commissions bear ample testimony to the need for the removal of discontentment and an improvement in conditions of service under the Government Labour legislation and the contribution of the Labour Tribunals and judiciary towards the amelioration of the service conditions of private employees have been considerable. There can only be two alternatives, if the relations between the employer and the employee are to improve, namely, a liberal increase in wages and improvement in conditions of service and stabilisation of price level through increased production.

(ii) *Fringe Benefits*. By this expression is meant the advantages which the employees get collaterally to the main consideration for services, namely, the wages. These wages-supplements save for the employee an expenditure which is inevitable. The benefits include vacations on pay, sick-leave with pay, medical service, and assistance to employees, when injured in accidents. Statistics of a survey, conducted by the Chambers of Commerce of the United States, showed that about 17 per cent to 20 per cent of the pay-roll is covered by these benefits.

The Personnel Department in any institution would do well to be on the lookout and forecast the direction which the increasing demands of the employees are likely to take and to be prepared to meet them or to convince the employees about the reason for non-compliance. Strained labour relations are often traceable to the unpreparedness of the management when a sudden demand arises.

(iii) *Service Programmes.* Plans and programmes, which may not be strictly germane to any phase of work of any particular administration, have often proved to be of considerable utility as an aid to efficiency, for instance, recreational, athletics and social programmes. They have a two-fold object. They contribute to the living of a well-rounded life by the employees and provide the institution with workers better fitted for their daily task. The extent of such facilities is necessarily governed by the peculiarities in outlook of the employers and the employees. It is said that the employees in general are interested only in salary, hours of work and working conditions, and hardly evince an interest in the above programmes. Barring such exceptional cases, the rule may be gradually laid down, that the employees' efficiency gets a fillip through such programmes.

Recreational and social programmes may include social gatherings, informal meetings, dramatic associations and music groups, picnics, flying clubs, holiday tours, chess and bridge gatherings, etc. Athletic programmes may include facilities for engaging employees in after-office hours' activities, volley-ball, basket-ball, tennis, golf, swimming facilities, gymnastics, hockey, cricket and some other varieties of sport activities which have been found popular.

(iv) *Equipmental Aids.* India's heritage of "all brains and no tools" can hardly be relied on for efficiency in modern administration. While the theoretical and scientific aspects cannot altogether be ignored, it is the field of practical and material aids that yields a harvest of efficient results. A well-equipped library, a study and a reading-room with facilities for quiet perusal are the necessary requisites. Congenial surroundings, air

and lighted rooms with stillness and silence pervading, certainly contribute to higher productive capacity. Minimisation of manual labour and substitution of automatic mechanical aids not only add to perfection of execution, but have far reaching effect on the economy and strategy of management. The recurring and overhead charges are brought down and they afford a solution, so far as it goes, to the problem of labour unrest. The larger the number of workers, the more is the propensity to pick holes in the management and to spread disaffection.

Almost everyday, we hear of new inventions in office equipment and factory work. An illustration would suffice. The modern dictaphones and tape-recorders obviate all need for note-taking by stenographers. The very art of stenography should have become obsolete a few decades back. But we have the sad spectacle of not even a single court or judicial tribunal from the Sub-Magistrate to the Supreme Court possessing even a single tape-recorder, while the expenditure on recruitment, training and salary of stenographers goes to the tune of several lakhs of rupees. Again, very few offices are using the automatic machines like calculators, data-processing equipment and electronic computers, or even penny-slot machines. In factory work, mechanisation and automation is at the minimum in our country. The reason is not far to seek. We have plenty of cheap manpower and the fear of a rise in unemployment through mechanisation is acting as a deterrent. Certain departments of Government would sooner engage half a dozen peons and messengers than sanction a telephone.

(v) *Supervision.* One of the indispensable factors, which contribute to the success of any undertaking involving an appreciable amount of labour, is the quality of supervision. The primary function of a supervisor is correction and co-ordination. In an organisation, where various individuals with varying degrees of aptitude, skill and diligence, are employed on work towards a common objective, there are bound to be errors and shortcomings which can be rectified only under the vigilant eye of a supervisor. Further, co-ordination of various units of work necessarily demands the attention of a common head.

Real and effective supervision requires exceptional qualities. The supervisor should be a man with intelligence, quickness of grasp, keenness of observation, an insight into human nature and its perversities, and above all, patience, sympathy and imagination. He should grasp the fundamental cravings of the employee which are summed up by Halsey as follows:

1. to feel more important, more worthy, more worthwhile;
2. to live safely, securely, and comfortably;
3. to find the right mate and to rear a family;
4. to explore the unknown and to satisfy curiosity;
5. occasionally to escape serious reality, to be entertained, to play;
6. to improve one's own prospects; and
7. to save something for a rainy day.

The ideal supervisor has to assess the intensity of such psychological factors and attune his own approach and behaviour to the required pitch of comment and correction. Supervision has really to be welcomed and not resented by a worker as a very helpful external aid to his efficiency.

(vi) *Incentives and Awards.* Of late, much attention is being given to the need for increased production in business and improved efficiency in administration. A number of aids to achieve this objective have been discussed above. The crux of the problem, however, is the attitude of the employees, and unless they take active and positive interest in improvement programmes, no solid progress can be made. How to secure such motivation on the part of the public official or the business employee is the problem we are concerned with here.

The worker is a human being. He has individual feelings and expectations. He acquires values, both material and non-material. His desires and satisfactions are related to his values, which shape his attitudes and behaviour. While these are largely the product of his character and education, they are significantly influenced and moulded by the group in which he works and by his society in general. The productive effort of a human being is related to his attitudes. It is by no means a mechanical process. Therefore, the worker cannot be treated as a machine. In order to create the maximum urge in the worker to give his best, the employer has to recognise that human effort requires motivation. He must concern himself with the attitudes of the worker to his work. Such attitudes must be the best possible. To create them and to utilise them to the utmost advantage, it is necessary to give the worker his greatest satisfaction. Incentives and awards may go a long way in this direction.

Incentives may be of two types—negative and positive. Negative incentives, in the form of fear and punishment, are merely directed at blocking the doing of wrong. It is true that fear of loss of employment or of reduction in emoluments or rank, or loss of prestige is a factor that drives human beings to work. Reward for the meritorious and punishment for the shirker are both necessary for healthy morale in services. But, as an incentive, fear has only limited use. It acts as a goad, and cannot create the satisfaction necessary for the generation of a self-motivating force for continuous and spontaneous effort required for maximum efficient output. Moreover, it is impossible to continue enough negative devices to block all the wrong paths.

Positive incentives may be general or special. There are certain well-known general features of employment which normally produce urges or drives in the worker towards the desired productive ends. They are: greater security, more income, due recognition and reward for achievement, opportunity for advancement, fair treatment as an individual, better social status and respect, pride of performance, voice in the control of results, etc. The general scheme of employment conditions should, therefore, lay due stress on all these incentives. In addition, the modern progressive employer provides a variety of "fringe benefits"—certain financial, health, food and other services. While these, no doubt, develop in the worker a sense of belongingness and loyalty to his organisation and serve to keep him in good physical and mental health, they soon begin to be looked upon by the employees as complementary to his basic emoluments. Such benefits may be just taken for granted.

In addition, there is a variety of special incentives in industry and in business. These have to meet the attitudes of workers and take into account their economic needs and capacity. Such incentives will, therefore, vary from one enterprise to another, and even from one period to another in its history of growth, development and expansion, as also from one level to another in an individual worker's career. An award that may be a real incentive at one time or in one place may have little or no effect in another. An award or expectation of an award, that might lead a worker to a strong endeavour, might have no attraction for another. The range of special incentives and awards should therefore, be sufficiently wide to provide a suitable recognition in various occupations at different levels. However, no formula of general applications showing relationship between various factors involved and equation thereof to quantum of performance can possibly be laid down, save in the case of normally measurable outputs and their related standardised wage structures, i.e., when it is possible to lay down an accepted system of payment by results.

In industry and in business, indirect workers do not play a less important part. Incentives for them are generally fixed on the basis of a fair ratio of indirect hours to direct hours or indirect contribution to direct contribution in such a way that the co-operative team spirit among the combined group of direct and indirect workers is well preserved.

The bottom level of management carries the responsibility of developing the workers and inspiring them to highest endeavour. Outstanding contributions by the workers are often due to high qualities of supervisory leadership. Such supervisors should be appropriately recognised and rewarded, and so should the executives in higher levels of management.

There will be the question as to the most suitable type of reward or management at different levels. Not everyone requires monetary recognition. Depending upon his age and position, the executive often feels proud and happy when he is conferred with an honorary award, well publicised. No hard and fast rule can, however, be laid down in this regard. To meet various types of particular cases, requiring separate treatment, there has to be some amount of flexibility in an otherwise standardised system of incentives.

The balance between general incentives and special incentives will depend upon the nature of work, the needs of the situation, i.e., workers' attitude, behaviour and responses, the economic stability and programme of the enterprise and above all, upon the outlook of the employer. In Government or local administration, the objectives, the nature and tempo of work done, the conditions and the atmosphere are different, and so the range of incentives and the method of recognition and quantum of reward must naturally be different. In purely administrative agencies, the first measures should doubtless be directed towards control of disincentives, which implies providing satisfactory work conditions and other welfare amenities that would ordinarily produce a feeling of satisfaction and loyalty among the personnel.

Generally, it might not prove fruitful to offer substantial extra cash benefits as positive incentives for more efficient work, particularly in view of the nature of duties the administrative personnel is called upon to perform. There would be considerable difficulties in accurate evaluation of performance on a scientific basis. The system could also result in undesirable practices, accusations of favouritism and jealousies which may ultimately lead to weakening of the morale.

Ordinarily, it should suffice if there is provision for recognition and reward through advance increments or accelerated promotion for sustained, outstanding for meritorious performance over a period of time, or for other personal outstanding effort leading to substantial, tangible or intangible benefits to Government in efficiency and economy, or in other respects. A suitable method of recognising good performance on special jobs would be making an appropriate entry in service record or issuing a letter of appreciation. It may be useful to recognise and reward in cash or by other appropriate manner outstanding suggestions or effects resulting in significant improvement in work methods and procedures or in economy, particularly when emanating from lower levels. Significantly, higher output with respect to certain mechanical types of work or easily measurable items may be encouraged by grant of small cash rewards and/or merit certificates. Long career with loyal service and praiseworthy conduct throughout may be rewarded by prestige awards, e.g. certificates of honour or medals. In addition, exceptionally outstanding performance or leadership may be recognised, as for any citizen, through special token cash reward or prestige award from the head of the State or other high dignitary presented on a national or ceremonial occasion.

In 1961, the Central Government announced important measures for strengthening the administrative machinery in order to ensure the 'vigorous and punctual implementation of the Plan'. (*Vide* the Prime Minister's statement, given ahead in the 'Appendix'). The drive for administrative efficiency was institutionalised with the setting up, in March 1964, of a full-fledged Department of Administrative Reforms in the Ministry of Home Affairs. The Department was made responsible for—

(i) locating important problems and initiating studies in respect of them;

(ii) examining the organisation and procedures of selected departments with the object of eliminating problems of corruption at different points of the administrative machinery;

(iii) examining the question of setting up machinery for the redress of grievances of citizens;

(iv) making a rapid scrutiny of past recommendation and conclusions of committees and individuals with the object of packing up points that can and should be implemented without further enquiry;

(v) preparing the ground for a comprehensive investigation of the entire administrative system in India; and

(vi) continuing the work of the O and M Division.

In February 1973, this Department and the already existing Department of Personnel were merged to form a composite Department of Personnel and Administrative Reforms (DPAR); and the latter was located in the Cabinet Secretariat. In 1977 the Janata Government transferred it to the Home Ministry, and the old Department of Administrative Reforms was given the status of a 'wing' in the new set-up. In January 1985 the DPAR was brought directly under the charge of the Prime Minister to highlight its importance. On 26 March 1985, the Department's functions were enlarged and since then it is called as the Ministry of Personnel, Training, Administrative Reform, Public Grievances, Pension and Pensioners' Welfare. The Ministry functions directly under the Prime Minister and a Minister of State is in charge of it. Under the new set-up there is the Department of Administrative Reform and Public Grievances headed by an additional secretary. The Department of Administrative Reform and Public Grievances in the Ministry of the apex body of the Government in the field of administrative reforms including O and M. It accordingly, advises the Government on policy matters relating to Administrative reforms, provides management consultancy services to public organisations of all levels and all sectors, imparts management education and disseminates information on administrative practices and administrative techniques, and helps in promoting management effort in the Government.

9

Executive Agencies

Under The Secretariat sprawls a network of agencies which are charged with the execution of policies. With the steady expansion in, and increasing complexity of, the governmental functions, the executive agencies have been variously organised to suit the requirements of the situation.

The expansion of public sector, for instance, has led to the emergence of two new forms of organisation, namely:

1. Company; and
2. Corporation.

The Registered Society has been constituted to handle, inter alia, activities involving research, training, and dissemination of information.

In short, the executive agencies may be classified into the following types:

(i) An attached office (e.g. Central Public Works Department);

(ii) Subordinate office (e.g. Sardar Patel National Police Academy, Hyderabad);

(iii) Departmental undertaking (e.g. Ordnance Factories);

(iv) A company registered under the Companies Act, (e.g. Hindustan Steel Limited);

(v) A Corporation or Board set up under a special statute, (e.g. Damodar Valley Corporation, Tea Board etc.);

(vi) A society registered under the Societies Registration Act (e. g. Institute of Foreign Trade).

There are also instances of executive agencies functioning as an integral part of the Ministry itself (e.g. Directorate of Exhibition in the Ministry of Commerce), but this is not a widely prevalent practice. The most important form of executive agency is the Attached Office and the Subordinate Office and these two forms are discussed in this chapter.

Attached Offices

"Office which are closely and directly associated with the Ministries of departments of the Government of India in the shaping of policies by furnishing essential technical data and advice and providing executive directions to the departments etc. Which are responsible for implementing the policies or decisions of the Government should be regarded as Attached Offices."

The Ministry is the policy-making body, but policy must necessarily be made in the light of technical information. The attached office is the repository of technical information which is utilised by the Ministry in the formulation of policy. The origin of Attached Office is interesting. "The development of these Attached Offices was apparently the result of a confusion of two distinct functions—the laying down of policy and the day-to-day implementation of that policy. The latter is normally the function of the executive head, who while he may also function as an expert adviser on matters dealt with by the Secretariat, can only dubiously be regarded as concerned with the enunciation of policy. The distinction between the Secretariat and Attached Offices seem to be connected to the status." Tottenham in his Report of the Central Government (1945 46) compared the function of the various elements of the Central Government to a human machine—the Minister representing the will, the secretary the brain and the executive head the hands. Another oft-quoted analogy is that the Secretariat is the brain, Attached Office is the trunk and the subordinate offices under them are the limbs of the body. It is necessary here to point out that not all Ministries have attached offices. The Attached Offices in existence at present are as follow:

Ministry of Education and Social Welfare

1. The Directorate-General, Archaeological Survey of India, New Delhi.
2. Office of the Commissioner for Scheduled Castes and Scheduled Tribes, Delhi.

Ministry of Finance

1. The Office of the National Savings Commissioner, Nagpur.
2. The Directorate of Inspection, New Delhi.
3. The Directorate of Inspection (Research Statistics and Publication), New Delhi.
4. The Directorate of inspection (Customs and Central Excise), New Delhi.
5. The Directorate of Inspection (Investigation), New Delhi.
6. The Office of Controller of Insurance, Simla.
7. The Directorate of Training (Customs and Central Excise), New Delhi.
8. The Directorate of Emergency Risks Insurance Scheme, New Delhi.
9. The Central Excise (Self Removal Procedure) Review Committee, New Delhi.

Ministry of Agriculture

1. The Directorate of Economics and Statistics, New Delhi.
2. The Directorate of Marketing and Inspection, Nagpur.
3. The Indian Council of Agricultural Research, New Delhi.
4. The Directorate of Plant Protection, Quarantine and Storage, New Delhi.
5. The Directorate of Sugar and Vanaspati, New Delhi.

Ministry of Foreign Trade

1. The Office of Chief Controller of Imports and Exports, New Delhi.

2. The All India Handicrafts Board, New Delhi.

Ministry of Health and Family Planning

1. The Directorate-General of Health Services, New Delhi.

Ministry of Home Affairs

1. The Intelligence Bureau, New Delhi.
2. The Office of Registrar General, New Delhi.
3. The Border Security Force, New Delhi.
4. The Directorate-General, Central Reserve Police Force.

Ministry of Industrial Development and Internal Trade

1. The Directorate-General of Technical Development, New Delhi.
2. The Office of Development Commissioner, Small Scale Industries, New Delhi.
3. The Office of the Economics Adviser, New Delhi.
4. Research and Development Organisation for Electrical Industry, Bhopal.
5. The Office of Salt Commissioner, Jaipur.

Ministry of Information and Broadcasting

1. The Directorate-General, All India Radio, New Delhi.
2. The Press Information Bureau, New Delhi.
3. The Publication Division, New Delhi.
4. The Directorate of Advertising and Visual Publicity, New Delhi.
5. The Directorate-General, Doordarshan.

Ministry of Irrigation and Power

1. The Central Water Commission, New Delhi.
2. The Central Power Commission.

Ministry of Labour and Rehabilitation

1. The Directorate of Employment and Training, New Delhi.
2. The Office of Chief Labour Commissioner, New Delhi.
3. The Directorate-General, Factory Advice Service and Labour Institute, Bombay.
4. The Directorate of Labour Bureau, Simla.

Ministry of Law and Justice

1. The Central Agency Section, New Delhi.
2. The Law Commission, New Delhi.
3. The Branch Secretariat, Bombay.
4. The Branch Secretariat, Calcutta.
5. The Branch Secretariat, Madras.

Ministry of Railways (Railway Board)

1. The Research, Design and Standard Organisation, Lucknow.
2. The Office of the Railway Liaison Officer with the Directorate-General of Supplies and Disposals, New Delhi.

Ministry of Tourism and Civil Aviation

1. The Directorate-General, Civil Aviation, New Delhi.
2. The Department of Tourism, New Delhi.

Ministry of Works and Housing

1. The Central Public Works Department, New Delhi.
2. The Directorate of Estates, New Delhi.
3. The Office of the Chief Controller of Printing and Stationery, New Delhi.
4. National Buildings Organisation, New Delhi.

Ministry of Communications

1. The Directorate-General, Posts and Telegraphs, (P and T Board).

Ministry of Steel and Mines

1. The Office of Iron and Steel Controller, Calcutta.

Cabinet Secretariat

1. The Central Statistics Organisation, New Delhi.
2. The Industrial Statistics Wing, Central Statistical Organisation, Calcutta.
3. The Computer Centre, New Delhi.
4. The Lal Bahadur Shastri National Academy of Administration, Mussoorie.
5. The Central Bureau of Investigation, New Delhi.
6. The Institute of Secretariat Training and Management, New Delhi.
7. The Central Vigilance Commission, New Delhi.
8. The Directorate of Enforcement, New Delhi.
9. The Directorate of Revenue Intelligence, New Delhi.

Department of Supply

1. The Directorate-General of Supplies and Disposals, New Delhi.
2. The Office of Senior Pay and Accounts Officer, New Delhi.
3. The Directorate of National Test House, Calcutta.
4. The Directorate-General, India Supply Mission, U.K.
5. The Directorate-General, India Supply Mission, U.S.A.
6. The Office of Chief Accounts Officer, India Supply Mission, U.S.A.

In development administration powers should necessarily gravitate towards the Attached and Subordinate Offices. In 1946 there were in all 31 Attached Offices in the Central Government. Today there are about 70 of them but there has not been an increase in their power commensurate with their operational responsibilities which obviously are great. This imbalance between responsibility and authority has been the refrain of various administrative reports as well as of successive Five Year Plans. The Secretariat has been increasingly taking up work of an 'original' nature. It is privately confessed even in the Secretariat circles that at least twenty per cent of the total Central Secretariat work could readily be passed on to the Attached Offices. As a cumulative result of all this, the relations between the Secretariat and the Attached office are not very cordial or harmonious. The principal criticisms are summed up below.

Arguments Against the Secretariat

1. The existence of Secretariat as an entity separate from the Attached Office is based on the belief that the task of policy-making must need be separated from that of its execution. But where one task ends and another begins one can never be determined in a categorical way. Each shades off into another.
2. The presence of two separate bodies entails duplication of work, which is avoidable. The Secretariat is involved in work part of which is of an infructuous nature.
3. The Secretariat is the begetter of delays.
4. This is an age of the technocrat. The generalist administrator presiding over the Secretariat has outlived his utility and should be replaced by the technocrat.
5. The attitude of the Secretariat is fault-finding and negative. Posing as experts, the Secretariat personnel often betray their ignorance while scrutinising the proposals and schemes emanating from the Attached Office.
6. The belief that the Secretariat scrutinises a scheme against national and international setting and in the light of governmental policies and programmes is not true.

Arguments in Favour of the Secretariat

1. The generalist secretary is an integral part of the political system we have developed in our country. The Minister is a

layman. He needs the advice of a man possessing detachment and objectivity, and capable of examining the emergent matters in the context of the Government of India as a whole. The Secretary is the Secretary to the Government of India, not to a particular Minister.

2. It is desirable that a specialist's proposals are scrutinised by a generalist. The former is normally an enthusiast, obsessed with the importance of his discipline. This enthusiasm needs to be controlled and this is possible by letting his schemes be scrutinised by a generalist.

3. The presence of the Secretariat as a body separate from the Attached Office ensures justice and fair play. Those aggrieved by the decisions of the Attached Office can appeal to the Secretariat and expect redress of grievances.

4. The Minister needs a staff agency to advise him on his multifarious activities. This is the function of the Secretariat.

Pattern of Relationship Between the Secretariat and the Offices

The foregoing discussion may probably create an impression that the Secretariat and Attached Offices are arrayed in opposite, clearly demarcated camps. The relationship between these two entities does not fall into a single pattern. Indeed, there are six principle pattern of relationship developed at the Central level. These may briefly be discussed here:

A. There is complete merger between the Ministry and the Attached Office. The examples are the Railway Board and the Ministry of Railways, the Posts and Telegraphs Board and the Ministry of Communications. This pattern is eminently suitable for organisations undertaking work of an operational or commercial nature.

B. A senior officer of the Ministry is concurrently appointed as head of the Attached office. In this way he becomes responsible both for formulation of policies and for its implementation with the assistance of the common office located in the Ministry. Thus, the Joint Secretary in the Department of Labour and Employment (Ministry of Labour,

Employment and Rehabilitation) is the Director-General of Employment and Training. Similarly, the Additional Secretary in the Department of Agriculture is the Director-General of Food. "The advantage of the system lies in the fact of total elimination of distance between the Secretariat and the Attached Office. But this very fact also provides the disadvantage which is that the system blurs completely the functions of the Secretariat and the head of executive department. A comprehensive projection of the system throughout the country could only take place if the view was held that the Secretariat as such has no longer a role to play apart from the executive head." Even the Central Cabinet considered that it was risky and undesirable to entrust the duties of chief of any organisation to any officer of the Secretariat.

C. The Ministry's office is merged in the office of the Attached Office. The common office serves both the Secretariat officers and the officers of the Attached Office. There is only one file bureau and, what is more, the same clerical staff puts up papers before both levels of officers. At the level of the Secretariat, the paper is handled at the officer level, the officer being given only stenographic assistance.

This pattern has been recommended both by the Estimates Committee and the Second Pay Commission.

The advantages of this arrangement are that the proposal is examined only once, thus expediting the disposal of cases, and, secondly, that it results in sizeable economy in expenditure.

D. The Ministry and the Attached Office continue to have separate offices but have common files and common file bureau, all located in the Attached Office itself. This arrangement was visualised by the Bengal Administration Enquiry Committee (Rowlands) which wrote:

(a) Duplicate noting in the Ministry and the Department should be abolished. In particular;

(i) The practice of communication proposals from the department to the Ministry by letter should cease;

(ii) All matters requiring both departmental and ministerial consideration should be dealt with in special files;

(iii) Proposals from the department should be as comprehensive as possible;

(iv) The Head of the department should send the special file with his proposals to the Ministry where it should be dealt with initially by an officer who should indicate the action to be taken if he is unable to pass final orders immediately.

(b) The References Section should be given greater importance; it should be better staffed and regarded as a stepping stone to promotion."

The above account is also an excellent definition of the single file system. The advantages of this pattern of relationship are obvious but it does not do away with problems of separate offices with duplicate staff and double scrutiny.

E. The Ministry and the Attached Office continue to have separate offices and separate files but the head of the Attached Office is given an *ex-officio* secretariat status. Thus, the Textile Commissioner is the *ex-officio* Joint Secretary in the Ministry of Commerce.

This pattern has the following advantages:

(i) The head of the Attached Office gets more closely involved in policymaking processes. Thus his field experience is projected more meaningfully into policy formulation;

(ii) As the head of the Attached Office is given an *ex-officio* secretariat status, he has authority to taken decisions on certain matters on behalf of the Government without involving the Ministry. Under this arrangement, therefore, their is considerable saving of time as well as of paper work, as the matter does not travel up to the Secretariat for finalisation;

(iii) Also, the accepted policy is implemented in a more efficient way as the head of the Attached Office, because of his secretariat status resulting in his closer involvement in policy

formation, is fully aware of the background in which the policy was framed.

Its major drawback, however, is that it does violence to the fundamental principle of secretariat system, namely, policy-making must remain separated from policy implementation. Indeed, this pattern is open to all those criticisms attributed to pattern 2 discussed above.

F. Both the Ministry and the Attached Office have separate and distinct offices and files of their own, and consultation between them occurs through self-contained letter. This is the standard pattern both at the Centre and in the States. This pattern is based on the dichotomy between Staff and Line. The Ministry is Staff: the Attached Office is Line.

An example is the Directorate-General of All India Radio in relation to the Ministry of Information and Broadcasting.

This pattern of relationship enables the scrutiny of a proposal against national and international setting. In other words, a wider perspective is brought to bear on the examination of a proposal,. Secondly, It is always desirable to have a specialist's scheme scrutinised by a layman. In this way the specialist's excessive enthusiasm is kept under healthy control. Thirdly, this arrangement provides for a division of work between the secretariat and the Attached offices. The former concentrates on policy-making and the latter on the execution of the policy. The disadvantages of this arrangement are as follows:

1. This scheme is processed twice in two different Offices . This involves duplication of work and causes delay;

2 The scheme submitted by the head of the department is first examined in the Secretariaft at the assistant's level. The assistant's notes on the scheme tend to confuse the issues and lead to unnecessary queries. In the process, the original intentions of the scheme get distorted and obscured;

3 The objective and detached view taken by the Secretariat which is regarded as an advantage is, in fact, another name for ignorance.

Each pattern has thus advantages as well as disadvantages. No hard and fast rules can be laid down regarding the pattern of relationship which could be appropriate to a particular sphere of governmental activities. The pattern has to be so tailored as to suit the nature of activities or the past experience of the organisation, Nevertheless, neither absolute separation nor absolute merger is normally desirable. These entities need to be brought closer to one another. This can be done by (i) housing both at the same place and (ii) providing common office and common file bureau, serving both the Secretariat Offices and the head of the Attached Offices, This is the model recommended by the second pay Commission as well, The mode, in brief, is "that the Secretariat and the Attached Offices are combined into a single headquarters organisation; a common 'offices' serves the Secretariat offices as well as the head of the department; there is only one file bureau, and all references, including precedents, whether required by the head of Department or by the Secretariat Offices are put up by the same dealing hand and section Offices are put up by the same dealing hand and section officer. At the secretariat level, noting is done by officers of and above the rank of under secretary who have no exclusive 'office' staff' apart from stenographers or stenotypists. Such an arrangement avoids duplication of work, economises on office staff and is conducive to speedy despatch of business."

Ex-officio Secretariat Status

Today, there is a marked desire among the personnel in executive agencies of the Government to get clothed with ex-officio secretariat status, Such a status empowers its holder to act and decide on behalf of the Government, thus enabling him to carry greater weight than he would otherwise, Secondly, there is a belief among non-secretariat personnel that an officer who in the course of his duties, has to correspond with Ministries, state Governments or other high public authorities, must necessarily have secretariat status. Thirdly, as the secretariat status carries with it special privileges and facilities, there is a general hankering after such a rank. While there must be maximum delegation of power, both financial and administrative, to the personnel in the Attached and Subordinate offices, it may not be very prudent or desirable to take recourse to such a line of action. Otherwise, the authority of all those not having *ex-officio* secretariat status is apt to get prejudiced and even whittled down. The Government's policy on conferment of *ex-officio* Secretariat status, formulated as early as 1948, has been that the Secretariat status should be conferred upon only those officers "who (a) sign communications, orders or notifications on behalf of the Government; or (b) within the limits of the Rules of Business or Secretariat Instructions take decisions on behalf of the Government".

Any easy conferment of *ex-officio* Secretariat status on the personnel in Attached Offices will violate the fundamental principle of the Secretariat system, debase the value of the Secretariat designations and, finally, undermine the authority of the functionaries of executive agencies not having *ex-officio* Secretariat status. All this must be guarded against. The demand for a Secretariat status is likely to lose its intensity if the privileges and facilities accompanying it are as a rule extended to non-Secretariat personnel as well. It is, after all, these unshared privileges and facilities which propels the non-Secretariat personnel to demand Secretariat status.

Subordinate Offices

As said, earlier, the Attached Office is the trunk while the Subordinate Office is the limb of the body. A Subordinate Office functions as the field establishment or as the agency responsible for the detailed execution of the decisions taken by the Government. The Second Pay Commission defines these as "Departments or Offices which are responsible mainly for the execution of policies and programmes of the Government."

The Subordinate Office is thus the cutting edge of administration. It normally functions under an Attached Office. But where there is no Attached Office under a Ministry, it operates directly under the Ministry. The example of the latter type is the Inspector of Explosives (Nagpur).

Why a particular organisation has been assigned the status of a Subordinate Office is not often clear. Even the criteria classifying a certain organisation as the Attached Office and another one as the Subordinate Office are neither well-defined nor consistently followed. Indeed, there are hardly any criteria in existence. It is not, therefore, surprising to find many organisations committed to a subordinate status although these are engaged in work of an intricate and arduous nature. Accordingly, the First Pay Commission regarded the distinction between the Attached and Subordinate offices as "artificial" and recommended its abolition. What it wrote in 1947 holds good even today: "A great deal of the present descontent among staff would probably cease if the Secretariat proper is kept distinct from the other offices at the headquarters of the Government, not by upgrading of Attached Offices to Secretariat status but by removing the distinction between Attached and Subordinate Offices. Once the notion of derogatory status is removed and the scales of pay of office staff, whether they serve in a secretariat branch, or in an office of chief executive head at the headquarters of Government or in a local office, are determined purely with reference to the nature of the work; the qualifications required and the field of recruitment necessary for getting suitable personnel, the classification of staff will rest on a proper and rational basis."

Although it is the Subordinate Office which is responsible for the execution of the policy or decision of the Government, and, therefore, for delivering the goods, it has been accorded a distinctly interior status, as is indicated by the label "Subordinate". The pay scales of personnel in the Subordinate Office are the lowest; their service conditions are not attractive; their future prospects are dimmest; and, treatment accorded to his tier needs much to be desired. Work in many Subordinate Offices is intricate and arduous. The employees in these offices do the same type of work and possess the same qualifications as the secretariat personnel. The Secretariat was accorded an unduly high place during the British rule in India, as it was a chosen instrument of imperial control. Reflection of this attitude was the following observation of the Meston Committee (1908):

"We wish to make it quite clear, however, that in our opinion the Imperial secretariat requires in its clerical staff a higher degree of intelligence, a broader outlook and a more discriminating critical than are expected in the office of any provincial government."

This is no longer a valid supposition under the altered political and administrative situation. But, the ghost of Meston is still haunting the corridors of the Secretariat. The Attached Offices have succeeded in acquiring parity in all matters with the Secretariat. The Subordinate Offices, however, continue to be committed to an unreasonably lower status.

10

Automation and Reduction of Paper Work

Need for Automation

The main objective of administrative reforms is to increase the efficiency and effectiveness of the government by increasing productivity. In this scenario, automation and computerisation play an important role, as obsolete office equipment not only leads to a wastage of time on account of difficulty in handling but also does not give the required quality of output. Automation is also important for installing modern communication systems in offices, which can prevent generation of a lot of unnecessary file movement and useless paperwork.

Automation—Existing Scenario

The existing level of automation in government offices is quite inadequate and haphazard. Government offices are still continuing with the traditional machines like manual typewriters, cylostyling machines, etc. Which do not give the required quality of output. Most of the office equipment is outdated and poorly maintained. The telecommunication facilities are insufficient or absent in most of the offices. Furthermore, the office equipment is provided on the basis of designation of the person. The best and most expensive equipment like personal computer is kept in the room of the senior most officer who may either have no knowledge of its operation, or inclination or time to use it. In any case, one single person may not be able to utilise the equipment to its capacity. Thus there is a need to split the equipment into individed and Pooled equipment.

Generation of Useless Paperwork in Offices

Presently government offices generate a lot of useless paperwork in the form of unnecessary report/returns, extended file movement-in many cases for clarification of some minor query which could have been avoided, tedious procedures for disposing of dak, improper filing and the tendency amongst officials to correspond only through the medium of the written word even in cases where requisite information could be easily gathered by phone, personal interaction etc. Such tendencies are a major cause of delay and reduce the level of efficiency in government offices.

COMPARATIVE POSITION

Level of Automation in Other Countries

Most of the other countries have realised the importance of proper office equipment and reduced paperwork in increasing the efficiency of government offices and initiated several steps in that direction. The developed countries of the world have had a very high level of automation with attendant reduction in useless paper work, during the past 2-3 decades. Currently, the United Kingdom invests more than 2 billion Pound Sterling a year and employs 20,000 staff (despite reduction in the overall size of the government) to install and operative various information and telecommunication system. In Canada a blueprint has been designed to substantially change the way in which technology is implemented throughout the government. A 'Software Exchange Service' (SFS) has been opened to promote and facilitate the sharing of government owned application software, and related system between different government organisations at all levels. The level of automation and technology in developing countries is also being upgraded continuously. In Bangladesh, computerisation of government offices has been taken up on a large scale. Alongside O and M techniques like modified personnel manual, standardised job descriptions with MIS are also being utilised. In Malaysia, government offices are increasingly being provided gadgets for image processing, electronic data interchange, work flow automation as an integral part of the endeavour to help government departments to carry out they daily operations more efficiently and effectively and with less amount of paper work.

RECOMMENDATIONS

Heralding Computerisation

The existing manual system of working should be replaced by an automated and computerised system. This change should be initiated from top levels of executives in the government whose commitment to the process of change should be total and visible. The various activities being taken up for computerisation should be prioritised and activities having a public interface, those involving a lot of legal complications and litigation or those that generate a lot of repetitive work should be computerised in the first leg.

The final objective of automation is the creation of the paperless office or the almost paperless office. Once of the fears expressed by officers is that there would be no record of who said what and therefore accountability would be diluted. It is now possible to use devices by which a Government file can be almost replicated on the computer, with sufficient safeguards to ensure that it would always be possible to fix responsibility for statements made by individual officials. We need to educate officials about these techniques, so that there are no unfounded fears on this account.

Proper Training

In the new office, the higher level management will have to be receptive to adopt new technology Proper training would therefore be essential for training the senior officers on both—the skills for operating computers and the appropriate attitude to implement information technology in the organisation. Simultaneously, the general staff would also have to be trained for using the office automation and also to accept technology as a facilitating and supporting system. Sometimes innovative technology programmes are initiated without informing the employees and their unions. This leads to rumours and misunderstandings about the reasons for their introduction. The first impression that the employees get is that they will lose their jobs due to computerisation. Their fears about information technology should be addressed properly through meetings and notices. JCM can play an important role in this respect.

Making the Existing Systems and Procedure Computer Friendly

The introduction of information technology would require changes in the systems and procedures. Each system and procedure would have to be studied in detail and suitable software and hardware implemented for each application. Present forms being used in government are cumbersome and not amenable to being fed in the computers. All such forms would need to be simplified and made both customer and computer friendly. Need to fill in multiple forms should be minimised and ultimately eliminated, once the entire government machinery is properly networked.

Creating Proper Data Base

Computers can be used effectively only if a proper and accurate database is available. Hence a proper database would have to be developed. All government departments should accordingly initiate compilation of available information in a proper format which can be used for building up an extensive database.

Ensuring Compatibility

While initiating computerisation, each ministry and department should design their system in consultation with expert bodies like NIC so as to ensure compatibility within the overall system of the government. The design should also take into account the present and future data volumes and must examine costs and benefits of various alternatives available. This should also be extended to all the field organisations as well. The overall emphasis should be to develop a network in the entire government machinery wherein immediate exchange of data through computers would be facilitated. The system should also contain hierarchical and functional level based codes so that appropriate confidentiality of data is maintained.

Other Office Equipment

Apart from computers, other office equipment which improve the effectiveness and efficiency of employees should also used.

These include Electronic Typewriters, Photocopies, E-Mail which enables the transmission and reception of mail, FAX or telex around the globe. Microfilming Equipment which make miniature copies of records on film and stores the film either on small reels or strip and can be used for reducing the number of files. Scanner which can be used to scan letters and text so that the need for typing the stencils is obviated, etc. Machines should also be utilised for enforcing punctuality in office through electronic recording of attendance and timing of disposal of cases etc.

Procedure to be Adopted

In the whole process of automation, care should be taken to ensure that modern equipment is provided on the basis of needs. Individual equipment should be provided to a person only if he needs its continuously or if work would be hindered or delayed otherwise. This can include equipment like calculator, computer terminal etc. Other equipment which is large and expensive should be kept in a common pool with timings for the use of individuals and sections decided in advance. Such pooled equipment would include fax, photocopier, telex, DTP facilities, NICNET, computer systems, franking machines, scanner, paper shredder, etc. All government offices should have a central pool of equipment like telex, fax photocopiers and word processors in an easily a accessible room which can be used by various officers to taken high quality print-outs for the purpose of correspondence, reports, etc.

Reduction of Paperwork

There are also several steps which need to be taken in order to reduce paperwork in Government. Some recommendations in this regard are as follows:

(a) All forms should be reduced in size and be pared to be barest minimum. Only one copy of the same should be asked for from the customer. More copies, if needed, should be generated in the Government office.

(b) Reports and returns should be reviewed every three months. All unnecessary reports/returns should be discontinued

forthwith. The periodicity of reports/return should be ruthlessly re-examined to see whether their periodicity could be made longer. If a monthly return is converted into a quarterly return, we immediately reduce paperwork by two-thirds.

(c) All officers should be authorised to destroy some incoming papers immediately on receipt. Sometimes the same representation is received from six quarters and adds to the volume of a file. The five extra copies should be destroyed immediately on receipt.

(d) No copy of a letter should be endorsed to any person, unless it is clearly known that it will be useful to him in some way. If such a letter is received by any one who is not concerned with it, he should destroy the same immediately on receipt.

Many such methods for reduction of paperwork can be devised, once one makes up one's mind and trains everyone in Government to think in similar terms.

Improving Productivity

INTRODUCTION

One of the major thrust areas in this Report is the need to improve productivity of Government employees. We have kept this at the forefront of our mind and many of our recommendations have been made with the sole purpose of raising productivity to an optimal level. In this chapter, we will give a few examples of such recommendations.

Three Major Ways

There are three major ways in which productivity is sought to be improved:

(a) By measures that ensure that employees have more time available for work;

(b) By measures that motivate employees to work more;

(c) By measures that improve the productivity of employees through organisational restructuring, use of information technology etc.

Making More Time Available

One of the most obvious ways in which employees can be made more productive is by making more time available for work.

Increasing the number of workings days

The first measure is increasing the number of days available for work in a year. Currently, there are too many holidays in Government and we follow a five days week in a number of

Government offices. Further, there is a tendency to declare a holiday on very flimsy grounds like the death of a VIP or the birth centenary of some departed leader and so on.

Six-day Week

We have recommended the promulgation of the six-day week instead of the five-day week. This single step immediately increases the number of working days by 40. The number of gazetted holidays have been reduced from 17 to 3. This gives another 14 days. We are suggesting that other holidays should be declared only on the death of an incumbent President or Prime Minister and on no other death. This will also increase the number of working days by at least 6 days in a year. Thus we have been able to add a total of 60 days or two months to the number of working days in a year.

Encashment of Leave

We have allowed employees to encash 60 days of earned leave in their service period. Assuming a total service period of about 30 years, such encashment would also increase the number of working days for an employee by an average of two days in a year.

Time Clock

In order to ensure punctuality in attendance, we have suggested the introduction of the time punching system, so that each employee right up to Cabinet Secretary has to punch in his time of arrival and departure. Such a system has worked wonders in Malaysia and it can do so in India too.

Transport Allowance

Punctuality in Government offices becomes a casualty also because employees cannot afford to travel from residence to office in their own vehicles, be these cars, motor bicycle, scooters or bicycles,. We have recommended the grant of a modest transport allowance that would permit most employees to meet at least some part of the heavy expenditure they are compelled to make on commuting to office. It is hoped that this would also promote punctuality.

Serving of Tea on the Table

One major irritant in Government offices is the tendency of employees to use the taking of tea as an excuse to absent themselves from their seats for as long as half an hour at a time. We have recommended arrangements that would ensure the service of tea, coffee, cold drinks and snacks on the table, so that no interruption to the work schedule takes place.

Changing Timings of Service Institutions

Another important recommendation is that Government should change the timings of hospitals and dispensaries, banks, shopping centres, etc. so that these are open in the mornings and evenings when Government employees (and all employees for that matter) are free. This can be done either by introducing a shift system and bifurcating the present staff, or through a split duty system in which case we can pay a split duty allowance to officers and staff. The idea is that Government employees should not have to leave office and transact the business of taking their children to a doctor, shopping or encashing a cheque, on official time.

Motivating Employees to Work More

Having brought the employee to the office in time, having prevented him from getting late in distraction like tea, bank transactions or shopping, and having increased the number of working days is only part of the battle. How is the employee to be encouraged to work more?

Output-based Budgeting

We are suggesting budgeting and financial reforms that will convert our budgets to documents outlining the outputs and outcomes of departmental work instead of being obsessed with inputs. If implemented in the right spirit, it will bring about management by objectives, with every employee knowing exactly what his duties are what kind of output is expected from him and putting in his best to meet the laid down targets.

Productivity and Bonus

All incentive schemes have to be productivity-linked. Bonus

is supposed to be so. Unfortunately, many of the bonus schemes currently in operation are linked to production and not to productivity. We have suggested certain modifications so that there is no automatic increase in the quantum of bonus merely by efflux of time, but there is a direct link established between productivity and bonus. We are also suggesting the conversion of ad hoc bonus schemes into productivity-linked bonus schemes.

Performance Appraisal

Performance appraisal is another area of reform. If we develop better methods of appraisal, which are linked to actual performance in qualitative and qualitative terms, and link promotion and other incentives to such objective appraisal, we would be creating the best motivation for higher productivity.

Weeding out of the Incompetent

As part of the appraisal system, we are suggesting a ruthless weeding out of the incompetent and corrupt elements at the time of promotion to the Senior Administration Grade. If this is linked to performance, it will have very salutary results.

Performance Related Increment

We are also introducing the Performance Related Increment scheme, under which an employee's performance during the previous year would determine whether be remains where he is, earns an increment or is given two increments instead of one. This is a precursor to Performance Related Pay, which can be introduced at a latter stage.

Appraisal of Group 'D' Employees

Group 'D' employees currently do not face an annual performance appraisal. This is because they had no promotion avenues so far. Having introduced the four-grade structure for these employees, we have also brought the ACR back. There will thus be increased pressure on them to perform.

Specific Suggestions on Productivity

In the case of certain departments we have made specific

suggestions for improving productivity. For example, 25 per cent of running allowance has been linked to the punctual running of trains. Similarly, if a pension payment order is delayed due to the negligence of someone in Government, he was have to pay interest to the affected employee for the period of delay. For the telephone department, we have suggested a coloured points systems, with red for bad work and green for good work, the points being added every months to arrive at a numerical assessment of the productivity of telephone mechanics. There is also a recommendation for customer opinion surveys to ascertain the views of customers of services provided by the Government.

Other Measures for Increasing Productivity

There are other measures that have a very direct and positive impact on productivity. Some of these are briefly mentioned in the succeeding paragraphs.

Organisational Restructuring

Organisational restructuring include a number of steps like amalgamation of Ministries and departments, delegation of administrative and financial powers, delaying, level-jumping, the introduction of the Desk. Officer system, functional multi-skilling and creation of new cadres like those of Executive assistants and Office Attendants etc. All these will lead to greater efficiency and thus to higher productivity.

Reducing Numbers

There are also numerous suggestions for reducing the numbers in Government employment through privatisation, contracting out of services transfer of functions, schemes and organisations to the State Governments, or their conversion into cooperative institutions, PSUs and autonomous bodies revision of norms etc. Many of these recommendations will lead to higher productivity per employee from among those who are left in the Government.

Simplification of Procedures

Office procedures prescribed in government organisations at present are very complex, cumbersome and time consuming. Such procedures often lead to a greater emphasis on observation of the prescribed norms rather than maintaining productivity. Procedures in all government offices need to be simplified and made less tedious and time consuming.

Accountability

A shift has to be made towards accountability in the positive sense where in a greater emphasis will be laid on achieving the end result rather than a mere adherence to rules and procedures. This will also provide government employees with the necessary impetus to try out various innovative approaches for increasing productivity.

Automation

Then there is the whole field of office automation, reduction of paperwork, computerisation, introduction of information technology etc. Which is likely to cause a quantum jump in the productivity of Central Government employees.

Ensuring Right of Redress

It is inevitable that the large size of the Government machinery and the plethora of services provided by it should generate grievances. These can be broadly divided into two types—grievances of customers and grievances of employees.

Withdrawal of Government

One major policy thrust that can reduce both is the withdrawal of Government from areas that can be transferred to the corporate of private sector. This option has to be pursued vigorously.

Need for Effective Redressal

But for areas that remain with the Government, an efficient grievance redressal machinery has to be an integral part of civil service reforms. It has to be effective, speedy, objective, readily accessible and easy to operate. It has also to be well publicised so that aggrieved parties are aware of not only the available recourse but also the forum for lodging the complaint.

EXPERIENCE OF OTHER COUNTRIES

Malaysia

Other countries have tried to build effective grievance redressal mechanisms. In Malaysia, a Public Complaints Bureau has been created in the Prime Minister's Office. It has the status of an independent organisation to look into complaints against public agencies. It is the main channel for the public to forward their grievances against public servants. Several steps have been taken to inform the public about their right of redress.

United Kingdom

In the U.K., the Citizens' Chapter (1991) introduced mechanisms for registering and redressing complaints made by customers. Government took steps to publicize the procedures for lodging complaints. A Complaint Task Force was created for setting up improved complaints systems. A telephone helpline called "charterline" was installed to help people to find out more about public services as also how to lodge complaints about them. A post of Ombudsman was created to deal with complaints of alleged injustice caused by Government's maladministration. If other attempts at redress failed, individuals could approach the Ombudsman through their Members of Parliament.

Canada

A Department of Public Works and Government Services was opened in Canada, in order to permit members of the public to lodge formal and informal complaints. The Canadian International Trade Tribunal was appointed in order to receive and decide upon complaints in respect of award of Government contracts to private parties.

Consultants' Advice

Tata Consultancy Services have suggested that all public grievances should be received and acknowledged only at one point. The Department of Public Grievances should function as a nodal department and forward the complaints to the respective departments for necessary action in a time-bound manner. Creation of a grievance committee for handling grievances of employees has also been suggested.

EXISTING SYSTEM

Department of Public Grievances

As in everything else, we already have a public grievance redressal machinery in place. At the apex is the Department of Public Grievances, under the charge of a full-fledged Secretary who reports directly to Cabinet Secretary. It registers all public grievances received either from individuals or from the newspapers and forwards the same to be concerned Ministries. Action taken thereon is monitored closely.

Special Cells

Individuals can also file their grievances with the concerned Ministry or Department directly. Most Ministries have special cells under senior officers for looking into such grievances. People also request their public representatives to intercede for them with the Ministers or senior officials.

Defect in Present System

The trouble with the present system is that it is not worked properly, due to the following reasons:

(a) The concept of customer orientation is almost non-existent;

(b) Government officials are not properly trained in effective grievance redressal;

(c) There is no pinpointed responsibility for each task;

(d) Responsibility for non-redressal of a grievance is not fixed there and then;

(e) No reward or punishment system exists;

(f) There is no systematic attempt to assess the customers' opinions;

(g) Multi-tier institutional mechanisms have not been developed;

(h) There is no institution outside the departmental machinery which could effectively intervene on behalf of the aggrieved person.

Our Recommendations

An effective grievance redressal machinery has to be put in place, so that each of the above defects is taken care of. Our recommendations try to achieve this objective.

Citizens' Charter

There has to be a Citizens' Charter, defining the rights of the customers of Government schemes and services. Each department has to publish its own Charter, defining its standards of performance, fixing time limits, setting out the grievance redressal mechanisms, stating what redress would be made. For example, the Department of Telecommunications will have to state how much time it will take to set a telephone in order. Suppose it stipulates 24 hours. If it fails to rectify a defect within that period, it will have to pay damages to the subscriber. Each Government employee has to understand that he is a public servant in every sense of the term and he has to serve the public. That is the only reason for his existence. The idea that Government employees dispense favours to members of the public has to be buried once for all.

Attitudinal Change

Officers have to be trained in effective grievance redressal. There are some basic principles for this. Each officer has to maintain an open door policy. His doors have to be always open to the members of the public, to listen to their grievances. Disposal of paperwork has to be second priority. So long as papers are given more importance than people, our administrative systems cannot improve. Intervention has to be personal, by calling the concerned official or by ringing him up. Deadlines have to be set for each task. The completion of each task has to be monitored. No backchat is to be tolerated from subordinates. Each person is to be trained in problem solving, and in fighting our innate tendency to pass the buck to someone else.

Pinpointing of Responsibility

The distribution of work in Government officers has to be done in such a way that you can always pinpoint responsibility on a single individual. No one who is called upon to perform a task should be able to claim that it is not his job. If he is held responsible for non-performance, he should not be able to wriggle out.

Performance Appraisal

Whenever a grievance is redressed or not redressed within the time limit prescribed by the organisation, there should be an automatic mechanism for recording of the performance there and then. It should be recorded for several purposes. It should go into a data bank which records the performance of the individual. That should enable the department to prepare a Monthly Performance Appraisal, which should be communicated to the individual. The other use to which the information can be put is the determination of the individual's entitlement to a financial reward or punishment.

Reward and Punishment

A simple system in the telephone maintenance wing of DOT could award green points for good work and red points for slipshod work. At the end of the month, all the green and red points could be totalled up, to give either a net green (plus) or red (minus) figure. That figure could determine whether the individual would be entitled to an incentive or a deduction. In other departments, it could be linked with (say) running allowance in the railways or performance-linked bonus in the postal department or a cash incentive in a defence workshop.

Customer Opinion Surveys

We require a well organised system of Customer Opinion Surveys, which could give us feedback about the performance of an organisation or individuals within it. These may be conducted internally, through units dedicated to the task of Performance Appraisal or by engaging private survey agencies on a contractual basis.

Institutional Mechanism for Redressal

A multi-tier institutional mechanism has to be developed for grievance redressal. This means that only grievances which cannot or are not redressed at a particular level will travel to the next higher level. A grievance will keep on travelling up the hierarchy, as long as it is not solved. There should be automatic mechanisms which alert each higher level about the unresolved grievances at the next lower level as soon as the stipulated standard time has elapsed. One of the methods could be that of Lok Adalat or Social Audit Group.

Sarvochha Lok Adalat

The highest tier of grievance redressal at the bureaucratic level should be the Secretary (Public Grievances), who should be one of the senior most Secretaries to the Government of India. He should be able to hold a monthly meeting to discuss unresolved grievances which need attention at his level. The meeting should have representatives of the administrative Ministry, and the Ministries of Finance and Law, all of whom are fully empowered to commit their Ministries to any course of action that may be jointly decided upon. In important cases, therefore, concerned Secretaries may attend the meeting personally. The aggrieved party should also have the right to make a verbal representation before this forum, which may be called the Sarvochha (Apex) Lok Adalat. Decisions of this Adalat should be final and binding on all the Ministries of Central Government.

Calling for Departmental Files

The Secretary (Public Grievances) is currently authorised to call for the file pertaining to any case of any Ministry and to pass any orders that he may deem fit, taking all the circumstances into account. It is not known how often or whether at all he exercises this power. But it would be salutary to have this power vest in him, and wherever necessary he could obtain the approval of the Cabinet Secretary or the Prime Minister, to lend the necessary weight and finality to his decision.

Ombudsman

We also need an Ombudsman outside the routine bureaucratic machinery. This could be a retired Judge or senior bureaucrat, who may be given a Constitutional or legal staus. He would be available for attending to unresolved grievances and could intervene in critical matters. His hearings could be public, but without there being any lawyers. The complaint and the representative of the Government department could be heard and an appropriate order passed either setting a time limit to the matter being resolved by the department or in the case of a dispute, even deciding what line of action should be pursued.

GRIEVANCES OF EMPLOYEES AND PENSIONERS

Machinery

The grievances of employees and pensioners will have to be mainly dealt with by having multi-level points of grievance redressal, starting from the immediate boss and travelling through the layers of head of office, head of department, administrative secretary and so on. Time limits for grievance redressal should be fixed and adhered to.

Grievance Committee

Each Ministry should have an Employees Grievance Committee chaired by the Secretary. This should be the apex of a hierarchy of such Committees, starting from the field level. Unresolved grievances should travel quickly up the hierarchy, so that matters are set right within the shortest possible time. Personal hearings should also be allowed at each level.

Pension Adalat

For pensioners, we must create a multi-tier effective Pension Adalat system, fully empowered at each level to take short cuts, short-circuit procedures, reduce paperwork and come to reasonable, commonsense decisions which resolve the matter in issue on the spot. For policy matters, SCOVA should be fully empowered in the manner of the JCM, as has been mentioned in another Chapter.

13

Administration and Control

In the most common sense, government consists of a group of individuals who share a defined responsibility for exercising power. In this sense, the definition refers to the cases where government is sovereign as well as to the cases where it is not so. But in case of the sovereign government with a 'defined responsibility' taking the shape of its legitimacy in the sense of the sanctified right to exercise power on behalf of others by means of decision making, the concept turn out to be a government being a group of individuals exercising legitimate authority, and maintaining, protecting and adapting the society by making and carrying out decisions along with exercising a practical monopoly of coercive powers.

Governance is the manner in which authority, control and power of government is exercised in mobilising a society's economic and social resources to address the issues of public interest. It is the art of governing, associated with the exercise of authority. Good governance is epitomised by, among other things, predictable, open and enlightened policy making. It can be secured by sound, responsive and competent administration, respect to basic human rights and values, strengthened democratic institutions and effective institutional as well as structural framework to ensure accountability and transparency.

Limits of Variation

There are at least two main limits of variation upon a sovereign government. The first is the *efficacy* of the government. It means the capacity of administration government to cater to the needs of society. The second is the *form* of the government. It refers to the internal structure of a given type of government. Both the efficacy and the form are related to each other in the sense that when one type of government is made to change into another, it is generally related to the efficacy or performance of a particular government. A limit upon government is evident when for any reason, for example, inability to take decisions, failures to comply with widely distributed but central values, it can no longer function. If the situation cannot be remedied by changing the incumbents of political office, in other words, if the political roles and supporting offices are no longer acceptable, then the legitimacy is withdrawn, indicating that the system of government is no longer deemed appropriate by the public. It means that the limits of the government have been breached. In that situation, change from one type of government to another is most certainly to occur.

Normative, Structural and Behavioural Aspects of Government

In general, the forms of government can be classified dichotomously in as follows with a considerable scope of overlapping: (i) democratic or totalitarian; (ii) presidential or monarchical; (iii) pluralistic or monastic; (iv) competitive or monopolistic; so on and so forth. Such distinctions are based on two important factors, namely, the organisation of government and the degree of control it exercises over the society. In other words, these factors combine the moral or normative dimension of government while the structural and behavioural aspects of government. Justice, equity, equality, etc., are the abstract themes under normative aspects of government. Though these aspects people define their lasting values, their ideas of right and wrong. It is these normative aspects by means of which speculations about the aims and activities of government are made in terms of the central values and ultimate aims of a political community, and thus defining the political legitimacy of the government. The structural aspects or principles of government deal with the arrangements and instruments involved in governmental decision making. These are also related to normative issues as far as the form of government is taken to be a means of attaining the ends of society. A study of structural dimension leads to the analysis or alternative forms of government along with normative considerations, in order to assess the most suitable form which can realise the goals of society by means of governmental decision-making. Both classicists (interested in normative issues) and structuralists assumed political/ governmental behaviour to be a condition of conflict. A propensity to conflict is regarded as the normal political expression of human nature by both groups of the thinkers. Hobbes treated this assumption as "the war of all against all". Thus both Plato and Hobbes sought authoritation governments to deal with the condition of conflict as the best means to control it. Other thinkers have suggested a division of power as the best way to regulate conflict. Some combinations of normative and structural theories have been called institutionalist approaches. Carl Friedrich, Harold Laski and Herman Finer as institutionalists concerned with the normative and structural relations between law, constitutional forms, and governmental procedures in wide historical, religious and economic contexts. In current times, studies in government are characterised by the refinement of structural theories into a system leading to a set of interrelated elements which can be integrated with behavioural theories.

ANALYSIS OF GOVERNMENT

Theoretically all forms of government in the world can be analysed through two basic approaches. There are: (i) Mechanistic; and (ii) organismic.

The Mechanistic Approach

The assumption underlying the approach is that the society is composed of competing and interacting interests (both individual and group) and these generate conflict, and it is the responsibility of government to resolve such conflict. Thus, government is an agency for finding solutions to remove tension in the political system. As government possesses a decision-making device, which responds to tensions in the system, the appropriate action is supposed to be forthcoming. A representative model in this approach takes behavioural tensions as "inputs" or stimuli affecting political leaders, who, while responding to them, make decisions or "outputs". Thus,

$$S \rightarrow G \rightarrow D$$

where S represents society (providing inputs), *G* government, and *D* policy decisions (outputs).

Here the social system is a national society and government responds to a variety of stimuli (inputs) generated in the society. These inputs may include customs and beliefs (normative characteristics), classes and interests (structural characteristics), and preferences and perceptions (behavioural characteristics). In this view, the government is cast in the role of mediator and judge in conflicts between contending parties. The law of the land embodies the principles of structural organisation. This law serves as the basic framework for all other forms of organisation. Normative consensus adheres to maintenance of this legal framework. Government supports and strengthens the consensus by ensuring utmost realisation of norms already held.

The normative assumption which underlies this approach indicates that a social system is composed of individuals or groups with an equal right for representatives. The structural assumption is that a government must reflect proper representation; and the behavioural assumption being that competitive conflict between the members of the social system gives thrust to representative forms imperatively. This approach presupposes following characteristics of the system:

1. The individual is the unit of which the social system is composed of;
2. The ends of the individual are maximised;
3. The structure of government is organised in such a way that a plurality of ends of maximised;
4. The decisions of government, by maximising a plurality of ends, maintain a balance or harmony in the system; and
5. The principle of legitimacy is equity.

The *mechanistic* basis in this approach reflects that government is a contrivance. Its origin is not organic, rather it is established. It is endowed with each structural principle with a predictable consequence. The Western democratic governments show a pattern of variants of this conception. The constitutions of many of the Afro-Asian nations were adopted with this general approach.

The Organismic Approach

Under this classical approach, both Plato and Aristotle related government to the evolution of human society from lower to higher forms; thus making government essentially an educational body, embodying a set of ideals and perfecting rationality. Hegel gave this conception its most powerful rationale, while Marx brought it into popular understanding. Marx saw in the evolution of man's higher purposes a relationship between change in the material world and the unfolding human consciousness. Government happens to be an instrument of this relationship. Thus, government has its own cycle; an instrument of revolutionary action, if successful, it represents the most dynamic class; it comes to power as the instrument which must transform revolutionary impetus into practical accomplishment; after this accomplishment, it is rendered anachronistic and vulnerable until the final stage, when government itself is no longer in need. "The ultimate aim of Aristo-democracy, Herder saw in the disappearance of statistical as an administrative 'machine' of government, and its replacement by an 'organic' way of ordering social life, in which active cooperation would render all forms of subordination obsolete and superfluous".

The orgasmic evolutionary concept implies a role for government, which directs society towards higher ends. This approach is also enriched by ecclesiastic and theocratic ideals. This emphasises the role of the society over and against the role of the individual. Modern organic conceptions elevate man to a central position; however, these emphasize that the society is the instrument of his perfection. It is in accordance with such views that revolutionary governments treat themselves as the instruments of social transformation. Thus, in this approach we have.

$$G \rightarrow D \rightarrow CS$$

where G denotes government (providing inputs), *D* policy decisions, and *CS* changes in the social system (outputs).

Here, the government is the instrument by means of which changes are produced in the social system. The government defines the objects and purposes of the changes (normative characteristics). The organisation of government (structural characteristics) is done in accordance as the best means for accomplishing the predetermined purposes; and the activities of the government include the symbolic manipulations which are carried on through education, media of communications, etc. This is imperatively needful to affect both the content and manner of policy decision-making which are required to achieve desirable changes in the social system.

In the mechanistic approach, government (*G*) is the dependent variable and social system (*S*) is the independent variable. Power is presumed to be inherent in the public, which creates the inputs of stimuli to which government must respond. In the organismic approach, government (*G*) is the independent variable and social system (*S*) the dependent one. Governments in this approach tend to the centralised in the form of their authority. They tend to convert their objects and goals into norms and treat them sacred and ethical precepts by means of which the legitimacy is defined. The mechanistic type of governments tend to be competitive, pluralistic, and democratic; while the tendency of organismic type of governments remains to be monopolistic, monistic, and totalitarian. *Normatively,* the mechanistic type is more secular than the organismic type. *Structurally,* the first type is less hierarchically organised. *Behaviourally,* the first type relies heavily on internalised norms and self-control, rather than on external authority. Both the types of governments in their various concrete forms are perpetually vulnerable to each other, and thus a continuous dialogue of conflict is obtained between them over time.

The dialogue of conflict referred to above itself renders some implications. To explore these implications the differences between the two political norms, namely, sacred and secular ones, happens to be very important, because it draws our attention to the normative basis of a government and, therefore, to its legitimacy. Normative conflict arises out of sacred and secular beliefs.

Sacred Political Norms

Sacredness does not apply only to theocratic or primitive societies; rather it applies as well to many modern states. The sacred qualities of Marxism-Leninism in the erstwhile Soviet Union were enshrined in an elaborate philosophical system. Even in modern China, Mao's prescriptive sayings assumed such a sacred characteristic as to define the basis of political legitimacy. Many nations betray this characteristic (though in a lesser degree) when an attempt is made to ritualise the authority of a charismatic or highly personalistic leader by endowing his words and teaching attaching special significance thereto. All governments, in general, possess some sacred qualities, either elaborate and ideological or tockenly symbolic such as a flag, a constitutional document, etc. These aspects of government may be ceremonial or may represent a means by which the solidarity and unity of a society could be properly expressed.

There are three main varieties of sacred attachments which may overlap each other. These are:

(i) The *primordial* attachments which refer to beliefs about race, language, and nationality (a typical expression of primordial attachment is nationalism);

(ii) The *philosophical* attachments (the most generalised moral and philosophical ideal in which a total synthesis is expressed relating to man to his environment and specifying the way of the future is to be found in socialism); and

(iii) The *religious* attachments (this refers to religious beliefs in which the origin of the society, moral purpose, and a particular pattern of transcendental beliefs are associated in a universal religious doctrine).

Secular Political Norms

Secular political norms generally rely on a framework of rules rather than on some lofty objects of State. Common examples of secular systems are those in which the sacred elements have diminished by means of institutionalisation. Although sacred norms do not disappear, but these become a part of the accepted pattern of right and wrong that these are ritually referred to on certain occasions. And the ceremony has taken place of the substance of belief for these sacred attachments. The governments adopting secular norms reserve 'higher' goals to the individual, and these goals are taken to be inherent in the individual's body of private beliefs. If governments should violate these norms, they run the risk of overstepping their *limits of variation* and of being eliminated.

Forms of Authority

There are two forms of authority to be considered here, which have relevance to government. These are centralised authority and decentralised authority.

Centralised Authority

The power under centralised form begins from the top and is applied downward through a specific delegation of authority. A bureaucracy or a military organisation represents this system of hierarchy for power flows. Government in this case may be represented by as single figurehead, a king or dictator, or by an oligarchy or junta. In such highly centralised system, the following types of characteristics are observed:

1. The concentrated power is subject to few checks;
2. The power inheres at the top;
3. The subordinate authority is derivative of the main authority; and
4. There is strong reliance on the personality of a particular leader.

Decentralised Authority

Under decentralised authority, power is generated by the public through the aggregation of their political wants. It is expressed through various groups, and is regulated by an abstract system of rules. The usual normative expressions of decentralised authority include the acceptance of the principle of majority rule, protection of rights, and representation. A democratic government is ushered in which such dencentralisation, with check and balances, and parliamentary control over the executive. The political recruitment to sensitive positions is undertaken by some form of election. However, such practices do not exhaust the forms of decentralisation. It may also be functional, in which case the allocation of the economic power in society is made among various groupings, such as industrial/commercial chambers, protective unions, professional association, and other interests groups.

Models of Government

Based on political norms adopted and the type of authority practised, governments in the world can be typologically categorised as follows:

Type A. Governments in this system are highly centralised and sacred. They represent modern populist totalitarian governments;

Type B. This type consists of the governments which adopt centralised authority with secular political norms, representing many autocratic systems of government;

Type C. In this system, governments follow sacred political norms with decentralised authority. This represents many early forms of theocratic society, spanning from the feudalism of the Middle Ages in Europe to religious or theocratic governments in America;

Type D. Almost all modern democratic governments practising secular political norms and decentralised power of authority comprise this type of the system.

Sacred and Centralised Governments

In this sacred-centralised type of the system *A,* government activities as the independent variable and is generally associated with a new moral framework. Countries where major revolutions have taken place or have gained independence in recent times, this system works well and fittingly applicable. Some variants of this system are described in paras that follows:

Communist Governments

The sacred-centralised type of communist governments have high degree of centralisation which encompasses the total society. The sacred goal of governments remains to transform the material conditions of life and the consciousness of the people. A Communist party providing a militant leadership and the spearhead of government seeks the evolution of the community in the sense of a moral objective. In the Leninist form of the communist regime, no competitive sources of power could be tolerated. This system formed the models of state organisation for all other communist systems for a long time. However, two important features may be observed in this system since the death of Stalin. First, the sacred quality of Marxist-Leninist ideology has declined, as younger generations find it less significant as a doctrine than as a ritual. Secondly, a trend towards decentralisation has started to pick up. A conflict is there between the communist political leaders and the technical specialists, economists, scientists, etc. Alternative structural transformations have taken place in Hungary, Yugoslavia, Poland and within the 15 constituents of the erstwhile Soviet Union. In the case of Hungary and Poland, cultural decentralisation, and in the case of Yugoslavia economic decentralisation represented the moves for providing greater freedom. However, the communist models became much attractive to governments in developing countries which wanted to follow the Soviet pattern of rapid industrialisation for several decades.

Fascist Governments

Notwithstanding the structural similarities between communist and fascist governments, particularly with respect to the roles of a powerful totalitarian political leader and a weak set of parliamentary institutions, one important difference is worth mentioning. Communist governments are monolithic, emphasising the evolution of the entire community; while fascist governments tolerated certain corporate groupings. The developmental or evolutionary sacred ideology around which communist governments try to organise their societies embodies certain universalised moral goals. In contrast, the sacred attachments of fascist governments showed greater attraction to primordial sentiments, such as race, nationality, etc. Germany, Italy, and Spain remained the three particular examples of fascist governments. Although all the three were highly centralised, but they varied considerably with respect to the sacredness and secularity of political norms.

There were important normative ambiguities in both the German and Italian systems for which they tried to resolve in the apotheosis of violence. This was clearly observed in their total repudiation of democratic, decentralised forms of government. Both the German and Italian fascism represented an authentic totalitarian populism, in which medieval ideas of corporation, organic concepts of the society, and primordial sentiments were interwinded within a highly centralised system of administrative government. The Spanish case has been less ideological and less centralised. It has been more autocratic than totalitarian, as it remains an extension of an old and established bureaucratic system which traces its roots to the imperial Spanish tradition, the Inquisition, and a centralised monarchy.

Secular and Centralised Governments

A secular-centralised system of government has several important features. These include autonomous power in the hands of a president or monarch, a single political party, whether in the form of an elite (a communist party) or a populist mass party with an elite centre (most nationalist parties), a truncated or largely ritualistic parliament which does not have a real veto power over the executive, and an election system which does not allow effective competition between candidates for political office. Several characteristic common problems are observed in all forms of such centralised governments except in the case of the institutionalised monarchies. Two most important problems are: succession to high public office (which is usually accompanied by severe struggles for power), and the institutionalisation of disagreement.

The cases of secular-centralilsed governments include Czarist Russia (notwithstanding some important theocratic elements incorporated in the role of the Czar), and Bismarck's Germany.

Some examples are colonial administrative governments in British and French Africa, South Asia, the Netherlands, the East Indies, and the Belgian Congo. Many of the newly independent nations have gone from one from of highly centralised system, under colonialism, to another, in the from of one-party government, but with a change in the quality of political norms. The norms often become endowed with intense attachment to primordial loyalties associated with race and nation and, to a lesser degree, with some aspects of socialism and public ownership all wrapped up in a particular ideological message, such as Nasserism in Egypt, Nkrumahism in Ghana, or Gandhism-Nehruism in India.

Sacred and Decentralised Governments

The genesis of Western democratic governments is traced to a synthesis of generally agreed religious values. This synthesis is linked with a generalised Christian ethic. The theocratic origins of democratic governments are very crucial in this regard. Successive American governments in the past adopted a unified set of Christian theological precepts. Law was based on the prior conception of agreed principles of political propriety. The formation of these principles can be found in many different theologically articulated forms, including the religious was between Catholics and Protestants and between various Protestant groups as well. These issues were so important to politics that much of the process of secularisation can itself be traced to the search for some mutually agreeable and satisfactory common denominator of precepts in order to render politics more secular. In the United States, this was clearly recognised in the works of Brooks and Henry Adams, both of whom saw the modern economic State, with its emphasis on instrumental values, economic exchange, and corporate finance, as destroying the implicit basis of the original Christian values. Where new constitutional governments have been most successful, they have evolved a shared set of political norms deriving from a previous period when such norms were explicitly sacred. The aforesaid account shows that almost all modern secular-decentralised governments are successive to their earlier various forms of sacred-decentralised ones.

Secular and Decentralised Governments

With the spread of secularisation in Western societies, theological obligations gave way to codes of civic regulations. Religion was substituted by law providing the basis for political norms. Increasing prosperity in Europe propagated the idea that beneficial political condition could be created by free and democratic governments with maximum political participation for all people. During the 19th century, preferential attempts were made to incorporate the entire membership of a society through constitutional democracy rather than modifying the structural principles of government. A government was widely viewed analogous to the approach of classical economics. In this view, the society is composed of voters, whose choice like that of consumers tantamounts to consumer sovereignty. Through the election system resembling the market system, voters choose their representatives in accordance with the stated preferences serving as the basis of their choice. Government, consisting of parliament and cabinet together with administrative bureaucracy is taken similar to the productive unit and manufacturing decisions. The evaluation of government is done by the public through electoral mechanism. The presence of the courts is to ensure that no violation of the rules of the system is committed. The principles on the basis of which the system works refer, among others, to a high level of information, rationality as an attribute of voting and decision making, and equal representation. Such principles underlie the American form of presidential government and the utilitarian systems advocated by John Stuart Mill and the Benthamites in England. Supporters of this type of system advocate improvement of information, provision of education to achieve rationality, and improvement of electoral systems to obtain the maximum placement of public wants in a representative assembly.

One of the important problems in this system is whether proportional representation should be preferred to simple majority voting or some combination of weighted balloting or some different criteria. Questions also arise about the role of political parties in government. The principle of majority rule implies in effect that the degree of support obtained by a particular doctrine is the true measure of power which is created by that support. Thus, majority rule is a principle of power which provides credit to the rationality of the majority and uplifts reason as well the numbers above abstract morality; and thereby the instrumentalities tend to take on their own moral obligations.

There are two alternative forms that have stressed the idea of the organic society rather than the mechanistic doctrine of individualism. The first is an extension of the medieval doctrine. It incorporates Catholic beliefs in the context of a decentralised State. Various specific approach to democratic government, such as Christian socialism and Christian democracy are upheld in this form. The second form is democratic socialism. It puts more emphasis on the democratic State as a means of fulfilling conditions of equality and freedom together with the development of the moral and material basis of the society.

NATURE OF DEMOCRATIC GOVERNMENTS

Functionally, the democratic governments can be classified into two different ways. First, they are categorised as unitary and federal systems. The unitary governments are based on the position that all powers, not otherwise reserved, belong to a central government; while the federal governments take the position that residual powers lie with the constituent geographical units which make up the federation. Secondly, they can be divided into presidential and parliamentary forms. Generally, in a presidential system, a president elected by the people is responsible to them, rather than to the legislature; while the legislature is also responsible to the people who elect it, and not to the president. Thus, a provision of checks and balances is made with the people acting as arbiters during periodic elections held at fixed intervals. In the parliamentary system, parliament is treated as supreme. A Prime Minister is responsible to it and holds his/her office at its pleasure. A government can fall through vote of confidence and changes in parliamentary party membership. In case of the fall of government, a new general election to parliament becomes imperative. The majority of plurality of seats won by a political party provides a mandate to form a government. Under parliamentary system of government, the President (or monarch) is largely a figurehead.

The concern of democratic governments lies with the problems faced in the growing complexity of modern life and fulfilling the expectations which individuals have from a secular government as such. While the problem in most of the decades of 20th Century remained in terms of improvement of electoral and representation methods, the present emphasis is on the work-load of parliaments, congresses or assemblies. Both the unitary and federal systems now accept the principle of one person, one vote. 'Popular sovereignty' Tends to mean a parliamentary representation embodying territorial and demographic bases. To maintain debate on important issues and to get through a heavy legislative workload have become a very ticklish job in modern parliament. Parliament divides according to the directions given by the party whips. A free vote (each member voting according to his/her conscience) has become rare in today's environment. Some form of cabinet dictatorship' is supposed to maintain discipline in parliament in these days. The quality of working of parliamentary or cabinet forms of decentralised democratic government depends on the quality of work of government carried out by the relevant political parties. This is affected by various kinds of structural rules. In multiparty systems, sometimes cabinet instability occurs, as all decentralised and democratic forms of government have some means to control the executive and this is not an easy mechanism. Therefore, the stability of such parliamentary governments depends on the stability of certain conditions. Where parliament is characterised by two political parties, instability is rare. This is partly on account of rigorous party discipline maintained by the parliamentary parties.

Presently, highly individualistic conceptions of democracy have been replaced by notions of group representation, block voting, and responsiveness of government to various groups, such as professional bodies; business lobbies; trade unions; cooperative movements; civic associations; veterans' organisation; religious organisatous; educational, cultural and welfare groups; etc. All these factors refer to the relations between society and government. Thus, some intervening variables function between society administration government. These intervening variables take the form of political parties, interest groups, subgroups within government itself, and other such entities. Symbolically, the whole political process may take the form of the following model.

$$S \rightarrow IV_1 \rightarrow IV_2 \rightarrow G \rightarrow DA$$

where S = Social system (providing inputs); IV_1 = Intervening variables in terms of political parties, interest groups, etc; IV_2 = Intervening variables in terms of electoral methods, political recruitment, etc.; G = government in terms of chief executive and cabinet, parliament and committees, senior bureaucracy (administrative machinery), etc.; and DA = Decisions and actions in terms of policy decisions, socialisation, amelioration and integration, etc. (The outputs).

GOVERNMENTS IN DEVELOPING COUNTRIES

The governments in those nations who achieved independence after World War II, have a tendency to include main characteristics of all the forms/models which have been discussed earlier in this analysis. In Africa and several parts of Asia, there are attachments to primitive governments, which remain in competition with central government for the loyalties of the people. Regional clusters associated with a religious or linguistic affiliation may represent powerful primordial loyalties, denying legitimacy to a central government or countering it with a preference for local primordial attachments; thus, creating serious problems for unity and legitimacy within the context of a nation. Moreover, these nations clearly emphasise the positive role of government as the main instrument of social change, actively intervening in all aspects of life, from family relationships to educational opportunities, from road building to the development of local airways. In this respect, government functions as an independent variable.

However, even among developing countries, most constitutional patterns follow the line of Western parliamentary government. Sufficient parliamentary control is maintained through the instrumentality of party discipline. It is also possible to retain popular government based on parliamentary practice and a cabinet system along with few formal checks on the executive.

Practically, the governments of the nations who became independent in the late 40s and afterwards in 20th Century have become various types of amalgams of the models which have been described earlier in this study in terms of theocratic, communist, fascist, and democratic. Their genesis in primitive government is identifiable in normative terms, with a mythical past providing a national identity. The communist emphasis on puritarnism, public ownership, and discipline is represented in recruitment of a developmental elite and in its method of exercising power; while fascist governments continue to give representation to corporate functional groups in some sense. Western democratic ideals and some of the procedures are accommodated commonly in the pattern of parliamentary governments with the populist democratic emphasis.

The various models of government analysed here appear to be so antithetical that it would seem very difficult to blend them into a viable and effective system of government. Thus, most of the governments in developing countries are in the process of changing into some more stable type. In most cases, what holds a government together is allegiance to a particular political leader, connected with a revolution or a mass movement. These governments generally depend on a personalised leader supported by a dominant political party. In certain cases, the crucial factors are the relationship between the leader of the government and the leader of the party, and the role of the party. Quite often, the first two are the same person, and the party exercises the power of the government. Hence, it can be inferred that these sorts of governments theoretically act as an independent variable *vis a vis* their respective social systems. However, functionally these governments reflect the expression of the elite which manipulates a large political party which itself represents a wide diversity of interests. In the process, government and social system tend to be incorporated into the broader concept of a single political party. Party becomes the independent variable, with government the intervening one, and the social system the dependent one. Even where there is more than one party, the situation is not very different. There may be several dominant national or regional (tribal, linguistic, ideological or otherwise influential) parties, rather than one party, however, none are deeply committed to a single ideology, and in this they differ sharply from communist or fascist parties. This model may be represented as:

$$P \rightarrow G \rightarrow SC$$

where P = Party (providing inputs); G = Government; and SC = Changes in the social system (as outputs).

The above mentioned type of situation is observable in conditions of radical transformation from dependent to independent status or directly after a revolution. The structural framework within which the parliamentary and cabinet systems operate remains there in some form; it intervenes between government and changes in the social system. The role of government, based on the formal decision-making process, remains the making of technical decisions, while the main contents of policy are entirely provided by governmental leaders, who also happen to the senior party leaders. Nasser's Egypt, Nkumah's Ghana, Nyerere's Tanzania, Algeria under Ben Bella, and India under Nehru are classic examples of the model specified in this section.

Most of the governments in today's time show behavioural weakness in their population *vis a vis* government. Changing allegiances and ritualisation of authority, the stresses and strains of rapid economic change and industrialisation, the creation of conditions under which individuals are able to establish a set of personality boundaries compatible with changing normative and structural conditions, etc., are the emerging problems which need to be dealt with reasonably and positively. A combination of political norms, nationalist primordial sentiments, and philosophical ideological expressions contribute to provide a basis for the motivational system of the society. Structurally these elements are organised more frequently in functional or corporate bodies with and around a political party rather than in parliamentary or representative institutions.

A THEORETICAL MODEL TO TEST GOVERNANCE

A general theory of government requires a model which is sufficiently explicit to account for the limits of variation, sufficiently flexible to handle diverse methodological emphasis, and empirical enough to be fully operationalised. Therefore, incorporating the various approaches in a single model, it is proposed to assume political behaviour (*PROBLEM*) as the independent variable; while treating political norms (*PN*) and political structures (*PS*) as intervening variables. The effectiveness of these intervening variables is bound and limited by the legitimacy pattern established by the relationships between political behaviour and political norms. Political structures can be considered in terms of their consequences for decision making, which in turn, are designed to maintain a sustained pattern of political behaviour in consonance with the maintenance of political norms. Thus, the model becomes symbolically as:

$$PB \rightarrow (PN \rightarrow PS) \rightarrow PD$$

where PB = Political behaviour (as inputs); *PN* = Political norms; *PS* = Political structures; and *PD*-Policy decisions (outputs).

The complexity of this model could be enlarged by rotating these variables for different purposes and to hold each of them independent in turn, for estimating their effects. The selection of variables to be held independent is arbitrary. However, it might be useful to treat political structure as the independent variable to estimate the effectiveness of different forms of government, such as democratic, totalitarian, centralised, decentralised, pluralistic, monopolistic, competitive, etc., along with the changes in political norms and political behaviour. Furthermore, in addition to rotating variables, some new intervening variables could also be added. The new variables may be normative ones in the form of ideologies as well as structural ones in the form of political parties, administrative organisations, and such other factors. The model could be used to test good governance of a modern government.

—D.P. Sharma

14

Openness

Definition

The simplest definition of openness is "easy and speedy access to right information". In the context of government functioning in the present era of economic liberalisation. "Openness" means giving everyone the right to have access to information about the various decisions taken by Government and the reasoning behind them.

Comparative Position in Other Countries

In most of the countries where large scale administrative reforms have been carried out, emphasis has been laid on liberalising the extent to which details of policy, performance and other information about government activities are made available to the general public. In the U.K., Citizen's Charter contains specific provisions for promoting increased openness about the reasons for decisions taken by the Government. In 1888, certain changes were effected in the Official Secrets Act, 1911 to narrow the scope of official information falling within the ambit of the Act. Besides, a While Paper guaranteeing a statutory right of access to personal records held by the government has also been implemented in April 1994. Canada has an Access to Information Act which gives all Canadian Citizens, as well as people and corporations present in Canada, the right to have access to federal government records that are not of a personal nature. The government has taken steps to ensure that information about its activities are broadly available to the people, with exception being limited and narrowly defined, and provisions for resolving any disputes over the application of such exceptions independently of the government. An information Commissioner has been appointed to investigate from members of the public arising from the above-mentioned Act. Government of Malaysia has also taken various steps of provide an open and transparent government in terms of decision making. These include publication of reports on public complaints, progress of administrative efforts undertaken by the government etc.

Recent Trends

As would be clear from the above, there is a trend worldwide to have increasing openness in the system of governance. Various factors like changing socio-economic milieu, increased awareness of the public their rights, the need to have a fully accountable and responsive administration and growing public opinion which views efforts at secrecy as enhancing the chances of abuse of authority by government functionaries, have led to a demand greater transparency in governmental functioning. However, openness is neither feasible ncr desirable. Accordingly approach to openness in government functioning has to.

OPENNESS WITH PUBLIC

Balanced Approach

All governments in the world practice studied concealment of information from the people though the nature, degree and extent thereof varies. While capitalist and democratic countries have a higher degree of openness *vis a vis* authoritarian regimes, nowhere in the world is government functioning totally open. The effort is to satisfy public demands as far as is reasonable and practicable. Transparency also has to be fully compatible with the constitutional and parliamentary system of the country and the cost of sharing information should be commensurate with the benefit to the public. It may also not be practicable to give information about any proposal under consideration while it is to be finalised, as this is likely to bring into play several pressure groups with attendant increase in corruption. Thus what we need in the country toady is a limited openness in government functioning, which would make available ex post facto information about various, but not all, government decisions to the citizens of this country. While anything that is detrimental to the interests of the nation, the security of the state or its commercial, economic and other strategic interests, may not be made public nothing should be held back just to subserve the interests of individual bureaucrats and politicians.

Right to Information Act and Setting up an Independent Authority

Experience of other countries shows that we will have to initiate the process by passing a Right to Information Act, somewhat on the lines of Canada and the United Kingdom. Adequate safeguards will have to be built into the legislation to ensure the primacy of the national interest as also the privacy of the individual citizen. At the same time, an independent authority will have to be constituted to decide whether a document can be made public or not. In this context, we recommend the creation of a National Information Authority which may be headed by a retired Supreme Court Judge or a retired Chief Justice of a High Court. In should also include independent and eminent persons as its members. The decision of this authority should be appealable only in the Apex.

Dissemination of Information

Public relations wings, which already exists in most of the government departments, should be converted into Public Relation-cum-Information Wings. Their functions should include dissemination of information to citizens on payment of a prescribed fee. People should be able to inspect Government papers and, if necessary, take photocopies of descried documents. No extra staff should be employed for this work, as the existing staff of R.R. Wing can take on these duties additionally. Departments should can take on these duties additionally. Departments should also publish information of general interest and keep copies of these in their libraries for general consumption. They should put information on computers with linkage to Internet and other global networks.

White Paper and Press Communique

Every important government decision involving a shift in policy should invariably be accompanied by a White Paper in the nature of an explanatory memorandum. Whenever a government decision brings about any pecuniary benefit of the value of Rs. 100 crores or above to any particular individual, group or company, whether in form of licences, tax relief or award of large projects, an elaborate 'press communique' explaining the origin of the issue, factors taken into account while arriving at the decision and names of the particular groups/individuals which it has benefited, should be released, within 24 hours of the decision.

Openness in Public Dealing Offices

A new kind of office structure, with a counter system, as in the case of banks, should be adopted in all field offices involving public contact. This has already been used with success in the Ahmednagar Experiment wherein the district office was restructured, demystified and made more open so as to facilitate the work of the general public. We have to move towards a government office which gives a clear-cut time-limit for disposing of any request of a member of the general public. An individual, if he so wishes, should be made aware about the exact stage of his case at any point of time. In such a system, an applicant is given a fixed time-limit, at the time of submission of his application giving the date on which the final decision on his request would be conveyed. The Passport Office has already initiated a system, where the status of an application can be ascertained at any point of time.

Cutting Out Discretion

Openness also implies that the reasons for Government decisions are placed on record in black and white. For this purpose formulation of criteria that would be used for decision-making is a must. Accordingly specific rules, criteria and norms have to be laid down for every activity of the government. The areas of discretion should be minimised and, in fact, eliminated. There should be no provision for Ministers, MPs or bureaucrats to dispense favours like medical college seats, Government accommodation, telephones, gas agencies, petrol pumps and the like. All such out-of-turn or discretionary quotes should be abolished. Wherever discretionary powers have to exist, these should be exercised by a group of officials with disparate backgrounds. In such cases, there should always be a recorded decision giving full justification for the stand taken. These groups should never be headed by ministers.

OPENNESS WITH EMPLOYEES

Transparency in Appointments, Promotions etc.

Presently, the procedures involving personnel management in government are kept so much under warps that even government servants themselves are not aware of them. Many of these activities like policy of transfers and postings, procedure for empanelment and even the list of persons who have made it to a panel remains closely guarded secrets. Transparency in dealing with matters relating to appointments, promotions, placements and personnel management is essential. We recommend that clearly defined criteria for all matters concerning promotions, transfers, appointments, etc. of government employees should be laid down. When a panel is drawn up, it should be published so that everyone knows where he stands. Apart from reducing frustration amongst government employees, this will obviate the need for fighting service-related cases in the courts.

Redress Against Superiors

Openness in governmental functioning has to extend to resolution of disputes among government servants. In the present hierarchical structure in the government, a subordinate does not have any avenue to air his grievance against his immediate superior to anyone. The official rules provide for representation through proper channel in which the first link is again the next immediate officer. Moreover, in case of a dispute, there is always a predilection among the top bureaucrats to go by the statement of the senior officer. It would be better if in such cases, the senior officer counsels both parties involved in the dispute to arrive at a mutually acceptable settlement. If difference still persist, efforts should be made to delink the two persons involved in the dispute, as they may both be good people, only temperamentally incompatible.

Relations with the Media

Openness should not means indiscreet leaks about Government actions, all of whose secrets are bandied abut in public. In fact, openness should do away with the every provocations for such leaks. By its very nature, the work of a government employee is faceless as it invariably flows out of efforts involving the entire system. The concept of anonymity of the public servant is good thing and should continue. Lately certain public servant have developed a tendency to acquire a false halo by cultivating the press and giving them friendly leaks. There is a need to suppress this tendency. The Conduct Rules already provide for departmental action in such cases. There is a need to implement this severely so that no more paper tigers amongst bureaucrats are created by the media. At the same time, the public relations machinery of different government departments should be trained to give out balanced stories to the media who should also be given sufficient opportunity to visit the places where good work has been done. Instead of issuing drab press notes giving dull statistics, the media should particularly be apprised of individuals who have been helped by the system, as human interest stories always evoke greater attention.

15

Planning

Planning of a rudimentary sort, is an inherent part of individual and, so, of co-operative or collective endeavour. It is "a rational process characteristic of all human behaviour." The need for planning has come to be widely recognised, and the prejudice against it is fast dying out even in the so-called capitalist or free-economy countries. Planning is no more equated with communist ideology and methodology. In brief, is has acquired respectability and has become even fashionable. Planning is of particular significance to an underdeveloped country where a lot has to be achieved with limited resources and within a restricted time. Thus, in our country and, for the matter of that, in all countries with developing economies, planning is perhaps the best way to pull up the economy to a self-sustaining and self-generating state. Verily, "all organisation must plan if they are to achieve their ends."

WHAT IS PLANNING?

Dimock defines planning as "the use of rational design as contrasted with chance, the reaching of a decision before a line of action is taken instead of improving after the action has started." Seckler-Hudson succinctly defines it as "the process of devising a basis for a course of future action." In the words of Millet, "Planning is the process of determining the objectives of administrative effort and of devising the means calculated to achieve them." In short, planning is the conscious process of selecting and developing the best course of action to accomplish a defined objective. It is a comprehensive term and involves a succession of steps:

1. *Determination of the objective*. This may involve collection of available data and an enquiry into all aspect of the problem. Various alternatives are examined and then a final decision is taken. It is a policy decision and is, therefore, political in nature;
2. *Consideration of possible course of action to achieve the objective.* Once the objective has been determined, the next problem in the finding out of the best means to achieve it. This implies the posing of possible alternative methods and examining each one of these. In may be necessary to test each of these alternatives through actual operations;
3. *Selection of the best course of action*. This implies evaluation of the result of investigations and test of the various alternative and finally choosing the best of them.

Planning is a rational, dynamic, and integrative process. In the first place, planning is not and cannot be haphazard and improvised. It is never the result of chance or unconscious effort, nor can it be acquired in a 'fit of absent-mindedness'. Planning is a rational, conscious and deliberate effort. "Planning is rational because it demands a systematic analysis of several possible means and ends, followed by a selection of those means thought best suited to the designated end." Secondly, planning is not a static process; it is dynamic and needs continuous adaptation in the light of experience. Constant evaluation, review, follow-up and redecision, if necessary, are *sine qua non* of good planning. Flexibility in a plan is, consequently, not undesirable. There should be no absolute rigidity about a plan. Thirdly, planning is a comprehensive and integrative process. It is not confined to any one branch of knowledge like politics, economics, sociology and engineering; it comprehends many disciplines. Planning is, above all, an exercise in coordination, integration and synthesisation of varied programmes and resources. Finally, a question is often asked if planning is a line or staff function. While some amount of planning is inevitable at all levels of administration, and while plan-consciousness at operating levels is essential for the due implementation of plans, planning, as a process of formulation and evaluation, is primarily a staff function.

KINDS OF PLANNING

Planning can be of many types—overall, limited and administrative. The first of these, commonly called socio-economic planning, is the most comprehensive, and it is in this sense that the term is used here. Socio-economic planning is more than laying down a few economic targets here and a few physical targets there. It is an overall effort to achieve an all-round development of the country. Four-year and seven-year plans are manifestations of this type of effort. Such far-reaching, long-range and overall planing often becomes the subject of controversy. Eyebrows are raised and suspicions aroused about such planning. Questions, like these, are asked: Is planning compatible with democracy? Does not planning, by its very definition, imply regimentation? Is not planning totalitarian, etc.? In reply, it may be said that planning is certainly the negation of *laissez-faire* both in political and economic spheres. But *laissez-faire* and democracy need not be regarded as interchangeable concepts. The 19th century liberal capitalist democracy is now obsolescent. All this is not to deny that planning in communist countries has often led to suppression of individual liberties and has been accompanied by drastic measures including terror. The fault may, however, be not of planing so much as of communism. Anyway, India is trying the experiment of attempting to establish a socialist society through planning by a democratic process.

Fulfillment of economic and physical targets, on the other hand, represents an isolated, separated, limited and up-coordinated programme of developing only certain sectors of the life of the community. Thus, in India, before 1947, the textile industry had reached a fairly high stage of development, and Tatas had set up a big steel plant at Jamshedpur, Similarly, the Government has taken in hand the programme of establishing schools, dispensaries, hospitals, etc. Construction of roads and provision of irrigation facilities are other examples of piecemeal attempts at development. In other words, the Government did take in hand and implemented many programmes of development in the fields of agriculture, education, public health, industry. public works, etc. Certain economic, and physical and financial targets were, undoubtedly, fixed and attempts were made to achieve them. But there was no planning as such in the sense in which the term is now used and understood.

Planning may, again, be governmental and non-governmental. Almost all big industrial businesses and commercial concerns, whether in India or abroad, draw up and execute their own plans of development. However, we are concerned here only with governmental planning of administrative planning. There are some who divide governmental planning into 'administrative' (policy and programme planning) and 'management' (operational planning). Such terminological controversies need not worry us here. As shown above, we regard planning as an important task of management. Administrative planning comprehends all the activities of government and "can be divided roughly into policy, programme and operational planning. This division is based on the level, the main objectives, and the subject-matter with which each type deals." No attempt, however, should be made to draw too fine a distinction between them as they are but phases of the single process of planning Policy planning occurs at top levels—the Legislature, the Cabinet, the President or the Prime Minister, and one of them or varying conjunctions of them. However much the public officials may help in and contribute towards policy-making, they do not make policies. Policies, being political in nature, should be formulated only by those who have political responsibility. A polity, as such, is ineffective unless it converts itself in the form of concrete programmes. The making of such specific programmes and projects, is the responsibility of the top and middle executives. In India, this role is played mainly by the secretariat helped and advised by the line department heads. The last, but by all means an important phase, is of implementing or executing the plan. This is the responsibility of the line or operational agencies which lay down the plan of action necessary to implement the projects or programmes. The test of the success of a plan is its right implementation, and it is not unoften that agencies involved in this task modify, and at times even subvert the policies enunciated at the top.

Plans may also be of varied durations, short-range or long-range. The annual Budget itself is one-year plan. Then there are four-year, five-year, six-year and seven-year plans. These plans of specific durations are made in the context of long-range of perspective plan. Such a plan projects itself 15 to 25 years hence, and attempts to determine the goals to be reached at the end of that period. The present projects and programmes are adjusted to realize these goals, and preparations are set afoot to create trained manpower and raise resources to meet the needs as they arise in future. Perspective planning, thus, helps in the formulation of present plans and in maintaining and continuing from one plan period to the other. The importance of perspective planning has been realised in India and the Planning Commission was provided in February 1957, with a Perspective Planning Division engaged in the task of assessing the requirements of the country in respect of various sectors of activity so that projection could be made into the future over a period of 20 to 25 years. Planning may, thus, be said to be a never-ending occupational problem for a manager.

PLANNING PROCESS

Planning is a succession of steps through which the planner must go. These steps are: understand the objective to be achieved; evaluate the situation or setting; consider possible courses of action and select the best course of action. Seckler-Hudson suggests six steps in systematic planning, namely: (1) a careful definition and limitation of the problem to the extent possible; (2) the exploration of all available information pertaining to the problem; (3) the posing of possible alternative solutions or methods of handling the problem; (4) the testing of one or more tentative solutions through actual operations; (5) the evalution of the light of experience, continuous research and new developments; and (6) reconsideration of the problem and the results, and redecision if justified.

According to Millett, planning embraces three broad steps: (1) the formulation of goals; (2) an assessment of the resources available to realize these goals; and (3) the preparation of a work programme designed to achieve the determined objectives. In short, the planning process includes three steps—the formulation, execution and evaluation of plans. We shall, now, briefly describe the existing machinery in India for the above three aspects of planning.

PLAN FORMULATION

We have in the Planning Commission a competent body for the purpose of drawing up a national Plan, and all the three plans drawn up so far, are well-written documents. The Commission's task is to assess the nation's resources, draw up a Plan to use them with proper priorities and allocations, determine the conditions, machinery and adjustments needed to make the Plan succeed, appraise the progress of the Plan from time to time and make any recommendations necessary to facilitate it.

The first step in the process of formulating the Plan in India is for the Planning Commission to prepare, on a rough basis, certain schemes and projects in consultation with the Central Ministries and the State Governments in the background of the perspective Plan: to determine some kind of priority; to take stock of the available resources; and to distribute these resources among the different agencies, central and state, on an approximate basis. These estimates and projections are then placed before the National Development Council. The schemes and projects, modified in the light of the NDC's recommendations, are then sent to the Union Ministries and the State governments in the form of preliminary instructions.

Then begins the second stage of each Union Ministry Department and each State Government preparing its own Plan. The machinery for planning is fairly well-developed at the State level. As a rule, there are whole-time Secretaries in charge of planning and development, many of whom also carry Community Projects. The Planning Departments in the State are co-ordinating in varying degrees the work of other Departments in the States in relation to the Plan. At State headquarters, co-ordination is achieved through an inter-departmental committee of Secretaries in charge of various development departments. The Chairman of the Committee is the Chief Secretary or the Secretary in charge of planning. Generally, the function of co-ordination for planning and for the implementation of district programmes are combined in a single officer, commonly described as the Development Commissioner. As a rule, a Committee of the State Cabinet under the Chief Minister provides overall guidance and direction. Leading non-officials are associated with the formulation and implementation of plans at the State level through the State Planning Boards. In addition, there is generally at the State level a State Development Committee consisting of the Chief Minister and Ministers in charge of Development Departments for lying down general policy and other matters concerning the Five Year Plan. In certain States, like Utter Pradesh, there is also a State Planning Board which includes non-officials.

It is understood that while framing the Second Five Year Plan, it was decided that planning had to be done from below. Detailed instructions were sent from the Planning Commission and the State Governments indicating how districts should prepare local and village plans within the general framework and how, within the district, the work of planning must be organised, plans being prepared for individual village and groups of villages, such as, tahsils, national extension development blocks, etc. It is stated that a serious effort was made in the initial stages to plan from below, but after the State plans were pruned, they were not adequately broken up into district and local plans and implemented as such. It has now been decided by the Standing Committee of the National Development Council that the general principle of giving responsibility for development to the representatives of the people within the district should be accepted. With the establishment of the new pattern of 'Democratic Decentralisation', the Panchayat Samitis and Zila Parishads will acquire in fuller measure the authority to draw up their own plan projects.

Learning from the past experience, two things have been done in the making of the Third Plan. First, the broad overall magnitudes have been determined before the process of village and block planning was initiated. Secondly, at the village and block level, particularly the latter, certain fields have been identified which appeared, on the whole, more appropriate for planning at that level rather than attempt to cover the entire range of development. The fields earmarked are agriculture, co-operatives, village industries, elementary education, rural water supply, supervision of certain minimum amenities to rural areas and works for mobilizing more fully the manpower of rural areas.

After the States and the Union Ministries have submitted their plans to the Planning Commission, there begins the process of dovetailing the various schemes, programmes and projects into an integrated plan. In the course of shaping the plan, the Commission consults representatives different in Parliament. At the end of these exercise, the draft Plan is published and thrown open for public discussion. The universities, the press, political parties, chambers of commerce, trade organisations and other groups and individuals are free to give their comments on the draft.

The next stage is a period of prolonged detailed discussions between the Planning Commission and the representatives of different Stage Governments as a result of which agreements as to the size and nature of State are reached. The Union Ministries are similarly consulted in finalizing the Central Government Plan. These tentative agreements are then placed before the Union Cabinet and after its approval are sent to NDC. The Planning Commission then gives the final shape to the Plan in the light of the NDC's recommendations. The Plan is then presented to Parliament and after getting its approval, it becomes the official Plan and published as such.

PLANNING COMMISSION

Origin

The origin of planning in India can be traced to 1933, when M. Visvesvaraya formulated a ten-year plan with the target of doubling the income of the country. Five years later, in 1938, at the instance of the Congress party, a National Planning Committee was set up with Jawaharlal Nehru as its Chairman. In 1941, the Government of India appointed a Committee for Planning, which was replaced in 1943, by the Reconstruction Committee of the Executive Council with the Governor-General himself in chair. Next year, separate Planning and Development Department was established. The same year some leading industrialists prepared Plan for the economic development of the country known as the Bombay Plan. Under the inspiration and guidance of the Planning Department, a number of development schemes were prepared by the Central and the Provincial Governments to be undertaken at the war. Problems of planning were reviewed towards the end of 1946, by the Advisory Planning Board, established by the Interim Government. The Board suggested the setting up of a Planning Commission, single compact authoritative organisation, directly responsible to be Cabinet and devoting its attention continuously to the whole field of development. The recommendation was accepted and the Planning Commission was established by a resolution of the Government of India, dated 15th March 1950.

Functions

The Planning Commission, with the Prime Minister as the Chairman, has emerged as a powerful and effective staff agency in India. The functions of the Commission are as follows:

1. To make an assessment of the material, capital and human resources of the country, including technical personnel, and to investigate the possibilities of augmenting such of those resources as are found to deficient in relation to the nation's requirements;
2. To formulate a Plan for the most effective and balanced utilisation of the country's resources;
3. To determine priorities as between projects and programmes accepted in the Plan;
4. To indicate the factors that retard economic development, and to determine conditions which should be established for the success of the Plan;
5. To determine the nature of the machinery to secure the successful implementation of the Plan;
6. To appraise from time to time the progress of the Plan and to recommend the necessary adjustments of policy and measures; and
7. To make recommendations either for facilitating the discharge of its duties or for a consideration of the prevailing economic conditions, current policies, measures and development programme; or for an examination of problems referred to it for advice by Central or State Governments.

Composition

The Commission at present (in 1985) consists of chairman, deputy chairman and six members. The Prime Minister is its Chairman. The Deputy Chairman is the full-time functional head of the Commission. Of the six members, three are ministers in the Central Government and the remaining three are full-time members. All cases involving policy are considered by the Commission as a whole. The formulation of the plans, adjustments in the plans, matters involving departure from the plan-policies, important cases involving disagreement with a Central Ministry or a State Government, and difference of opinion between members of the Commission are some of such cases.

There is a close liaison between the Cabinet and the Commission. The Chairman is the Prime Minister himself. Other members of the Commission are invited, as and when necessary, to attend the meetings of the Cabinet and its Commission. On the other hand, important economic issue arising in the Ministries are generally discussed in the Commission before they are considered in the Cabinet. Thus, there is a regular system of ideas and suggestions flowing from the Commission to the Union Government and *vice versa*.

Organisation

The Planning Commission works through three major divisions—Progrmme Advisers, General Secretariat and Technical Divisions.

Programme Advisers. Thus are four senior officers designated as advisers having the status of *ex officio* Additional Secretaries to the Government of India. They assist the members of the Commissions in matters concerning field-study and observation of various schemes and projects and the progress of their implementation. The advisers also pay specific attention to the problem of finance, public co-operation and administration connected with the implementation of the plans.

General Secetariat. It has four branches, namely, Administrative Branch, Plan Co-ordination Branch, General Co-ordination Branch and Information and Publicity Branch.

Technical Divisions. The Commission has 20 Technical Divisions and Sections which fall broadly under two groups, namely- General Divisions, and Branch or Subject Division. The General Divisions are concerned with the problem of overall economic and social planning, each examining some specific aspects of these problems. The Subject Divisions, on the other hand, deal with specific sectors of the economy like Irrigation and Power, Food and Agriculture, Education, Housing etc. The Technical Divisions are responsible for scrutinizing and analysing various schemes and projects to be incorporated in the Plan; conducting technical studies and research regarding Plan Projects and programmes; preparing study material and reports on the Plan; following up of Plan Projects, etc. The heads of these Divisions are generally subject-specialists designated as Chiefs or Directors who are assisted by Deputy and Assistant Chiefs and some research staff.

Advisory Bodies. Some of the important advisory bodies functioning in the Planning Commission are; Committee on Irrigation and Power Projects, Co-ordination Committee, and Research Programmes Committee.

NATIONAL DEVELOPMENT COUNCIL

Origin

One of the most important problems facing any effort at planning on a nationwide scale is the difficulty of co-ordinating the policies and programmes of autonomous State comprising the Indian Union. The constitution has made no provisions for such a co-ordinating agency. It was to fill up such a gap in the planning process that the National Development Council was created in 1952. In fact, it was the Advisory Planning Board set up in 1946, under the chairmanship of K.C. Neogi, which first suggested the setting up of a consultative body representing the provinces and the princely states as well as some other interests to help in the work of the Planning Commission. Later, the Planning Commission itself fell the need for such a body. Said the draft outline of the First Five Years Plan (July, 1951): "In a country of the size of India where the States have under the Constitution full autonomy within their own spheres of duties, it is necessary to have a forum, such as, the National Development Council at which, from time to time, the Prime Minister of India and the Chief Ministers of States can review the working of the Plan and its various aspects." The Government accepted the suggestion and the N.D.C. was born as a result of a resolution on August 6, 1952.

Functions

The objectives of the Council, as specified in the Resolution itself, are "to strengthen and mobilize the efforts and resources of the nation in support of the Plan, to promote common economic policies in all vital spheres, and to ensure the balanced and rapid development of all parts of the country on the recommendation of the Planning Commission." In fulfillment of these objectives, the Council has been charged with three functions:

1. To review the working of the National Plan from time to time;
2. To consider important questions of social and economic policy affecting national development; and
3. To recommend measures for the achievement of the aims and targets set out in the National Plan including measures to secure the active participation and co-operation of the people, improve the efficiency of the administrative services, ensure the fullest development of the less advanced regions and sections of the community, and, through sacrifice, borne equally by all the citizens, build up resources for national development.

It was envisaged that the N.D.C. would advise and make its recommendation to the Central and State Governments. It has been functioning since its inception as a high consultative body wherein the frame of the Five Year Plans, the important problems facing the Indian economy, and the policies but have to be adopted for tiding over the urgent problems, have been discussed and solutions arrived at. Thus, in addition to the Plan, the Council has concerned itself with problems like food, creation of the State Trading Corporation, and land reforms.

Composition

The Council consists of the Prime Minister who is the Chairman, the Union Ministers for Home, Finance and Defense, members of the Planning Commission, and the Chief Ministers of States. If a Chief Minister is unable to attend the meeting, he can send his substitute. In addition, ministers, subjects pertaining to whose ministers find place on the agenda, are also invited to attend. Moreover, there have been occasions where the Governor of the Reserve Bank, economists and other experts have been invited to address the meetings. At the outset, due to the large number of A, B and C States, the membership of the Council had risen up to 50. With the decrease in the member of States as a consequence of reorganisation, the usual attendance now stands at 30. The large membership reduced the utility of the Council for discussion as a compact body, and in November 1954, a Standing Committee was established with only nine Chief Ministers a few Union Ministers as members. In addition, the Council has been appointing Committees from time to time to make detailed examinations of certain problems. Thus, the Council, at its meeting in March 1960, set up a Committee on price control. The Secretary of the Planning Commission is also the Secretary of the Council and the Commission furnishes the Council with administrative and other assistance.

The Council ordinarily meets twice a year but there is no rigidity about it, and it has met more than twice a year on many occasions. Till the end of 1960, the Council had met 16 times. The agenda is prepared by Planning Commission Secretariat and includes matters of national importance, on which it is necessary to obtain the views of the State. The Secretarial prepares a memorandum on such subjects and submits it to the Vice-Chairman who obtains the approval of the Prime Minister. The agenda is then circulated among the members of the N.D.C., and the Union Cabinet Ministers. The meetings begin with an address of welcome by the Chairman who usually gives his views on the items included in the agenda. A few other persons may then give their exposition of the problems and then there is free and frank discussion. It is interesting to note that ordinarily no formal resolution is passed. The practice is to have a complete record of discussion and gather out of it general trends pointing to particular conclusions. Decisions are usually unanimous.

Evaluation

The first function of the Council is to act as a kind of bridge between the Union Government, the Planning Commission and the State Governments. It helps in the co-ordination not only of policies and programmes of plans but also other important matters of national importance. Secondly, it provides a good forum for discussion and full and free exchange of views. There is no other comparable forum. Thirdly, it is also a device for sharing of responsibility between States and the Union Government.

Many and varied are the criticisms levelled against the N.D.C. There are some who charged the N.D.C. with usurping authority and functioning as a virtual super-cabinet. Thus, M. Brecher, Nehru's biographer, referring of this body, observes: "The National Development Council was established as a supreme administrative and advisory body on planning....Since their inception, the N. D.C. and its Standing Committee have virtually relegated the Planning Commission to the status of a research arm." In a similar vein, H.M. Patel, a retired member of the Indian Civil Service, remarks: "Among the Advisory Bodies to the Planning Commission is included the N.D.C. This is surely inaccurate, as is clear from its composition. The N.D.C. is a body obviously superior to the Planning Commission. It is, indeed, a policy-making body and its recommendations cannot but be regarded as policy decisions and not merely as advisory suggestions." Santhanam goes even further: "The position of the N.C.C. has come to approximate that of a super-cabinet of the entire Indian Federation, a Cabinet functioning for the Government of India as well as for the Governments of all the States." Late A. P. Jain ex-Food Minister in the Union Cabinet, had charged the Council for acting arbitrarily. According to him, the Council infringes upon functions which under the Constitution, are assigned to other bodies and attempts to do what the Council of Ministers at the Central and the States' levels should do. Thus, in 1956, the target of food production in the Second Plan was raised suddenly by the Council without consulting the Food Ministry. Similarly, in 1958, the Council took a decision on State Trading without considering whether the State had either the capacity or the will to enforce controls, the logical corollaries of State Trading. In Jain's opinion, the Council, neither by law or by nature of its composition, is a body competent or studied to take decisions on national issues. It is suited to talk, debate and advise, but decisions should be left to the Cabinets at the Centre and the States.

To appreciate the above criticism, it is necessary to know that the Council has neither constitutional nor statutory position; it is the creature of the Union Cabinet. It is listed as an advisory body to the Planning Commission and its recommendations are not binding on anyone. It is true that, in practice, the Council has become a high-ranking policy-making body and its recommendations are usually accepted. This is due to the nature of its membership. The Council may well be said to be a summit conference of the chief executives of the States and the Centre; and it is no wonder if its decisions carry weight. "There is no harm if the Council sometimes functions as super-cabinet so long as it reaches decisions after full deliberations." In fine, due to the status and stature of its membership and to the role it plays, the Council is bound to gain more and more influence and presetting, and *de facto* authority.

There are, however, two possibilities of marring the effectiveness of the Council. In the first place, the Council may turn out to be a forum for the ventilation of grievances of the part of the spokesmen of the States. It will be a bad day for its future if the Council forgets its main role of co-ordination and integration of State policies. A reading of the proceedings of the Council will, however, reveal that such a trend is not completely non-existent. Secondly, if and when the present one-party character of all the State and Central Governments changes, it is sure to have repercussions on the working of the Council.

Implementation

The Plan, as finally adopted, is implemented by the Central Ministers and the State Governments in their respective spheres. The Planning Commission is an advisory body and has no executive functions. In the beginning, it has some executive responsibility when the Community Projects Administration, supervising the implementation of the programme of Community Development and National Extension Services in the States, was a wing of the Planning Commission. This work has since been transferred to a separate Ministry of Community Development, and the Planning Commission is now only a national organ for planning and a staff body to advise the Union Cabinet.

It has no direct responsibility for the administration of Plan programmes which are the responsibility of the Union and State Governments. The Commission, however, has advisers on programme administration who tour the States and assess progress on a continuing basis and make recommendations necessary to move the programmes ahead. The Commission also undertakes information and publicity work to acquaint the people with the Plan and to stimulate public co-operation in its implementation. Two organisations that assist Commission in the implementation and evaluation of the Plan Projects and programmes, are the Committee on the Plan Projects and the Programme Evaluation Organisation.

Much of the criticism against planning in India falls in the field of implementation. Our experience with the working of the various Plan has shown that the effective implementation of Plan Projects has been the weakest link in the chain of the entire planning process. This has been particularly true regarding the execution of programmes in the rural areas where an overwhelming majority of our people live. Effective implementation of a small Plan is perhaps more conducive to public good than indifferent execution of a big Plan. In the words of the Planning Commission itself. "The success of the Third Plan will rest very largely on the efficiency with which it is implemented." Examples of indifferent of Plan Projects are legion, for instance, grow-more-food campaign, distribution of seeds, manure and *taccavi* loans, social education provision or irrigation facilities, etc., etc. What is this due to? It is not enough to blame the ignorance of the villager or the lack of ethics of the part of the public officials. A close examination of the situation reveals that five factors are involved in it, namely-lack of enlightenment on the part of the people, character of official personnel, insufficient and ineffective supervision, want of educate communicate among the officials, and the criterion of the evaluation of work of the officials.

Evaluation

One of the functions of the Planning Commission is to appraise from time to the progress achieved in the execution of each stage of the Plan and recommend the adjustment of policy and measures that such appraisal might show to be necessary. The Commission makes this appraisal, (i) through monthly reports of selected projects, quarterly reviews of the working of the Plan, the annual progress reports obtained from the Central Ministries and the State Governments; (ii) through the Advisers (Programme Administration) who visit the State within their charge throughout the year, and study at first hand the working of the development programmes giving special attention to the more important projects; and (iii) through the machinery of the Committee on Plan Projects. In addition, there is a Programme Evaluation Organisation which assesses the work of National Extension Service and Community Development Programmes.

There posts of Advisers (Programme Administration) were created in 1952. A fourth adviser was added later. There posts are filled by senior officers of suitable administrative experience with State. The functions of the Advisers are to keep the Planning Commission in close touch with the progress of the planning in its various aspects and to give the fullest possible assistance to State Governments and the Central Ministries in matters concerning implementation of various projects. They help to effect co-ordination between the State and the Planning Commission in regard to (i) preparation of the Five Year Plan, (ii) preparation of the annual Plan, (iii) provision of adjustments in the Plan, and (iv) watching the progress of the Plan and attending to the problems of implementation which they come across during their visits to the States. As regards the implementation of the Plan, the Advisers hold discussions, during their visits, with the various development departments and the State Planning and Finance Departments and review the progress of the Plan in different sectors and projects. Particularly, they look into those projects which are assisted by loans and grants from the Central Ministries, and also note the States' efforts to raise resources. In the course of these discussions and field inspections, problems relating to bottlenecks due to non-availability of steel, technical personnel, allocation of foreign exchange, procedural delays in the approval of schemes and the sanctions for financial assistance by the Ministers of the Government and other such matters come to the notice of the Advisers and are dealt with in their reports. The Planning Commission draws the attention of the Ministries concerned to those problems through personal discussion, and suggests that an immediate solution is necessary. The Advisers sometimes lead teams of expects from different Ministries to examine particular problems and make recommendations to the Government of India. They check the estimates of projects and assess the expenditure incurred on the projects in terms of the Plan. They also offer advice to State Governments for improving the implementation of the projects and the Plan in different fields of development.

COMMITTEE ON PLAN PROJECTS (COPP)

Origin

A checkup of the Second Plan indicated that the traditional view of economy, namely, reduction in the staff strength, was outmoded in the context of the Plan. The real issue in the Plan expenditure is the speed with which projects can be executed which requires a great deal of thought and effort in standardizing practices and procedures of execution in order to make estimation of costs realistic; to achieve basic economy based on scientific development of techniques from the inception of the project; and to set up norms and standards for evaluation. It was against such a background that the Committee on Plan Projects was set up in 1956, in pursuance of a decision of the National Development Council, for exploring the possibility of achieving economy consistent with efficiency in the projects included in the Second Plan. The COPP, as a separate entity was wound up in 1970.

Organisation

The Committee on Plan Projects (COPP) had the Home Minister as Chairman, and the Ministers for Planning and Finance, and the Deputy Chairman, Planning Commission, as members. In addition, two Chief Ministers of State for each category of projects were nominated to the Committee by the Prime Minister in his capacity as the Chairman of the National Development Council. Besides, the Union Minister concerned with the project under investigation was also a member.

Activities

The functions of this Committee, as envisaged in the Second Plan were:

1. To organize investigations, including inspections in the field, of important projects, both at the Centre and in the States, through specially selected teams;
2. To initiate studies with the objective of evolving suitable forms of organisation, methods, standards and techniques for achieving economy, avoiding waste and ensuring efficient execution of projects;
3. To promote the development of suitable machinery for continuous efficiency audit in individual projects and in agencies responsible for their execution;
4. To secure the implementation of suggestions made in reports submitted to the Committee on the Plan Projects, and to make the results of studies and investigations generally available; and
5. To undertake such other tasks as the National Development Council may propose for the promotion of economy and efficiency in the execution of the Second Five Year Plan.

For convenience of investigation, the Committee had divided the projects under certain heads—irrigation and power, public works and buildings, agriculture and communications, public industrial and mineral enterprises, and social services. For each set of projects, the Committee worked through groups composed of Ministers from the Centre and Chief Ministers of States. Reports of investigating teams were disussed with the Chief Ministers of States concerned with the execution of projects under study, and the normal procedure was for investigating teams to discuss and obtain the views of the Central or State Departments and authorities in charge of projects on their draft reports before submitting them to the COPP. Matters of general policy connected with the investigation of projects were considered from time to time in meetings of the Standing Committee of the National Development Council.

By way of illustration, let us examine the working of the team for the evaluation of selected building projects. It was clear to the COPP early enough that construction costs should be the major target for analysis with a view to economy and efficiency and that, among them, the buildings alone would account for nearly Rs. 800 crones out of a total outlay of Rs. 4,200 crores for the Second Plan. In was, therefore, decided to set up a team for the evaluation of building projects. The team was composed of the Minister for Food and Agriculture as leader, a well-known Consulting Engineer, the present and a former Director of the National Building Organisation as members, and a Superintending Engineer of the Central Public Works Department as Secretary. In addition, the Director, Central Board of Research in Irrigation also attended important meeting of the team and had access to all its working papers. Since the team had to investigate various projects of highly technical nature, it had set up technical panels consisting of qualified persons in different fields. Thus, there were separate panels for Grain Godowns, Slum Clearance, Factory Buildings, Bridge Structure, etc. So far, the evaluation team has taken up the investigation of various types of buildings representing an estimated plan outlay of Rs. 550 crores, namely Grain Godowns, Multi storeyed Buildings, Factory Buildings, Slum Clearance Schemes, Residential Buildings. Small Storage Structures, National Water Supply, Sanitation Schemes, and Bridges. The report of the team of Multi storeyed Buildings has own won encomiums in all quarters and has become a regular book of reference. Subsequent to the publication of the report, a proforma was prepared which brought out the actual performance of any particular building compared to the standard laid down by the team. The team had also undertaken the study of the organisation at some of the building sites to evolve a pattern which would be conductive to greater economy and efficiency. The team had also made detailed study of the Public

Works Organisation at the Centre as well as some of the States', and came to the conclusion that certain changes were necessary in the organisational set up in order to make it conducive to speedy and economical execution of works.

Similarly, the team for the study of Community Projects and National Extension Services did a remarkable work under the Chairmanship of Balwantrai Mehta. In its three-volume Report (1957), the team made a thorough and detailed study of the working of local bodies and development blocks, and recommended a new three-tier organisation of local and development administration in the district which has since come to be known as 'democratic decentralisation'. These recommendations have been adopted with minor modifications in different states. The Committee also submitted a report on the working of Social Welfare Agencies in the country.

PROGRAMME EVALUATION ORGANISATION

The Organisation was established in October 1952, simultaneously with the inauguration of the Community Development Programme. It was set up under an agreement between the Government of India and the Ford Foundation dated the 12 August, 1952. It is an independent unit for assessing the work of the National Extension Services and Community Development Programmes, but functions under the general guidance of the Planning Commission.

Organisation

The Organisation at the headquarters consists of a Director and two Deputy Directors, eight Research Officers and other staff. In the field, there are three Regional Evaluation Officers, one for Eastern Zone with headquarters at Calcutta, a second for Southern Zone with headquarters at Bombay, and a third for Northern Zone with headquarters at Delhi. Each of these three officers has 6 to 7 Project Evaluation Officers under him, twenty of them in all. The centres where these officers are posted were selected by dividing the country into major economic and agricultural regions. The choice of the particular centre was guided by the objective of obtaining area's representatives of the different environmental, agricultural and economic conditions in different regions so that the rural development programme might be studied under varying conditions. Regional Officers tour and guide the Project Officers in their surveys and act as intermediaries between them and the State Governments. The Project Evaluation Officers are expected to be in the know of all the changing conditions in the Blocks. They have also to conduct surveys in order to assess the impact of the Plan Projects on the community. For this purpose, they have the assistance of an investigation staff. They work in close contact with the Project staff. Among the Research Officers one category is in charge of tabulation units and the other of processing. Other officials put the reports together coming in from the field, scrutinize them and prepare final reports.

The present set up of the PEO enables in to work independently of the Minister dealing with community development. It works under the general direction of the Planning Commission. These directions are informal and, as the Director of the Organisation told the Estimates Committee, "There has not been a single instance where the Planning Commission or Projects Administration has even asked the PEO to do a thing in a particular way."

Functions

The main functions of the Organisation, as laid down in 1952, are:

1. Making a systematic recurring evaluation of the methods and results of the Community Development Programme by keeping all concerned apprised currently of the progress being made towards accomplishing the programme objective;
2. Pointing out those extension methods which are proving effective and which are not;
3. Help in explaining why some recommended practices are adopted while others are rejected by the villagers; and
4. Furnishing an insight into the impact of the Community Development Programme upon the economy and culture of

India so essential to anticipating emerging obstacles to continuing economic and social progress.

The present work of the PEO is of two-fold nature: (1) a general appraisal of the progress of the programme with detailed examination of those aspects which may be of particular interest, and (2) field surveys to assess the impact of the programme on economic and social conditions. In the initial stages greater emphasis was placed on the general assessment. After the programme evolved a more settled organisational pattern, it was possible for the PEO to devote more time to analytical examination of particular aspects. It should be noted that the Organisation is not designed to make a check like an engineer which is an administrative function. It never takes upon itself the responsibility of checking the figures. The organisation in merely concerned with indicating the methods which are being adopted and to what extent they are adequate or otherwise. It is not interested in examining if the amount spent on development work is commensurate with the success achieved and progress made. Similarly, it does not test the technical efficiency of any improvement measure. It only brings out the fact that certain methods was not proving successful.

The Evaluation Reports are compiled on the basis of the data supplied by the Project Executive Officers, Block Department Officers or the District Officers, as the case may be, and there is no independent machinery of the PEO to check the basic data. However, the Project Evaluation Officers sometimes make on-the-spot check and make their own surveys to assess the impact of the Community Development Programme and are in frequent contact with the villagers who supply them the data for their observations. Moreover, these officers maintain contact with local non-officials and members of States and Central Legislatures at the Project and Block level in many cases and their views are duly considered by them, but the contact is informal. Evaluation Reports are of two types—Survey Reports and Main Evaluation Reports. Survey Reports, for example, 'Community Project Reactions', and 'Cotton Extension in PEPSU', are purely study reports and are circulated to the State Governments, the Ministry of Community Development and the Planning Commission. These reports are based on facts as brought out by surveys and are of great value to the field-workers. The main Evaluation Reports are sent to all Heads of Departments, Deputy Commissioners, or Collectors, and Block Development Officers in State. These are also translated in Hindi and other regional languages for wider circulation:

The PEO has produced sight Annual Evaluation Reports which make a general review of the programme and give a detailed discrimination of its work in certain specified evaluation centres. Besides, it also conducts surveys and enquiries. Among the important surveys are: a Survey of Initial Reactions towards the Community Projects, a Bench-mark Survey, the Acceptance and Practice Enquiry, and Study of the Role and Function of Gram Sevaks. The Organisation does a follow-up of its recommendations and keeps a record of the suggestions and recommendations made by it, and regularly checks the action taken by the Community Development Ministry and the State Governments on them. At times the PEO even makes in objective test of finding out as to what is actually happening in the field, and directions are issued to the field officers to see as to, to what extent the weaknesses in the programme pointed out are remedied or not remedied. The recommendations are not always accepted.

Bureau of Public Enterprises

The Bureau of Public Enterprises functions, since 1964, in the Department of Co-ordination (Ministry of Finance), and is headed by the Special Secretary—designated as Director-General, Bureau of Public Enterprises-and manned by experienced technical, industrial, economic and other experts and staff. The Bureau acts as a centralised co-ordinating unit in the Government for providing policy and overall guidance to public undertakings, and for making a continuous appraisal of the performance, organisational set up, manpower requirement, etc., of various public undertakings. It is a service, coordination and evaluation agency, performing the following functions:

1. To provide a central point of reference and consultation on and to deal with matters of general interest, like organisational patterns, methods of management, personnel policies,

collaboration arrangement, training programmes, project planning, economic, social and financial policies etc.;

2. To explore all avenues of economy in capital costs of projects (including townships) by scrutiny and analysis of elements of such costs in projects of different types;

3. To devise steps for improving the productivity and profitability of public enterprises by keeping under constant review their performance through suitable methods of reporting and analysis of the performance data;

4. To undertake appraisal and evaluation of selected area in the performance of public enterprises or in individual units as may become necessary from time to time; and

5. To prepare for presentation to Parliament annual report on the working of the central government undertaking or such other reports as may be called for by the parliamentary committees or other government agencies.

ADMINISTRATIVE IMPLICATION OF PLANNING IN INDIA

The Indian experiment in Planning for a socialist society through democratic process is unique in the contemporary world. Russia and China are both attempting to achieve socialism through planning but they do not use the democratic process. The Labour Party in Britain aims at bringing about a socialist society through democratic procedures but has no centralised planning machinery. The U. S. A. is a democracy but believes neither in socialism nor in planning. It is only India which has attempted to combine all the three—planning, socialism and democracy. We want to bring about democratic, cooperative, socialistic pattern of society with mixed economy under a parliamentary system without modifying traditions a great deal. This is a challenging, albeit difficult task.

The advent of planning, since 1950, has affected the nature, scope and scale of administration of the Union and State Administration in India. This impact has mainly arisen as a consequence of three major forces at work: (1) the assumption by the Government of developmental functions including those in the field of welfare; (2) the increase in the scale and variety of administrative operations; (3) the need for the greater association of the people with, and their participation in, the administrative process to facilitate planning from below and effective implementation of the Plans.

Both the First and Second Plans as also the Third Plan (Draft) have recognised the significance and role of public administration in the successful implementation of the plans. Said the First Plan: "In all directions, the pace of development will depend largely upon the quality of public administration, the efficiency with which it works and the co-operation which it evokes." In the words of the Second Plan: " If the administrative machinery both at the Centre and in the States does its work with efficiency, integrity and with a sense of urgency and concern for the community, the success of the Second Plan would be assured." Emphasizing the importance of administration in the successful implementation of the Plan, the Third Plan (Draft) says "The need for securing efficiency and speed in execution and widespread confidence in the integrity of the administration at all points affecting the general public has always been stressed as vital problems in economic development. With the increase in the tempo of development activities and in the functions of Government, these aspects of administrative reforms have assumed even greater urgency." Verily, all planning resolves itself into a set of administrative tasks.

ADMINISTRATIVE ORGANIZATION AND MANAGEMENT

The First Plan placed emphasis on administration leadership; integrity; machinery to enquire into cases of misconduct on the part of persons who hold any office, political or otherwise; efficiency; staffing arrangements for management of State industrial enterprises and for dealing with matters of economic policy and administration, development in land reforms and food administration; improvement of quality of recruits to the administrative service and of the procedures for their selection; establishment of joint 'development' cadres and similar other co-operative arrangements between the Centre and the States; improvement of in-service training arrangements, the importance of careful grounding in revenue and development administration for the probationers of the administrative services, the organisation of refresher courses for senior administrative officers, etc.; establishment of O and M units at the Centre and in States; improvement of supervision and inspection; better human relations; review of methods of financial control; greater attention to financial implications at the stage of planning of projects, and allocation of priorities; improvement of efficiency rating methods so as to facilitate promotion of outstanding officers; and systematic evaluation of result as a normal administrative practice.

The Second Five Year Plan enumerated the principal administrative tasks as follows: ensuring integrity in administration; building up administrative and technical cadres, and providing incentive and opportunities for creative services; continuously assessing requirements of personnel in relation to the tasks to be undertaken; organizing large-scale training programme in all fields and mobilizing the available training resources; devising speedy, efficient and economic method of work, providing for continuous supervision and arranging for objective evaluation of methods ands results at regular intervals. It also emphasised the need for affording opportunities to officials at all levels for exercising the maximum responsibility; schemes for executive development; an attitude of speed and urgency; administrative talents to be drawn from all fields; and emphasis on correct human relations.

The Third Plan lists the principle objectives to be realised in public administration as; (1) formulation of policies in clear-cut terms by Government and ensuring continuity in giving effect to them; (2) clear assignment of responsibility for implementation with full appreciation of the objectives to be achieved at every level including Minister, Secretary and Head of Department, and no interference with the decision of the individual public servant within the field assigned to him by law and regulation; (3) ensuring everyday efficiency with speed and prompt disposal, including (i) proper training of personnel, especially middle-grade, (ii) simplification of procedures through systematic work studies, and (iii) effective supervision of workout each level; (4) continuing administrative leadership for securing steady improvement in administrative efficiency and standard; and (5) ensuring in respect of important construction projects that the best results accrue for the expenditure incurred, and there is integrity and economy at all points.

16

Comparative Public Administration

Comparisons of administrative systems has had a long tradition. But a focus on this aspect of administrative studies is about forty years old. Only after the Second World War and with the emergence of new nations in Asia and Africa, a vigorous interest in comparative studies of Public Administration has evolved.

Comparative Public Administration, in simple terms, refers to a comparative study of government administrative systems functioning in different countries of the world. The nature of Comparative Administration has vast ramifications and ranges from the narrowest of studies to the broadest of analysis.

To understand the meaning of Comparative Public Administration, it would be desirable to look at the types of comparative public administration studies undertaken by scholars in the field. We Shall examine the meaning, scope and nature of Comparative Public Administration. We shall also discuss its conceptual approaches.

WHAT TO COMPARE?

In comparative (public) administrative studies, the unit of analysis is an administrative system. Therefore, the focus is either on the whole of an administrative system or on its various parts. Briefly, the subject matter of comparison would be one or all of the following phenomena:

(i) Environment of the administrative system;

(ii) The whole administrative system;

(iii) The formal structure of the administrative system with a focus on the pattern of hierarchy, division of work, specialisation, authority-responsibility network, decentralisation, delegation, control mechanisms, procedures, etc;

(iv) The informal organisational patterns existing in an administrative set-up, including the nature of human groups, the relationship among individuals, motivational system, the status of morale, patterns of informal communication and the nature of leadership;

(v) The roles of the individuals;

(vi) The interaction between the personality of individuals and the organisational system;

(vii) The policy and decisional systems of the organisation that link its various parts;

(viii) The communicational system, which also involves the feedback mechanism;

(ix) The performance of an administrative system.

You would notice from the foregoing discussion that an administrative system is not a simple entity. There are intricacies of its functioning which will be highlighted in any comparative analysis.

Comparative administrative studies can be conducted at three analytical levels: macro, middle-range and micro.

Macro studies focus on the comparisons of whole administrative systems in their proper ecological contexts. For instance, a macro study would involve a, comparison of the administrative systems of India and Great Britain. It will comprise detailed analysis of all important aspects and parts of the administrative systems of the two nations. It will be comprehensive in its scope. Though the studies of macro level are rare, they are not impossible to be taken up. Generally, the relationship between an administrative system and its external environment are highlighted in the macro level studies. The middle-range studies are on certain important parts of an administrative system that are sufficiently large in size and scope of functioning. For instance, a comparison of the structure of higher bureaucracy of two or more nations, a comparison of agricultural administration in two or more countries on a comparison of local government in different countries will form part of middle-range studies.

Micro studies relate to comparisons of an individual with its counterparts in other settings. A micro study might relate to an analysis of a small part of an administrative system, such as the recruitment or training system to two or more administrative organisations. Micro studies are more feasible to be undertaken and a large number of such studies have been conducted by scholars of Public Administration. In the contemporary Comparative Public Administration, all the three types of studies co-exist.

Another relevant question that arises is what is the range of comparative administrative studies? What type of studies are generally included in this realm? In fact, the scope of Comparative Public Administration studies is so wide that a variety of analysis form part of this branch of knowledge.

THE RANGE OF COMPARATIVE STUDIES

Broadly three are five types of studies. They are:

Inter-institutional Analysis

It involves a comparison of two or more administrative systems. For instance, a comparison of the structure and working of the Home Ministry of the Government of India with the Defence Ministry will be a case of inter-institutional analysis. Such comparisons could involve the whole of an administrative organisation or its various parts.

Intra-national Analysis

When an analysis in a comparative perspective is taken up among various administrative systems functioning within a country, it would be an intra-national analysis. Comparison of district administration in Bihar and Punjab would be an example of such an analysis.

Cross-national Analysis

When two or more administrative system (or their parts) are compared in the settings or different nations, this would be cross-national analysis. For example, comparing the recruitment of higher civil service of China. Thailand and Tanzania will form an example of a cross-national analysis.

Cross-cultural Analysis

A cross-national analysis of administrative system involves countries forming part of different "cultures", this would be called a cross-cultural analysis. For instance, comparing the administrative system of the USSR (a socialist state) with the U. S. (A capitalist system) could be termed a cross-cultural analysis. Even a comparison between a developed country (e.g. France) with a developing country (e.g. Algeria) or between a developing democratic country (e.g. Philippines) and a developing Communist regime (e.g. Vietnam) will be covered in a cross-cultural comparison. Thus the word "cultural" in the category "cross-cultural" has a broad connotation and involves an aggregation of distinctive political, economic and socio-cultural traits of a particular system and its environment.

Cross-temporal Analysis

Such a comparison involves different time-frames for analysis. For instance, a comparison between the administrative system prevailing during Ashoka's reign and during Akbar's regime would be a cross-temporal analysis. Likewise, comparisons between the administrative systems of ancient Rome and modern Italy, or between the administrative practices prevailing during the period of Jawaharlal Nehru and Indira Gandhi would fall under the rubric of cross-temporal analysis.

A cross-temporal analysis may be inter-institutional, intra-national, cross-national or cross-cultural. For instance, a comparison of the administrative control mechanisms prevailing during the times of Julius Caesar. Alexander, Harsha. Attaturz and Nasser will be cross-national as well as cross-cultural. Exactness in cross-temporal studies is not possible because of differences in the nature of historical sources available for various periods. But some broad conclusions on the basis of existing sources can be reached through such studies. Nimord Raphaeli has defined Comparative Public Administration as a study of Public Administration on a comparative basis. The Comparative Administration Group referred to Comparative Public Administration as the theory of Public Administration which belongs to diverse cultures in the national settings and the body of factual data by which it can be expanded and tested. Robert Jockson has defined it as the phase of study which is concerned with making rigorous cross-cultural comparisons of the structures and processes involved in the activity of administering public affairs.

NATURE OF COMPARATIVE ADMINISTRATIVE STUDIES

Some scholars believes that comparison is an inherent part of any social analysis and whenever we examine any social problem or issue, we cannot do so without employing the comparative approach. Famous social scientist, Durkheim, subscribed to this approach.

Further, Elsenstad believes that there is no distinction between comparative research and general social research, for the methods of the two are similar. On the other hand, there are other scholars who believe that comparative inquiry has special focus and techniques.

Before the Second World War, there were several studies on comparative politics and administration but such studies were primarily descriptive and normative. Fred Riggs, the foremost scholar of Comparative Administration had observed that there were three trends which were noticeable in the comparative study of Public Administration. These were: (1) "normative" to "empirical". (2) "ideographic" to "nomothetic" and (3) "non-ecological" to "ecological". We shall now briefly refer to these trends.

Normative to Empirical

Traditional studies of Public Administration were very much influenced by the classical approach. These studies emphasised upon 'good administration' which was based on following certain ideal principles. Efficiency and economy were considered to be the primary goals of all administrative systems and there were certain principles of formal organisation which helped in the achievement of these goals. Therefore, a few models of administration, primarily of the western democratic world, were considered to be useful for all other administrative systems. As a number of developing countries emerged on the scene and with the success of the communist systems in various parts of the world, it became clear that a limited culture-bound normative approach to the study of Public Administration was not adequate. The behavioural approach highlighted the value of studying the facts and reality in a significant manner and therefore the comparative studies of Public Administration after the Second World War started assigning greater importance to the study of administrative "reality" existing in different countries and cultures. These studies were more interested in finding out facts about structural patterns and behaviours of administrative systems rather than in describing as to what was good for each system.

In this context, it may be mentioned that two important trends have influenced the character of some administrative studies in the past two decades or so. First, the concept of "Development Administration" which focuses on the goal-orientation of administrative system is basically a normative concept. Though it considers reality as the basis of such goal-orientation, the emergence of Development Administration as a focus inquiry since the early sixties, Comparative Public Administration (encompassing the field of Comparative Development Administration) has evolved a synthesis between the normative and the empirical elements of analysis.

The second movement that has influenced the nature of Comparative administrative studies is the New Public Administration which stressed the idealistic goal to be achieved by an administrative system and thus tried to bridge the gap between the "is" and "should" aspects of Public Administration. In the late sixties, the New Public Administration marked the "post-behavioural" trend and its impact on most administrative analysis has been profound.

Ideographic to Nomothetic

The words "ideographic" and "nomothetic" have been used by Riggs in specific contexts. An ideographic approach concentrates on unique cases, e.g. a historical event, study of single agency, single country or even a single cultural area.

Nomothetic approach, on the other hand seeks to develop generalisations and theories a which are based on analysis of regularities of behaviour of administrative systems. Thus earlier studies of Comparative Public Administration which were ideographic in character focused on the study of individual nations or institutions and their approach was primarily descriptive. No serious attempt was made to compare various nations and systems. Generally, within a volume on comparative government administration, there were separate characters on different nations, without any attempt to look at the similarities or differences among such nations, in terms of their administrative systems. These studies, therefore, were 'comparative' only in name and did not help in the process of theory-building or in developing generalisations concerning the functioning of administrative system in different settings.

Nomothetic studies analyse various administrative systems in comparative context in a manner that will help in the generation of hypothesis and theories. The objective of such studies is to look at the similarities and differences of various administrative systems existing in different nations and cultures and then draw certain generalisations relating to administrative systems functioning at various levels and in different settings.

It maybe noted that the emphasis on nomothetic comparative is more noticeable in the United States of America than in Europe or Asia. Presently, a large number of comparative administrative studies are ideographic in character. Even these studies, it must be admitted, contribute to knowledge in Comparative Public Administration. Analysis or theory-building has to be based on facts and description. And therefore, in the present State of comparative administrative studies, a co-existence of ideographic and nomothetic studies may have to be accepted.

Non-ecological to Ecological

The traditional studies of Comparative Public Administration were mainly non-ecological. These studies mentioned about the environment of administrative system only in a casual manner. There was no serious attempt to examine the relationship between the administrative system and its environment. Thus, it had become very difficult to identify the sources of differences among various administrative system. However, studies undertaken after the Second World War have been specifically looking at similarities and differences among environmental settings prevailing in different nations and cultures and have been attempting to examine the impact of environment on the administrative system on the one hand and the influence of the administrative system on the environment, on the other. The well-known ecological approach relates to the study of interrelationship between the system and its environment. This approach, popularised by Fred Riggs, has been regarded as an important development in the study of Public Administration.

It may be noted that most of the comparative studies of Public Administration after the Second World War have been referring to the environment of the administrative systems, but the main emphasis is still on analysing the impact of the environment on Public Administration. The analysis relating to the influences of the administrative system on the environment is still inadequate. Nevertheless, a change in emphasis is noticeable and the ecological orientation is gaining stronger footing in the contemporary comparative administrative analysis.

At this stage it may be pointed out that when Riggs presented the above three trends in 1962, he was conscious of the fact that there is bound to be a co-existence of older as well as the newer emphasis in the comparative studies. Accordingly, today there are normative as well as empirical, ideographic as well as nomothetic and non-ecological as well as ecological approaches co-existing in the literature on Comparative Administration.

Scope of Comparative Public Administration

The scope of Public Administration has increased enormously during the twentieth century. The importance of Public

Administration has grown substantially with the success of the Russian Revolution, increased role of state during and after the Second World War, measures of welfare adopted in most of the countries and growth of large number of developing countries.

Today, Public Administration influences almost all aspects of human life. Even in a capitalistic country like the USA, the role of government has expanded in an effective manner. The net result of this increased role of state or government has been that large number of specialised branches of Public Administration have come up on the scene. Some of these branches are economic administration, social administration, educational administration, health administration, transport administration, space administration, etc.

Besides, there are areas such as state administration, urban administration, rural administration, financial administration and personnel administration which have become integral parts of the vocabulary of government. Therefore, when we compare administrative systems existing in various nations or cultures, we can compare either the whole of the administrative systems or some important parts of such systems. Today, we find a number of studies on comparative educational administration, comparative health administration, comparative economic administration, comparative social administration and other related areas.

Further, there are a very large number of publications on comparative urban administration and comparative rural administration. It becomes clear that the scope of Comparative Public Administration is as vast as that of its mother discipline, *viz.* Public Administration. Anything that is 'administrative' can be compared.

While discussing the scope of Comparative Public Administration, not only the specialised branches of administration have to be taken into account. Further it also needs to be stressed once again that comparative studies can be conducted at macro, middle-range and micro levels. These studies can be inter-institutional, cross-national, cross-cultural and cross-temporal.

Here an interesting question arises: what do we include under the rubric of "nature" of Comparative Administration and what do we put under the heading of "scope" of Comparative Administration? The best advice than can be given to students of Public Administration is that to attempt a neat distinction between the 'nature' and 'scope' of comparative Public Administration may not be a very useful effort. There two aspects are overlapping and have common stress on the types, levels, and range of comparative studies.

Significance of Comparative Public Administration

The importance of the study of Comparative Public Administration is well accepted today. There are two factors that make comparative studies significant. The first factor relates to the academic study of Public Administration. It is believed that through Comparative Public Administration hypotheses, generalisation, models and theories can be constructed which can collectively help in the scientific study of Public Administration. The old orthodoxy of principles of administration is not considered valid anymore and therefore now it is believed that generalisations relating to administrative structures and behaviour emerging out of comparative studies in different nations and cultures can help in formulating theoretical constructs which can provide a scientific basis to the study of Public Administration. It may be mentioned that way back in 1947, a very eminent political scientist, Robert Dalh had observed that a science of Public Administration cannot be conceived of without adopting a comparative approach.

The study of Comparative Public Administration also contributes to a greater understanding of the individuals characteristics of administrative systems functioning in different nations and cultures. Besides, comparative studies also help in explaining factors responsible for cross-national and cross-cultural similarities as well as differences in the administrative systems.

The second important function of Comparative Public Administration relates to its relevance to the empirical world. Through a study of Comparative Public Administration, administrators, policy makers and academicians can examine causes for the success on failure of particular administrative structures and patterns in different environmental settings. It is interesting to find out through comparative analysis as to which important environmental factors help in the promotion of administrative effectiveness and which administrative structures function appropriately and successfully in what type of environmental settings. Lastly, an administrator or policy maker can, though comparative studies of Public Administration, have greater insight into the process and strategies of administrative reforms. He can look at the structures of administrative reforms adopted by various nations and examine those strategies and methods which can be helpful in his own country. In other words, through Comparative Public Administration we learn about the administrative practices followed in various nations and then we can endeavour to adopt those practices which can fit in our own nations and systems.

The importance of Comparative Public Administration lies in its academic utility in terms of scientific and systematic study of Public Administration and in improving the knowledge about other administrative systems so that appropriate administrative reforms and changes can be brought about in different nations.

Conceptual Approaches in Comparative Public Administration

There are a number of approaches, models and theories presently characterizing the subject-area of Comparative Public Administration. Particularly after Second World War, number of approaches have emerged in comparative administrative analysis. Much of this effort is based on an adaptation of the developments in comparative anthropology. Comparative sociology and comparative politics. We will now study different approaches.

Bureaucratic Approach

The most influential of the approaches is Max Weber's ideal-type bureaucratic model. This has structural characteristics of hierarchy, specialisation, role-specificity, recruitment by merit, promotion by seniority-cum-merit, career development, training, discipline, separation between personal and official means, etc. The emphasis in the model is on rationality and efficiency.

There have been a number of studies conducted in a comparative context employing the bureaucratic model of Weber. Notable scholars in this area include Michael Crozier (on France). Roy Laird (on the Soviet Union) and Morroe Berger (on Egypt). The methodological limitation of an ideal-type model and specific context of a legal-rational authority systems poses constraints in the application of Weber's model model to the comparative study of bureaucracies: Nevertheless, for an analysis of the bureaucracies, of the developed countries, the model it still considered eminently useful. Dwiht Waldo views Weber's bureaucratic model as a "paradigm" of Public Administration.

Particularly after Second World War, a number of approaches have emerged in comparative administrative analysis. Much of this effort is based on an adaptation of the developments in comparative anthropology, comparative sociology and comparative politics.

Behavioural Approach

The behavioural approach emphasises "facts", rigorous scientific methods of data collection and analysis, quantification, experimentation, testing, verification and an interdisciplinary orientation. It focuses on the analysis of human behaviour in administrative settings.

General Systems Approach

Further, the general systems approach views an administrative system as a subsystem of the society. It looks at various parts of an administrative system (formal organisation, informal organisation, roles, individuals) and examines the interlinkages among various parts. Besides, the approach analyses the dynamic interactions between the administrative system and its external environment.

Ecological Approach

One of the most poplar approaches in Comparative Public Administration is the ecological approach which has been stressed considerably by Fred Riggs. This approach examines the interactions between an administrative system and its external environment. Thus the impact of the political system, economic system, social system and the cultural system, on the structure and behaviour of the administrative system as well as the influence of the administrative system on these environment structures is highlighted in the ecological approach.

Structural—Functional Approach

A related approach, drawn mainly from Anthropology and Sociology, is the structural-functional approach. A structure according to this approach, is a pattern of behaviour that has become a standard feature of a social system. Further, a function denotes the impact of a structure on another structure and the interrelationships among various structures.

Fred Riggs has successfully applied the ecological and structural-functional approaches in his analysis of societies and their administrative systems. His typology of "agraria-transitia-industria" systems, developed in 1957, was superseded by the typology of "fused-prismatic diffracted" societies that was constructed in 1959. For the past thirty years or so. Rigg's model of prismatic society and its administrative system known as "sala" has ruled the comemporary model-building scenes in Comparative Public Administration. Despite criticisms and certain inherent methodological limitations, the prismatic-sala model has fascinated the students and practitioners of Public Administration in "developing" countries. A prismatic society, according to Riggs, is charactersed by a growing degree of structural differentiation but not matched by an equal degree of integration (coordination). This integration lag is reflected in almost all aspects of the functioning of a prismatic society.

A prismatic society and its 'sala' are characterised by 'heterogeneity', formalism and overlapping. Further overlapping has five dimensions: poly-communalism, poly-normativism, bazar-canteen model, authority versus control and nepotism. These features relate to the social, cultural, economic, political and administrative systems of the prismatic society. The details of these characteristics are found in all important books on Public Administration.

Development Approach

A very well-known conceptual approach in Comparative Public Administration is of 'Development Administration' which has been elaborately dealt with in a separate unit. This approach focuses on certain characteristics of a dynamic administrative system, e.g. goal-orientation, change-orientation, progressiveness, innvoativeness, participation and responsiveness.

Besides, the above, there are a number of other less-known approaches to comparative administrative analysis. These include 'information-energy' model of John Dorsey and decision-making model of Martin Landau. Nevertheless, other models have not been able to match the comprehensiveness and acceptability of Weber's bureaucratic model. Rigg's prismatic model and of course, the construct of Development Administration.

It appears that the experimentation phase in model-building in Comparative Public Administration is not vigorous anymore. However, the enthusiasm for understanding the varieties of administrative patterns is alive in the scholarship of Public Administration. This is why, one can hope for newer dimensions of Comparative Public Administration emerging on the scene in the times to come.

17

Perspectives on Public Administration for the 21st Century

FUTURE OF INDIAN PUBLIC ADMINISTRATION

"Ideas are the spectacles with which we look at facts", said Edward De Bono. What we see depends on what ideological spectacles we wear. To peer into the future of public administration in the 21st century is difficult, as one can't predict anything about the future. Imagine someone trying to give a talk on the perspectives on public administration for the 20th century in the year 1896! One wonders whether he would have been able to anticipate cataclysmic changes that took place in the 20th century resulting in India becoming an independent country, the disappearance of the 600+states and so on.

We can therefore approach the whole issue of perspectives for the 21st century from different angles. One would be to look at the inherent dynamics of public administration and draw conclusions about the likely trend of developments in the years to come. The other would be to assume that there would be a vision and a systematic effort at realising that vision which means that the dynamics of public administration will be focused in certain directions. Ultimately the perspectives depend on whether we are going to assume a mode of drift in which case certain inherent factors will come into play or whether we are going to have a vision and work towards it in which case there will be certain specific directions of development.

So far as the drift mode is concerned, we can look at external factors and those within the administration. After, all public administration is closely linked with development of society and therefore when we talk about the external factors they will relate to some of the broad trends for which we can offer analogies from geology an well as biology as has been done by Lestor Thurow.

Lestor Thurow has borrowed two concepts from geology and biology in his attempt to look into the future of capitalism in his recent book *"The Future of Capitalism"*. From geology he has borrowed the concept of plate tectonics to perceive and describe massive changes which are parking place and which have developed a force of their own. As regards to biology, he draws inspiration from the concept of the "punctuated equilibrium" in describing evolution. The disappearance of dinosaurs as a result of the catastrophe that took place 65 million years ago is an example of punctuated equilibrium. Of course, one commentator has pointed out that dinosaurs have really not been eliminated but have evolved into the birds we see today. Even if this is true, the scenario from when dinosaurs ruled the earth has undergone a sea change.

It is always good to remember one important principle of scenario planning and futurology. We have to think of the unthinkable or the showstopper. That will be the catalyst for punctuated equilibrium. Otherwise we will be like the futurologist who, looking into the 20th century in the 1890s, speculated that the roads of London would have seven feet of horse dung covering them by the year 1920. He had just extrapolated the figures of horse drawn carriages, which were quite common in the late 19th century in London. He never anticipated the automobile, the houseless carriage that was the showstopper in this case.

When it comes to internal dynamics of administration perhaps the laws of physics will apply. Newton's Law, particularly the first and third law of motion are relevant in this context. The first law is the Law of Inertia. Anybody who has dealt with large bureaucracies knows about Inerta. Unless there is a strong force to change it, the inertia is not going to change. This is where perhaps the pace of development will depend upon whether we are in the drift mode or in the focused vision mode. The third Law of

Newton "every action has an equal and opposite reaction" is also relevant. This will explain the difficulties and resistance in any process of reforms. While the bureaucracy and public administration will be subject to these laws, there is also another Universal Law, the second Law of Thermodynamics according to which in any system there is a tendency for entropy to increase. In other words, there is always a movement from order to disorder unless we are careful, and unless we intervene.

THE DRIFT MODE: PLATE TECTONICS

We can begin our exercise by looking into three broad sets of issues. The first: What are the major forces shaping our society today, which will have an impact on public administration? There will be the plate tectonics aspect of administration. The second set of issues would be to see what would be the features that will continue in any administration irrespective of the state of the society or the perceived role of the government. These are the internal factors of administration. The third aspect will be to speculate on the showstopper signifying the punctuated equilibrium.

Let us look at the first aspect of plate tectonics. The most significant aspect of public administration is the public, the people. We have already a population of about 1 billion and in the 21st century it may be stabilize at around 1.5 billion. Another aspect of our demography is that with the growing improvement in health services, the population is greying. The population of old people will become increasingly significant. After all, the average life expectancy for an Indian has gone up from 32 in 1947 to 56 today. So, in the 21st century we can reasonably hope that the average life expectancy of an Indian may even go up to 65. This has to be seen in the context of the other sociological phenomenon of the breaking up of the joint family and the growth of unclear families. We can therefore, visualise new pressures on our public administration in the social sector in the form of old age care and assistance. This aspect also has to be considered in the context of the progress made by the Asian Tigers vis-a-vis the western countries. One of the reasons given for explaining the success of the Asian tigers is that thanks to Asian values, the elders are taken care of by their families. Hence the burden of social insurance, which developed social economies have to bear, is not there in the societies of the East. This has helped the Asian countries to chalk up faster rates of growth than achieved in the West.

Another demographic fact of our population will be the significantly large population of those below 25 years of age. We can expect hopefully that the family planning and the family welfare initiatives of the government will succeed. If we are moving towards a stable population by mid-21st century, we can expect for the next say 20 years or so, a large percentage of those below 25 or 30 years in the population. This may gradually reduce as the greying to India becomes more significant.

The importance of this large young population and the pressures it will bring will be in the following areas:

(a) *Public Health:* As it will be directly linked with the effort at controlling the population and the need for any modern society to provide basic health services. One showstopper in the public health area will be AIDS. There was a recent report in TIME, which said that India was likely to become the AIDS capital of the world. If this happens, it will pose a major challenge in public administration.

(b) *Public Education:* The danger we are facing is that as we enter the 21st century we may have the notoriety of having the largest illiterate population in the world. At present, we are only 52 per cent literate. The challenge of achieving universal literacy has already been taken up by the government. The additional challenge in the 21st century will be the challenge of technological literacy and creation of technology through effective R & D.

(c) *Law and Order:* We have already seen the continuing low intensity warfare or terrorism in the Northeast, J & K, in some parts of Andhra Pradesh in the Naxaite movement, etc. The danger of such violent local disturbances will increase if we are not able to ensure that economic growth does not lead to greater disparities in income and quality of life. The Human Development Report 1996 highlight five types of defective growths: jobless growth, the rootless growth, the ruthless growth, the voiceless growth and futureless growth. So far as we are concerned, we face the danger of all these types of defective growth except voiceless growth. For nearly five decades we have imbibed the democratic tradition and our people will continue to have their voice and so the danger of voiceless growth is not there. The HDI report also indicates one of the long-standing challenges to the public administration, which will continue well into the 21st century—that of continuously trying to improve the quality of life.

The second factor in the plate tectonics shaping the future of public administration is the geo political forces. The end of the Cold War signifies that in the future, geo-politics is going to be dominated by economic competition on the one hand and tensions arising from nationalities and ethnic groups on the other. We are now living in a period when in our politics the regional parties are having an increasing say in the Centre. Will this trend continue regional forces become more dominant? Or will the economic process of integration bring a new perspective by which India will become India Inc. And the economic factors play a dominant role?

The 21st century will definitely be influenced by the GATT agreement and the WTO. Up to the year 2005 also we will see coming into force of some important aspects relating to the intellectual property rights. This means that in the area of economic administration, the role of the government will change from being an active player to being a catalyst. It will have to do more of steering than rowing. At the same time, the government will also have to increasingly play the role of an objective umpire and ensure a level playing ground for competitive market forces to operate.

The third important aspect of plate tectonics is the area of technology. In fact, the world has already become a global village in the 20th century. This process will be further accentuated in the 21st century. For public administration, the advances in technology will pose two types of challenges. For example, in the area of communications and broadcasting, already we see the impact of satellite communication and how this had an impact on the aspirations, culture and thinking of the emerging generation. Perhaps we will see more and more of a global culture. Of course, there will be those who would like to preserve Indian culture and will rail against cultural colonisation. However, technology being what it is, to what extent will they be successful? For example, even in France they are finding the American influence more dominant as a result of the impact of electronic media.

The other dimension of technology is the growing application of information technology and computers. Simultaneously with the liberalisation process there will be greater demand for more transparency in government operations. Hopefully an act like the Freedom of Information Act may be enacted in due course of time. We will then face the issues of national security and gurading national secrets on the one hand and also ensuring privacy of the individual on the other. However, the social tensions that will be created as a result of the electronic media is a public administration issue that will probably be posed with greater acuity in the 21st century.

There will arise new technology related issue in specific areas like energy. As move towards the next century and as fossil based fuels are consumed, energy will become an increasingly dominant issue. Energy is vital for growth. Alternative sources of energy will have to be developed. Necessary is the mother of invention. We will have to focus on technologies like solar energy and biotechnology. The green revolution saved India in the 60s. Biotechnology may be the method by which we feed our large population in the 21st century.

While these factors relating to plate tectonics of public administration will have their own dynamics, another important factor would be the political pressures of the day. But politics is ultimately the reflection of the social pressures and the demographic changes that are taking place. It is not possible to visualise the lines on which these factors are going to affect public administration. A safe assumption will be to think in terms of an oscillation theory or continuous action and reaction (Newton's third law). Our politics generally so far has been based on the distributive approach. We started with land reform, wealth and jobs. Perhaps this has had mixed results. We can create a better future if we focus on the positive approach of creating more jobs and wealth. Again, the recent possibility of genderising Indian politics by providing 33 per cent reservation of seats in the political institutions if rightly implemented will have a dramatic impact not only on politics but also on society as a whole. The neglect of the girl child will hopefully become a thing of the past.

Apart from the factors that are external to the public administration, changes in public administration also may come from internal factors, i.e. change agents within the public administration system who may be able to provide the leadership and make the administration perform more effectively and make it better suited for tacking the problems of the day.

One issue that will be relevant at any time in the future would be the perennial issue of corruption. Another would be the issue of efficiency and effectiveness of the government and this in turn would mean to what extent the government is able to change its systems and internalize emerging technologies. This will essentially depend on the leaders within the government, the bureaucrats (though political pressures will continue) and as the demographic analysis shows, the focus will have to be given in the immediate few years to the issue of social justice. But as the years go by, other issues perhaps relating to environment and old age will become significant. In view of the continuous growth in population, the pressure on urban cities will continue and urban management will increasingly become a key factor especially for effective administration.

As regards punctuated equilibrium in public administration one showstopper may be AIDS. Another could be an environmental disaster arising from some of the major projects under implementation about which the environmentalists are raising objection. Murphy's Law can operate in a vicious manner. Yet another disaster may be large asteroid strike on the earth or some phenomenon like the one at Tungustu early this century (1908) in Russia when a vast area in Siberia was devastated. By their very nature the punctuated equilibrium will be the blind spot in our exercise.

A VISION FOR THE FUTURE: INDIA AS A SUPERPOWER

When we look at the perspectives for the 21st century, we can be more confident of the directions in which public administration will evolve if we had a vision of what our country would be like in the years to come. Unfortunately in our country we do not seem to have any vision. A small country like Singapore has a vision of "Singapore as an intelligent island by the year 2000". Malaysia looks a little beyond and by 2020 wants to be a fully developed country. South Korea wants to join the G-7. We in India lack such a super ordinate goal. With our population, we should think of India emerging as an economic super power by the year 2020. Such a vision will give us ideas on how we can make public administration evolve to achieve this goal. In the absence of such a vision, we will only be drifting and be subject to the blind plate tectonic forces as mentioned above.

The government of India started the process of economic liberalisation in 1991. It has initiated a process by which the activist role played by the government in the economic administration will sooner or later be replaced by a more catalytic role. But there are certain areas where the government, whatever the political complexion, can never abandon its responsibility and as a result it will always be significant in administration. These are the areas:

(a) We are nation of poor people and public health is one issue, which the government will have to look after for the simple reason that if public health fails we may have disasters like the plague we had in 1994. Further, many people cannot afford private doctors. Even the medical insurance system invented in the United States is also leading to problems of funding and this is an issue they are wrestling with. For us, running public health institutions would be a major area of challenge in public administration. We must see how we can make hospitals and the public health system effective by using the resources that are available. Imaginative use of Information Technology would be very useful in this area both in terms of collecting information about the health of the population and also in terms of providing excellent medical care. Nearly 20-30 per cent of the costly equipment

in most of our hospitals is out of order. A systematic programme of seeing that our hospitals are not sick and that our equipments have the maximum uptime will bring about substantial improvement. In this we will be facing the problem of AIDS and other diseases like TB and malaria, which probably are once again becoming challenges at present. So, public health is going to be one major area of challenge in the 21st century.

(b) The next impairment area is education. It has already been mentioned that India will have the largest population of illiterate people at the beginning of the 21st century. At least we must try to see that we make our country literate as quickly as possible. In this effort we must be able to use all the techniques of modern technology of distance education and also make widespread use of the NGOs that have been effective in spreading the literacy movement.

(c) Creating adequate productive employment will be another major area of concern. With the growing population and better education would arise the challenge of getting adequate productive employment. This is where the role of the government will be very critical. On the one hand, the government will be playing a catalytic role in the economic development. We need not visualise a larger number of public sector enterprises growing but at the same time, we will have to think of innovative methods by which the employment in this country can be enhanced. We must think of new opportunities for growth. The employment opportunities provided by electronics whether it is in software or techno coolies by way of bibliographic database industry is a case in point. Another area would be to focus attention on industry based on waste because as industrial and economic development takes place, we will see that the red tape will be replaced with the green tape. A strategy were every waste product including even the municipal waste is utilised for productive purposes will be a challenge for the administration.

(d) The fourth area will be the area of law and order. The pressures of the population, the aspirations of the people leading to greater demands on the society and the increasing

accentuation of the ethnic and regional identities will pose problems of tackling the perennial problems of law and order. If we look at the past 50 years after Independence, we have tackled theses issues as and when they arose. Many a time one gets a feeling what the movements exhausted themselves. It is not clear whether the movements for regional separation and regional identity have a dynamics of their own but a lot of life, tension and unhappiness can be reduced if we able to handle intelligently and anticipate the growing tension. Simultaneously, we will also need to look into our entire legal system and maintenance of law and order for better results. When we look at our legal and criminal administration system, it appears as if the criminal has an advantage because our legal process is so slow. The blatant manner in which Charles Sobharj escaped punishment from Thailand through our inefficient legal and judicial system is a glaring example. We will have to think of effective handling of law and order problems. Of course, there will be the related issue of human rights. This is an area where there will be continuous challenges for all time to come.

Education, public health, employment and law and order will definitely be the areas of concern in public administration. The government will have to think of taking initiatives to ensure productive employment of people because if there is failure on this front, there will be greater tension with political consequences like separatism, violence and so on.

We can now look at some of the specific areas where initiatives will have to be taken if we want India to be an economic superpower. The first requirement is that we have to strengthen our infrastructure and ensure for example that we have to requisite energy to power the process of growth. As the conventional source of energy will become increasingly difficult in the 21st century, we will have to focus attention on non-conventional energy sources. We should particularly try to exploit solar energy because India is well placed with perhaps the maximum number of sunny days.

The other area where we have to focus would be the area of technology. As we will be living in an era of world intellectual property rights and as Indians have shown marked capacity particularly in hitech areas like electronics and biotechnology, we will have to think increasingly of joint R & D with institutions and countries abroad. As Dr. Mashelkar says, we must try to see whether India can become a platform for global R & D.

We will have to look at the whole network of our laws to see whether the pace of administration can be stepped up. If today our administration can be blamed, it is for corruption and delays. Delays can be eliminated if we can review all the various procedure we have and see how red tape can be eliminated. We must increasingly realise the value of time. This itself can eliminate to some extent petty corruption. Checking of corruption will be successful only if we are also able to evolve systems for prompt punishment and exposure of the corrupt elements. Our media is performing that role today but the administration will have to elvove its own internal system to weed out the corrupt.

One aspect of the liberalisation policy, which will become increasingly prominent relates to regional disparities. If has been said that perhaps if we draw a vertical line across the map of India, the states in the west seem to be doing better than those in the east. Liberalisation has introduced a feeling of competition among the states. Those who are in charge of less developed states will have to think of particularly innovative strategies to attract investment and growth.

In this connection a report appeared in Business Today, some time back, giving a gist of the Global Competitiveness Report 1996, points out that "India ranks 45th among 49, ahead only of Russia, Brazil, Venezuela and Hungary. From 35th in 1994 to 39th in 1995 and now 45th India's declining position is a mocking commentary on its liberalisation and reform. Equating competitiveness with the likelihood of sustaining growth in per capita income over a period of such in between next 5 to 10 years, the GCR clearly implies that India's prospects are dim.

The factors that determine the management ranking in the GCR experts report India's ranking in this area as follows. In overall management ranking out of the 49 countries India is 43rd. In entrepreneurship India is no. 19, risk taking and initiatives 13,

> *willingness to delegate 38, use of Infotech 44, customer orientation 43, time to innovate 47, time to market 44, TQM 42, strategy implementation 43, absence of monopoly 32, global managerial experience 44, managerial breadth 28, strong corporate boards 46, diffident corporate boards 45, work place organisation 47, availability of managers 18 and non wage incentives 18.*

To achieve the goal of India as an economic superpower by the year 2020, we will also have think of making public administration more effective. We will have to in a way re-invent the government. One starting point in this exercise, which has been mentioned before, for reinventing the government may be to consider the ten ideas mentioned by Ted Gaebler and David Osborne in their book *Government.*

Broadly we can look at the entire issue from two angles. The first is to take note of the massive plate tectonic forces, which shape the administration. The other is to have a focused vision to make our country an economy superpower by 2020 and start the systematic process of re-inventing the government and take specific measures to see that we improve our position as a country from the human development index point of view and the competitiveness index point of view.

The future scenario of public administration in terms of the organisation is also worth looking into. Logically, if public health, education and law and order are going to be the basic functions of the government, these should carry maximum prestige. However today for example, the economic ministries and the relating to regulatory functions seem to have greater glamour than those dealing with the social sector. Will a change in perception come about? Definitely, as the role of the government decreases in economic administration, perhaps the social sectors may become more attractive for the bureaucrats advancing in their career.

Another issue would be to what extent the governmental systems and procedures will start using modern technology. This depends essentially on the leaders within the government. For example today it is possible to use Information Technology extensively in administration but the forces of inertia seem to be more dominant. If we really want to become an economic superpower, perhaps the system to Public administration ought to be modernised by simplifying procedures and speeding up the decision making process and using Information Technology extensively.

Another related issue would be the degree of centralisation and decentralisation. Information Technology helps in both. In the Indian context, this will also depend on the equilibrium of forces between the regional forces and the central forces, between the regional polity and the national polity. In the mechanisms of the Constitution, the present constitutional framework should continue unless very severe developments distort the system. This type of punctuated equilibrium, which will propel such a development cannot be foreseen at this stage.

What will be the skills required from the bureaucrat and what will be the role of the bureaucrat in the 21st century? In his book *The Shape of Things to Come,* Peter Drucker said that in the next century, the Chief Executives would have to be more like the collectors, presidents of the universities or the superintendents of the hospitals. They will have to coordinate the work of many specialists. For this there has to be a massive changes in the type of skills of the bureaucrats in the different services and the organisations to met the emerging challenges. Innovativeness and creative thinking should be inoculated in all civil servants so that public administration does not suffer from massive inertia.

After all, the future is what we make if to be.

CIVIL SERVICE: A NATIONAL PERSPECTIVE

The Indian Civil Service was called the steel frame and looking into the future about the shape of things to come, Peter Drucker says that the type of management needed in society where there is going to be so much technology and specialisation, must be like the old ICS. The British had, with less than a thousand people, run the administration of a country of 300 million people. The Indian Administration Service is the successor to the Indian Civil Service. It was the vision of Sardar Patel who saw to it that this framework.needed for the administration of the country was nurtured properly. On the eve of the 21st century we need to address the question as to what are the perspectives of administration? We can look at the past and we can look to the future. A look at the past can give us concepts about the sound principles that have prevailed, how deterioration has crept in and what should now be done. While if we look at the future, we can try to anticipate the shape of things to come.

One of the doyens of the India Civil Service, B.K. Nehru, had made some remarkable observations. The first point he made was that we Indians have never really been democratic. If at all there was a democracy, it was only at the level of panachayats or at the level of the castes. The concept of the parliamentary democracy, which we adopted in our Constitution, is a direct result of our experience with the British where Indian leaders also became aware of the working of this system. The division between the political executive and the permanent bureaucracy was also appreciated. In the early years, thanks to visionary leaders like Jawahrlal Nehru and Sardar Patel, we were able to build the administrative service and maintain this fine distinction between the responsibility of the civil servant and the role of political leadership.

Nehru gave an interesting example of the role played be the civil servants in the early days. T.T. Krishnamachari was a very powerful Finance Minister and he wanted to see the confidential file to income tax relating to individuals. A.K. Roy, who later on become the Controller and Auditor General of the India, was the Chairman of the central Board of Revenue. When the minister asked for this file, Roy politely declined saying that he could not see the file. When the minister retorted that Roy as the chairman of the central board of revenue could see the file, why not the Finance Minister, Roy pointed out that under the rules, the files were confidential and only an income tax officer could see it and therefore the chairman, central board of revenue could see the file and not the Finance Minister. At the end, T.T. Krishamachri fell in with this argument. Therefore, the rules were modified later on to permit access to files for ministers as well.

Another example given by Nehru related to Jawaharlal Nehru himself. Jawaharlal had a servant called Hari who was very faithful to him and worked with he for a long time. He wanted a piece of land in UP and he could not get it. When B. K. Nehru asked him why he could not talk to the Prime Minister who would support him, Hari replied: "The Prime Minister supports me but the government does not support me." Hari made a distinction between the views of the political leader and the will of the government. The point made by B. K. Nehru was to indicate how in the early years of the civil service this distinction between the role of the bureaucracy and the political leadership was maintained and even at the highest level, powerful politicians like JLN and TTK had to operate within the system. In fact BKN added as a polite afterthought "JLN could make Hari an MLA because that was within his powers but he could not get the piece of land which he wanted so badly.

Over a period of years, according to BKN, our Indianness has asserted itself in our administration. He said that Indian tradition states that the ruler is absolute. The king can do no wrong. Emperors and kings might have had Maulvis or Brahmin pundits to advise them but ultimately the decision of the ruler was final. True to this tradition, in today's context, every MLA or MP thinks he is a ruler. Therefore, if the civil servant were to quote the rules to him, he feels that his right are being violated. This is a major change that has come about in the four decades of administration after Independence. BKN gave a very telling story to bring out a change in the political perspective. It seems a young IAS officer of the UP cadre was transferred from Delhi to Arunachal Pradesh and he was taken by one of the senior civil servants of H K L Bhagat who was a very powerful political in Delhi in those days. Bhagat asked him: "What category of officer are you?" The young man was confused and he said that he belonged to the UP cadre and gave the year of his allotment. Bhagat said: "Look, I am not interested in that. I want to know which of the category of officers you belong to. According to me there are three categories. Category A are those type of officers who when told to do a thing bring to our notice the legal position and the rules and conventions and say it cannot be done. Category B are those who point out the legal difficulties and resist but if we press for a certain time they carry out our orders. Category C are those who carry out whatever we say. If you belong to the first or second category, you have no chance. You have to go to Arunachal Pradesh. If you belong to the third category, I can see that your transfer gets cancelled." This is typical of the problem, which many civil servants face even today. We have seen some officials associated with certain political leaders and like the American spoil System in civil service in our country also such a system has come to prevail. This is visible whenever there is a change of government.

It would be ideal if the civil servants could focus on developing their professional skills and not be identified with the political leadership. Unfortunately the craving for plum postings is such that independent professional IAS officers may be a rarity. Officers who are idealistic and try to be professional may not get plum postings and get posted in secured or social sectors, which are not considered prize postings. Saxena, director of the LBSNAA has been highlighting the fact that in the IAS the craving is for posts which are connected with economic ministries, posts connected with regulations like law and order. On the other hand, if you look at the future of our country, it is areas like public health, education and rural development which are important in the long run and where one can do a lot of good work for the benefit of the people. A positive attitude, a creative approach and sound common sense are the basic skills a civil servant should have if he wants to have a successful career and also make a contribution in the process.

Looking to the future, one feels that the administration in the states will become even more important. We are witnessing the increasing role of regional parties at the Centre. We are also noticing that one consequence of the economic liberalisation process is that the state governments today have a lot more scope for showing an initiative and are competing for investment and development. Therefore, the application of managerial skills in the state government administration becomes very important. Application of Information Technology should be a very high priority because it is IT that can ensure that the common man has better services. IT also can be useful in bringing in a more transparent process of governmental working as well as direct and easy access to governmental information.

Ultimately, the motto of the IAS is efficiency in work—"*yogah karma su kausalam.*" Efficiency in work is considered as the yoga according to Lord Krishna. If we could bring in effectiveness and efficiency to whatever task is entrusted to us, and if we approach it imaginatively, we would be making a small contribution in the effective administration of the country. For real effectiveness not only should we master the techniques of administration and apply modern technologies like IT but we would also be rooted in certain basic values like commitment to the public good and absolute integrity—both financial and intellectual.